High Availability Network Fundamentals

Chris Oggerino

Cisco Press

Cisco Press
201 West 103rd Street
Indianapolis, IN 46290 USA

High Availability Network Fundamentals

Chris Oggerino

Copyright© 2001 Cisco Press

Cisco Press logo is a trademark of Cisco Systems, Inc.

Published by:
Cisco Press
201 West 103rd Street
Indianapolis, IN 46290 USA

Printed in the United States of America 1 2 3 4 5 6 7 8 9 0

Library of Congress Cataloging-in-Publication Number: 00-105374

ISBN: 1-58713-017-3

First Printing April 2001

Warning and Disclaimer

This book is designed to provide information about predicting high availability for Cisco product-based networks. Every effort has been made to make this book as complete and as accurate as possible, but no warranty or fitness is implied.

The information is provided on an "as is" basis. The author, Cisco Press, and Cisco Systems, Inc. shall have neither liability nor responsibility to any person or entity with respect to any loss or damages arising from the information contained in this book or from the use of the discs or programs that may accompany it.

The opinions expressed in this book belong to the author and are not necessarily those of Cisco Systems, Inc.

Trademark Acknowledgments

All terms mentioned in this book that are known to be trademarks or service marks have been appropriately capitalized. Cisco Press or Cisco Systems, Inc. cannot attest to the accuracy of this information. Use of a term in this book should not be regarded as affecting the validity of any trademark or service mark.

Feedback Information

At Cisco Press, our goal is to create in-depth technical books of the highest quality and value. Each book is crafted with care and precision, undergoing rigorous development that involves the unique expertise of members from the professional technical community.

Readers' feedback is a natural continuation of this process. If you have any comments regarding how we could improve the quality of this book, or otherwise alter it to better suit your needs, you can contact us through e-mail at feedback@ciscopress.com. Please make sure to include the book title and ISBN in your message.

We greatly appreciate your assistance.

Publisher	John Wait
Editor-In-Chief	John Kane
Cisco Systems Program Manager	Bob Anstey
Managing Editor	Patrick Kanouse
Acquisitions Editor	Amy Lewis
Development Editor	Christopher Cleveland
Copy Editor	Chuck Gose
Technical Editor(s)	Scott Cherf, Oliver Day, BJ Favaro
Team Coordinator	Tammi Ross
Book Designer	Gina Rexrode
Cover Designer	Louisa Klucznik
Production Team	Steve Gifford
Indexer	Tim Wright

CISCO SYSTEMS

Corporate Headquarters
Cisco Systems, Inc.
170 West Tasman Drive
San Jose, CA 95134-1706
USA
http://www.cisco.com
Tel: 408 526-4000
        800 553-NETS (6387)
Fax: 408 526-4100

European Headquarters
Cisco Systems Europe
11 Rue Camille Desmoulins
92782 Issy-les-Moulineaux
Cedex 9
France
http://www-
europe.cisco.com
Tel: 33 1 58 04 60 00
Fax: 33 1 58 04 61 00

Americas Headquarters
Cisco Systems, Inc.
170 West Tasman Drive
San Jose, CA 95134-1706
USA
http://www.cisco.com
Tel: 408 526-7660
Fax: 408 527-0883

Asia Pacific Headquarters
Cisco Systems Australia,
Pty., Ltd
Level 17, 99 Walker Street
North Sydney
NSW 2059 Australia
http://www.cisco.com
Tel: +61 2 8448 7100
Fax: +61 2 9957 4350

Cisco Systems has more than 200 offices in the following countries. Addresses, phone numbers, and fax numbers are listed on the Cisco Web site at www.cisco.com/go/offices

Argentina • Australia • Austria • Belgium • Brazil • Bulgaria • Canada • Chile • China • Colombia • Costa Rica • Croatia • Czech Republic • Denmark • Dubai, UAE • Finland • France • Germany • Greece • Hong Kong • Hungary • India • Indonesia • Ireland • Israel • Italy • Japan • Korea • Luxembourg • Malaysia • Mexico • The Netherlands • New Zealand • Norway • Peru • Philippines • Poland • Portugal • Puerto Rico • Romania • Russia • Saudi Arabia • Scotland • Singapore • Slovakia • Slovenia • South Africa • Spain Sweden • Switzerland • Taiwan • Thailand • Turkey • Ukraine • United Kingdom • United States • Venezuela • Vietnam • Zimbabwe

About the Author

Chris Oggerino has been employed by Cisco Systems, Inc., for over five years and is currently a Serviceability Design Engineer. As a Serviceability Design Engineer at Cisco Systems, Chris spends his time improving the reliability, availability, serviceability, and usability of Cisco products. Prior to his employment with Cisco Systems, Chris spent six years doing technical support of UNIX and internetworking products, three years in microcomputer corporate sales, and four years as a programmer at a variety of companies in the Bay Area. Chris currently resides in Los Gatos, California. You can reach Chris Oggerino at chris@oggerino.org.

About the Technical Reviewers

Scott Cherf is a Technical Leader in Cisco's IOS Technologies Division. Scott pioneered the measurement and estimation of Cisco's IOS software reliability in 1996. Since then he has presented his work both to Cisco's customers and to professional organizations. In 1999 he was invited to present this work at the IEEE's 10th annual International Symposium on Software Reliability Engineering. Scott was recently awarded a U.S. patent in the area of high availability systems design and continues to provide direction to Cisco engineers working on highly available Systems. Prior to joining Cisco in 1994, Scott spent 12 years as an engineer for Tandem Computers, Inc., where he participated in the design and implementation of the first commercial fault tolerant operating system. Scott has authored several internationally published papers on software metrics and has served as a technical editor for *IEEE Computer* magazine. Scott lives with his wife and two children in the town of Jackson, Wyoming.

Oliver Day is the founder and CTO of Digital Knox, a high security storage service provider. Oliver's research focuses on NAS, SAN, encryption, and network security. He has spent the last four years deploying enterprise solutions for Fortune 1000 companies.

B.J. Favaro Jr., ASQ Certified Reliability Engineer #4642, is a Senior Quality Engineer in Cisco's Manufacturing organization. B.J. is responsible for reliability prediction methods, reliability testing, and field reliability analysis at Cisco. Prior to joining Cisco in 1997, B.J. worked in a variety of management and engineering positions at Seagate Technology and taught mathematics at the high school and college level. B.J. was the principal developer of the SHARC spreadsheet tool provided with this book.

Dedication

This book is dedicated to Annette, Alex, and our soon-to-be-born daughter.

Acknowledgments

I want to thank B.J. Favaro and Scott Cherf first. Without their technical help and mentoring, this book would not have been possible. Scott's work on Cisco IOS Software availability was the catalyst for going from some availability research to an actual book. B.J.'s subject matter mentoring was a crucial part of the preparation and research for this book. B.J. and his team in Cisco Corporate Quality created the SHARC spreadsheet included on the CD.

Thanks to Terry Mar, Michael Shorts, and the other members of the Serviceability Design Engineering Team that supported my efforts.

Additional thanks go to Amy Lewis and Chris Cleveland from Cisco Press for their assistance in the production of this book. Amy, I think I could have kept this on the back burner for another year or two if you hadn't convinced me to get it done in time for the tradeshows. Chris, thanks for the graphics ideas and the solution to our e-mail problems!

I should also thank all the technical and grammatical editors that took the pieces that were delivered and made a book out of it.

Finally, a special thanks to my wife, Annette, for all those times she couldn't get my attention while I worked on this book—thanks for your patience.

Contents at a Glance

Part I   **Introduction to Availability**

Chapter 1   An Introduction to High Availability Networking

Chapter 2   The Basic Mathematics of High Availability

Chapter 3   Network Topology Fundamentals

Part II   **Predicting Availability**

Chapter 4   Factors that Affect Network Availability

Chapter 5   Predicting End-to-End Network Availability: The Divide-and-Conquer Method

Part III   **Examples of Analyzing Real-Word Availability**

Chapter 6   Three Cisco Products: An Availability Analysis

Chapter 7   A Small ISP Network: An Availability Analysis

Chapter 8   An Enterprise Network: An Availability Analysis

Chapter 9   A Large VoIP Network: An Availability Analysis

Appendix A   The Contents of the CD

Contents

Part I   **Introduction to Availability   3**

Chapter 1   Introduction to High Availability Networking   5

Why Do We Need High Availability?   5
What Is High Availability? 6
Attracting and Keeping Internet Customers   7
High Availability and Government Regulation   8

Presenting and Describing High Availability Measurements   8
The Percentage Method   9
The Defects per Million Method   10
MTBF, MTTR, and Availability   11
Relating the Percentage and DPM Methods   13

Additional Considerations in Measuring Availability   14
Analyzing Time Spent in Network Outages   15

Chapter 2   The Basic Mathematics of High Availability   19

Determining the Availability of Network Device Components   19
Estimating MTTR of a Network   20
The Availability Equation and Network Device Components   21
Availability and Uptime/Downtime   21

Determining the Availability of a Single Component   22

Determining the Availability of Multiple Components   23
Serial Availability   24
Simple Parallel Availability   25
N + 1 Parallel Availability   27
Serial/Parallel Availability   28

Determining Data Flow in a Network: Path Analysis   29
Using Reliability Block Diagrams for Path Analysis   29

Chapter 3   Network Topology Fundamentals   33

Serial Topology   33

Parallel Topology   35

Serial/Parallel Topology   36

Summary   39

Part II   **Predicting Availability   41**

Chapter 4   Factors That Affect Availability   43

    Predicting Hardware Availability   46
        MTBF and MTTR   46
        Calculating the Availability of a Simple Network Device   48
        Calculating the Availability of a Redundant Single System   51
        Calculating the Availability of a Network Segment   55

    Predicting Software Availability   57
        Calculating Software MTBF   57
        Examples of Including Software Availability   67

    Predicting Availability Considering the Environment   70
        MTBF and MTTR for Electrical Power   70
        Mitigating Power Loss   72
        Power Loss Summary   78

    Including Human Error and Process in Availability Calculations   79
        Historical Downtime Due to Human Error and Process   80
        Creating a Map of Downtimes Caused by Process Issues   81
        Incorporating Process Issues in Network Availability Predictions   82
        Mitigating Human Error Through Operations Process   85
        Human Error and Operation Process Summary   92

    Network Design   92
        Load Sharing Redundant Fail-over Mechanisms   93
        Standby Redundant Fail-over Mechanisms   93
        Examples of Fail-over Mechanism Calculations   93

    Summary   98

    References Used in This Chapter   99

Chapter 5   Predicting End-to-End Network Availability: The Divide-and-Conquer
                Method   101

    The Divide-and-Conquer Steps   101

    A VoIP Network Example   102
        Step 1: Determine Scenarios and RBDs   104
        Step 2: Calculate the Availability of the Network Components   106
        Step 3: Scenario-by-Scenario Redundancy Computations   106
        Step 4: End-to-End Availability Calculations for Each Scenario   109
        Section Summary: The End-to-End Network Availability Results   110

    Designing Networks for Availability Goals   111

    Summary   114

Part III   **Examples of Analyzing Real-World Availability   117**

Chapter 6   Three Cisco Products:An Availability Analysis   119

        Cisco uBR 924 Availability Calculations   119

        Cisco uBR 7246 Availability Calculations   122

        Cisco 12000 Availability Calculations   125

Chapter 7   A Small ISP Network: An Availability Analysis   131

        The Small Internet Service Provider Network   131

        Scenario 1 of The Small ISP Example   135
           System Level Calculations for Scenario 1   135
           The Network Availability for Scenario 1   147
           Summary of Scenario 1   152

        Scenario 2 of The Small ISP Example   152
           System Level Calculations for Scenario 2   153
           The Network Availability for Scenario 2   158

        Summary   161

Chapter 8   An Enterprise Network: An Availability Analysis   163

        System Level Calculations for an Enterprise Network   165
           The Cisco 3600 Availability Calculations   165
           The Cisco 1538 Availability Calculations   167

        The Downtime from Lost Power for an Enterprise Network   167

        Network Calculations for an Enterprise Network   168
           The Parallel Component Calculations   168
           The Serial Availability Calculations   169

        Human Error and Process Contribution to Downtime in an Enterprise Network   171

        Summary   171

Chapter 9   A Large VoIP Network: An Availability Analysis   173

        A VoIP over Cable Network   173

        The Availability Scenarios of VoIP over HFC   178
           Scenario 1: Data to the Internet   179
           Scenario 2: On Net Local Calling   180
           Scenario 3: Off Net Local Calling   182
           Scenario 4: Off Net Long Distance Calling   183
           A Final Note About Scenarios   183

The System Level Calculations for VoIP over HFC 184
The CPE Router System Level Calculations 184
The Head-end Router System Level Calculations 187
The Backbone Router System Level Calculations 189
The Switch (8540) System Level Calculations 193
The PSTN Gateway System Level Calculations 198
The Assumed Availability Figures 200

Network Level Availability Calculations 201
Calculating Smaller Redundant Segments 202
Small Serial Network Component Calculations 202

Major Network Service Construct Availability 213
The Internet Access Service Availability 213
The Network Control Service Availability 214
Power Contribution to Downtime 214
PSTN Gateway Services Availability Computations 217

Calculating Scenario Availability 217
The Scenario 1 Calculations 218
The Scenario 2 Calculations 219
The Scenario 3 and 4 Calculations 220

Summary 221

Appendix A The Contents of the CD 223

Computer Requirements 223

Basic Instructions for Using the CD 224

Chapter by Chapter Contents 224

Using the SHARC Spreadsheet 226
System Configuration Worksheet Procedure 227

Index 228

Introduction

Modern day networks have become crucial to our pursuit of life and happiness. Police departments, hospitals, businesses, and virtually anything we depend on runs on their networked computer systems. The more we depend on these networked computer systems, the more it affects us when they stop working.

For those of us that are involved in the planning, designing, building, and operation of these networks, the more we depend on the network, the more we need to predict problems in advance. Predicting problems in advance allows us to reduce the impact of these problems. With predictions of network availability, we can make sure our networks are going to service people satisfactorily before we build them.

Goals and Methods

The most important and somewhat obvious goal of this book is to show you how to predict availability of proposed network designs. Armed with that knowledge, you can make excellent decisions between alternative designs.

Historically, the methods used to compute availability include the use of advanced mathematics and complex processes. Those methods are the most accurate and provide the best results. However, most people that are responsible for networks do not have that mathematical background or the inclination to follow such complex, advanced processes.

This book presents simple methods for predicting availability that are acceptable in accuracy. By using only arithmetic, algebra, and a small amount of statistics, we can predict availability accurately enough to make good network design decisions

The CD included with this book includes examples and has built-in equations in order to allow you to perform network availability prediction with the least possible amount of math. What you will need to retain from the book will be the method to put your numbers into the spreadsheets.

Who Should Read This Book?

Anyone that is involved with the planning, designing, implementation, or operation of highly available networks is an appropriate reader for this book. The only exception to this list would be those that are already experts on high availability prediction and measurement.

If you are responsible for running a highly available network, you will find that this book includes only introductory material on operations. Operating a network for high availability is a science all by itself and the single section in this book is merely to remind the readers that the subject exists. Other authors are likely writing entire books on that subject.

Measuring the availability of a network is another area that deserves an entire book. Predicting the availability of a network on paper and measuring a real-life network are two completely different things. If your primary goal is to learn how to measure a network's availability, you will get only introductory material in this book. People measuring network availability, however, should definitely understand how to predict network availability. Comparing predictions with measurements enables identification of weak components in the network.

Useful References

Some of the books that I referred to for information about reliability/availability during the writing of this book targeted the advanced reliability engineer that really wants to be an expert (and use lots of calculus). In addition, I also referred to a couple of books that simply provided great information about how to build or run networks for availability (and don't use so much math). The first two books cited in the list that follows are for the advanced reliability engineer, while the second two books are geared more to building or running networks for ability.

- Lyu, Michael R., Editor. *The Handbook of Software Reliability Engineering*. McGraw Hill (ISBN: 0-07-039400-8)

- Kececioglu, Dimitri. *Reliability Engineering Handbook*. Prentice Hall (ISBN: 0-13-772302-4)

- Marcus, Evan and Hal Stern. *Blueprints for High Availability*. Wiley (ISBN: 0-47-135601-8)

- Jones, Vincent C. *High Availability Networking with Cisco*. Addison-Wesley (ISBN: 0-20-170455-2)

How This Book Is Organized

This book is divided into three major sections. Chapters 1 through 3 are introductory in nature. They introduce the reader to the concepts of predicting availability at relatively high level. Chapters 4 and 5 represent the tutorial portion of the book. These two chapters present the basic mathematics and processes for predicting availability and are presented in detail. Chapters 6 through 9 are increasingly complex examples. Chapter 6 takes the reader through the availability analysis of some routers. Chapter 9 takes the reader through the availability analysis of a fairly complex network.

Because many of the chapters in this book call upon concepts presented in previous chapters, I recommend reading the entire book in the order presented. Chapters 6 through 9 should be useful as reference material and reminders of how to perform a variety of common tasks in predicting network availability.

Summarized on a chapter-by-chapter basis, the book covers the following topics:

- **Chapter 1, "Introduction to High Availability Networking"**—This chapter introduces the reader to the basic concepts used in the book. "Availability," "Mean Time Between Failure," "Mean Time To Repair," "Parallel Redundancy," and "Serial Redundancy" are the key concepts the reader should understand after reading Chapter 1.

- **Chapter 2, "The Basic Mathematics of High Availability"**—This chapter introduces the reader to the equations that will be used in the book. "The Availability Equation," "The Serial Availability Equation," and "The Parallel Availability Equation" are presented in this chapter. This basic presentation about the mathematics used in availability analysis should prepare the reader for the tutorial sections presented in Chapters 4 and 5.

- **Chapter 3, "Network Topology Fundamentals"**—This chapter is intended to refresh the reader on network topology as related to high availability. Network design that represents parallel and serial network design is presented to remind the reader of what a parallel construct looks like in a network and what a serial construct looks like in a network. These basic building blocks will be used to create larger and larger network designs as the reader moves through the book.

- **Chapter 4, "Factors that Affect Availability"**—This chapter examines each of the five major things that contribute to network downtime. All too often, laypeople consider only hardware contributions to network downtime in their availability analysis. This chapter shows concrete methods for including hardware, software, environmental (power), human error and standard process, and network design issues in availability predictions.

- **Chapter 5, "Predicting End-to-End Network Availability: The Divide-and-Conquer Method"**—This chapter presents a method that enables a layperson to take a large network and divide it up into conquerable sections. When faced with analyzing the availability of a large network, dividing it into smaller easier parts will be required. This chapter presents the specific processes to perform this work.

- **Chapter 6, "Three Cisco Products: An Availability Analysis"**—This chapter begins our example section of the book. Starting with the simplest of devices, we work through example calculations showing how to perform the math and processes learned in the previous section. This chapter is meant to start the reader with the simplest of analysis and prepare the reader for the subsequent example, which will be more complex.

- **Chapter 7, "A Small ISP Network: An Availability Analysis"**—This chapter takes our reader beyond the calculation of individual boxes and into the analysis of a small network. While the network is fairly simple, the chapter takes the reader through the basic process of analyzing the individual boxes and then combining the results in the network calculations. Subsequent chapters will use the techniques in this chapter. This chapter also introduces the use of the SHARC spreadsheet in order to speed up the simpler calculations previously done manually.

- **Chapter 8, "An Enterprise Network: An Availability Analysis"**—This chapter presents an example that is similar in difficulty to the example in chapter seven. This example, however, is based on an enterprise type network as opposed to a service provider type network. While similar in process, networks for businesses look different from networks for large service providers and this chapter merely shows that a different looking network can be analyzed using the same tools and techniques.

- **Chapter 9, "A Large VoIP Network: An Availability Analysis"**—This chapter presents the culmination of everything in the book. The analysis completed in this chapter uses every equation, tool, and process learned in the book. A full understanding of the availability analysis in this chapter will enable the reader to analyze virtually any network for predicted network availability.

- **Appendix A, "The Contents of the CD"**—Appendix A describes the contents of the CD included with this book. The instructions for using the SHARC spreadsheet, included on the CD, are presented so that the reader understands how to use this application.

Icons Used in This Book

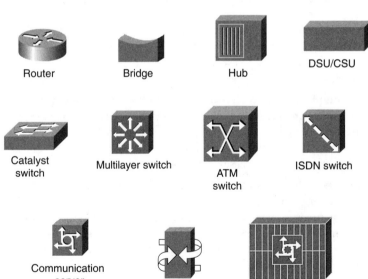

Router

Bridge

Hub

DSU/CSU

Catalyst switch

Multilayer switch

ATM switch

ISDN switch

Communication server

Gateway

Access server

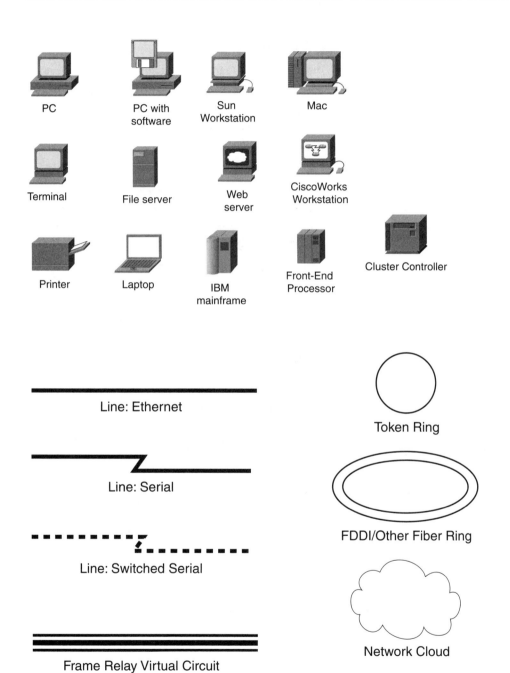

PC

PC with software

Sun Workstation

Mac

Terminal

File server

Web server

CiscoWorks Workstation

Printer

Laptop

IBM mainframe

Front-End Processor

Cluster Controller

Line: Ethernet

Line: Serial

Line: Switched Serial

Frame Relay Virtual Circuit

Token Ring

FDDI/Other Fiber Ring

Network Cloud

Command Syntax Conventions

The conventions used to present command syntax in this book are the same conventions used in the IOS Command Reference. The Command Reference describes these conventions as follows:

- Vertical bars (|) separate alternative, mutually exclusive elements.

- Square brackets [ ] indicate optional elements.

- Braces { } indicate a required choice.

- Braces within brackets [{ }] indicate a required choice within an optional element.

- **Boldface** indicates commands and keywords that are entered literally as shown. In actual configuration examples and output (not general command syntax), boldface indicates commands that are manually input by the user (such as a **show** command).

- *Italics* indicate arguments for which you supply actual values.

Introduction to Availability

Chapter 1   Introduction to High Availability Networking

Chapter 2   The Basic Mathematics of High Availability

Chapter 3   Network Topology Fundamentals

Introduction to High Availability Networking

Recently, the growth of the Internet and the use of computing systems to run businesses have blossomed in a way that few would have expected. In 1990, contacting individuals at some companies (mostly computer companies) via electronic mail was possible. Just a decade later, thousands of highly reputable companies were offering consumers the ability to actually purchase products from their web sites on the Internet. This fantastic growth of the Internet and networking has and is changing our lives in many ways.

As the Internet and networking become more a part of our lives, we are becoming dependent on them. We rely on them, and thus, we need them to be highly reliable. When you say that you want a *highly reliable network*, you are saying that you want your network to work all the time—you want it to be *highly available*.

As you proceed through this book, you will find that I have attempted to cover the subject of high availability using only arithmetic and algebra. This is by design and is the key reason I believe many people will be able to understand the material. All the other books I have read about reliability and availability use advanced mathematics such as calculus. While most of us can perform calculus when absolutely required, calculus is not easy to remember, nor is it something most enjoy. I hope that you, the reader, appreciate that what we give up in accuracy and process, we make up for in ease of understanding and accomplishment.

For those of you that want to move on to advanced reliability and availability topics, references in the front of this book will guide you.

Why Do We Need High Availability?

We have come to depend on the use of computers, access to the Internet, and the help of our favorite Internet sites. Many people regularly shop for things on the Internet. They expect to be able to go Internet shopping 24 hours per day, seven days per week.

If you have ever purchased anything online, you have probably felt a bit worried as you typed in your name, address, and credit card number—you feel as though you are giving out information that will result in yet more junk mail and the addition of your name on even more lists that cold callers use. The first-time registration process at most Web sites involves entering a wealth of personal information. On subsequent visits to the same Internet merchant, only a small portion of this information is normally requested. If you go back to the same merchant, you are unlikely to be added to more of those lists. Your privacy is retained. This first-time registration is a small but important barrier to closing the deal for the Internet merchant.

Imagine that you are a merchant on the Internet and someone visits your site and your competitor's site while shopping. Subsequently that person decides to purchase an item that you and your competitor are offering for a similar price. If the person registers on your site and buys the item, he or she very likely will be back to your site the next time a similar item is needed because he or she has already gone through the registration process. If the person registers with your competitor's site, then it is likely that he or she will buy that item from your competitor the next time it is needed. Now imagine that the consumer decided to buy from your competitor because your site was down. You not only lost the sale during the downtime, but you also lost the customer. In sales, this is about as bad as it gets.

Customers don't care why they were unable to access your site to place an order. Whether it was a Web server, network, service provider, or some other problem means nothing to them. All they care about is the fact that your site was unavailable and your competitor's site was available. Keep this story in the back of your head, and you will have no trouble understanding the cost of downtime. When the time comes to make the decision between price and availability, it will be much easier when you understand both the cost of downtime, as well as the cost of making downtime go away. You might say that competition is only a mouse click away!

Today's networks don't just carry sales transactions and business information. In fact in some places, you can pick up a telephone, dial a telephone number, and never even realize that the telephone call went over a data network instead of through the traditional telephone company infrastructure. Voice traffic is becoming yet another part of data networks, and data networks are becoming part of the telephone system.

In some cities, consumers can purchase their telephone service from a cable company instead of a traditional telephone company. These people depend on networking equipment to deliver emergency services. Imagine if you picked up your telephone to dial 911 and didn't get a dial tone. When someone's life depends on a network, network availability is crucial—it can be a matter of life or death. Network availability is now a member of an exclusive club, consisting of hospitals, ambulances, and doctors—things that can save your life.

What Is High Availability?

Have you ever been surfing the Internet and had to wait for a Web page for a minute or two? Have you ever noticed what seemed like a few minutes before anything happening? Now I don't mean waiting for a page to load because of your slow connection and pretty pictures on the page; that is a result of a slow connection. I am talking about those times when everything is going just fine and then, all of a sudden, things just seem like they stopped for a minute.

If you have experienced this, then you understand what it is like to notice some sort of network downtime. Of course, we all know this sort of thing happens all the time. A minute here, a minute there, and nobody actually worries about it too much. But imagine how you would feel if the page stopped loading and didn't budge for an hour. Imagine this happened while you were doing research for a project that needed to be done in 30 minutes. If you are like most folks, a minute here or a minute there won't bother you very much, but an hour might be a different story. An hour might irritate you enough to call someone and ask him or her what is happening with your Internet service.

Now think about your telephone. Do you remember the last time you picked up your telephone and there was no dial tone? Do you remember the last time you were on the telephone and you were disconnected? Some folks remember these things. However, most people have a hard time remembering the last time they had telephone trouble. It's hard to remember because it doesn't happen very often. If you do remember the last time you had no dial tone, how did you feel during that experience? In most cases, the feeling of having no dial tone is considerably more traumatic than having no access to the web. No dial tone equals no help in an emergency. No dial tone is a big deal to everyone. No web access is usually a minor inconvenience.

If you are about to build a network that provides dial tone, then you are going to have to build a highly available network. People will not stand for loss of dial tone because dial tone is something that they require all the time. Networks that provide dial tone must be highly available, or they will not be used. The customer will find a way to replace the network with something more available if they sense the network is not reliable.

Attracting and Keeping Internet Customers

Imagine that you are the customer and that you have a choice of buying your telephone service from your traditional telephone company, your cable television company, or your Internet service provider (ISP). Most people would say that they want to buy their telephone service from the telephone company. After all, the telephone company has been the most reliable service of all their services. The telephone company is even more reliable than the power company in most cities.

Now let us complicate the issue. Say that you can buy your phone service from your ISP for 60 percent less money than you have been paying for your phone service from the phone company. Most people will consider changing services for that much of a discount. The offer is even more attractive if you have two telephone lines. Maybe you can move the second line to the ISP, but leave the first line with the older, more established service. Perhaps you want to just try out the new discounted service, but only on your extra line.

Everyone I know would be willing to put his or her second line on the alternate source for a while. But everyone I asked said that he or she would switch back to the telephone company if the new service proved unreliable. Even at a 60 percent cost discount, high availability is a requirement. Reliability is not something that most people are willing to give up, no matter how much less money they have to spend for their phone service.

High Availability and Government Regulation

In the United States, telephone service is regulated by the government. Telephone companies are required to report downtime of their systems to the Federal Communications Commission (FCC). If a phone company has been negligent or had too much downtime, the government imposes a fine.

Life or Death and High Availability

A friend of mine used to work for a telephone company as a manager of a team that fixed the telephone network whenever it broke. He was under pressure to fix the network very fast whenever it wasn't working.

He once told me, "You haven't ever felt pressure and pain until you've been standing in front of an FCC review panel explaining why the phone system was down when a citizen needed to use it for a 911 phone call. There is no feeling as bad as knowing that someone died because your network was not working."

If you are planning to build a network that carries 911 traffic, you can expect that the government is going to be regulating the network at some point. For now, data networks are not regulated. But someday soon as more data networks carry voice and more of them make it possible for people to call 911 over them these networks will be regulated. Network repair folks and network managers are going to have to report downtime to the government.

Network downtime is going to be a big deal—yet another reason why high availability has to be designed into a network.

Presenting and Describing High Availability Measurements

There are two main ways to state the availability of a network: the *percentage method* and the *defects per million method*. Once you understand the basics of these methods, you will understand what you are reading when you get an availability analysis report. Both of these methods use figures like MTBF (Mean Time Between Failure) and MTTR (Mean Time To

Repair). The following sections describe these two methods as well as the terms MTBF and MTTR.

The Percentage Method

You have probably heard the term *five 9s* in relationship to the availability of a network. When someone says this, he or she is really saying that the device or network is 99.999 percent available. In fact, *99.999 percent availability* is a sure sign that the person is using the percentage method.

NOTE   When you are actually doing the math of calculating availability, you are likely to see a number that looks like 0.99999, rather than 99.999 percent. Remember that you have to multiply by 100 to come up with a percentage, which is how most people are used to seeing availability described.

The essential use of the availability percentage is to figure out how much downtime you are going to have over a year-long period. You determine downtime by multiplying the number of minutes in a year by the percentage of availability. This gives you the minutes per year that you will be operational. The balance is the downtime you can expect.

Because there are 365 days per year, 24 hours per day, and 60 minutes per hour, we can calculate that there are 525,600 minutes per year. However, this does not account for leap years, which have an extra day. The way that we will account for leap years, since they happen every fourth year, is to add one fourth of a day to every year. This results in 525,960 minutes per year, which is the number that is used in all the calculations in this book. 525,960 minutes per year is important enough, in availability calculations, that you will likely have it memorized before long—as you become well versed in performing availability calculations.

In addition to the number of minutes per year, *annual reliability* should be understood. Annual reliability is the number of times each year that a device fails. When you know the MTBF for a device, you can divide that MTBF by the number of hours in a year (8766) to predict the average number of failures per year. We will be using this knowledge when we predict how many minutes a network is out of service while it switches from a broken device to a working device in a redundant situation.

Because we know the number of minutes in a year and because we now understand that availability is a percentage, we can calculate downtime for a year based on the availability number. Table 1-1 describes how the number of 9s relates to uptime and downtime.

Table 1-1   *Number of 9s; Uptime and Downtime*

Number of Nines	Availability Percentage	Minutes of Uptime per Year (Percentage * 525,960)	Minutes of Downtime per Year (525,960 – Uptime)	Annual Downtime
1	90.000%	473,364	52,596	36.5 days
2	99.000%	520,700.4	5259.6	3.5 days
3	99.900%	525,434.0	525.96	8.5 hours
4	99.990%	525,907.4	52.596	1 hour
5	99.999%	525,954.7	5.2596	5 minutes
6	99.9999%	525,959.5	0.52596	32 seconds

As you can see, for each 9 in the availability percentage, a significant increase in performance is achieved. It is often rumored that after the second 9, each additional 9 costs twice as much. That is to say, if you want to go from three 9s to four 9s, the amount of money you spend building your network is going to double! But remember, double the money buys you 10 times more availability.

The Defects per Million Method

The second way to state availability is by using the defects per million (DPM) method. Using this method, we describe the number of failures that have occurred during a million hours of running time for a device or a network. It is common to see this method used for existing large networks.

With the DPM method, we can report issues of reliability that the percentage method would have difficulty tracking. Because DPM is often used for existing networks, we can use it to measure partial and full network outages. We can also measure the million hours in terms of hours of operation of the network, the hours of operation of the devices (added together) that comprise the network, or perhaps even the hours of use that the users get from the network.

In order to clarify the DPM method, let us work through a couple of short examples. Assume that your network consists of 1000 hubs, switches, and routers. Assume that you count any degradation in performance as an outage. Also assume that we base our figures on 8766 hours per year (accounting for leap years) and that our failure reports are done monthly. To determine hours of operation per month, multiply 1000 devices times 8766 hours per year and divide by 12 to compute 730,500 hours of operation each month. As you can see in Figure 1-1, you compute one million hours divided by the number of operating hours to get the number of defects per million hours for a single defect. Then you multiply this result by the number of defects to get the total defects per million hours. So if we had two failures during a month, we would report that as 2.74 DPM for the month.

Figure 1-1   *Determining Availability Given Two Failures in One Month*

Hours per year = 8766 (Accounts for leap years)

Number of Devices = 1000

Accumulated Hours per Year = 8,766,000 hours

Accumulated Hours per Month = $\dfrac{8,766,000}{12}$

= 730,500 hours

Converting 2 Defects per 730,500 hours:

$$\frac{1,000,000}{730,500} = 1.3689$$

2 * 1.3689 = $\boxed{2.74 \text{ Defects per Million}}$

Another way of reporting failures using the DPM method would be to base the million hours on network use. Let us assume that our network is large and constantly growing. Let us also assume that we bill our customers for each hour they use the network. Let us say that we have several thousand customers and that over the period of a month, they accumulate 1,200,000 hours of operation. In this network, if we had two failures, then the resulting DPM would be 1.67 DPM. Figure 1-2 shows you the calculations.

Figure 1-2   *Another DPM Calculation Example*

Total Network Hours = 1,200,000

Total Network Failures = 2

$$\frac{1 \text{ million}}{\text{Actual time}} = \frac{1,000,000}{1,200,000}$$

= .83333

DPM   = .83333 * 2

= 1.67

MTBF, MTTR, and Availability

So far, you have learned about failures per million hours of operation and about downtime as a percentage. In order to have a feeling of the health of a network, relating the number of failures and the length of each failure to each other is helpful.

MTBF is a number that you have probably seen on product documentation or in some other specification for a product. It describes the number of hours between failures for a particular device. A similar term is Mean Time to Failure (MTTF), and it describes the amount of time from putting a device into service until the device fails.

Many people confuse these two terms. Using MTBF instead of MTTF and MTTF instead of MTBF in most situations makes very little difference. Technically, the mathematical equation for calculating availability that we will use in this book should use the term MTTF, according to the historic standards on the subject. You will nearly always be able to get an MTBF number about products you wish to purchase. Finding MTTF numbers about products is difficult. Technically, the companies stating MTBF about their products are very likely to be giving you MTTF and not even know it.

In keeping with this minor industry oversight and to simplify our lives, this book uses MTBF in place of MTTF and discards MTTF completely because it will make very little difference in our calculations. Before getting into an example that shows exactly how little difference it makes to switch MTBF and MTTF numbers, you have learn about MTTR and the availability equation.

MTTR is the amount of time (on average) that elapses between a network failing and the network being restored to proper working order. In most cases, MTTR includes a little bit of time to notice that the network has failed. Then it includes some time to diagnose the problem. Finally, MTTR includes some time to perform the appropriate action to fix the network and a small amount of time for the repairs to bring the network into proper working order. In an ideal world, the timing to detect, diagnose, and repair a network problem will be measured in minutes. However, sometimes things happen in the night and no one notices for hours. Sometimes the first diagnosis is wrong and several hours are wasted fixing something that isn't broken. The key point here is to remember that there are three phases to fixing a network problem:

- Detection
- Diagnosis
- Repair

You can calculate percentage availability directly if you have both the MTBF and the MTTR numbers for a particular device, as shown in the availability equation in Equation 1-1.

Equation 1-1   The Availability Equation

$$\text{Availability} = \frac{\text{MTBF}}{\text{MTBF} + \text{MTTR}}$$

If we use Equation 1-1 to work a couple small examples, you can easily see how the difference between MTBF and MTTF makes no difference for our purposes.

Let us assume that a device we want to measure for availability has an MTTF of 200,000 hours. Let us also assume it has an MTTR of six hours. Let us further assume that the MTBF would be 200,006 hours, which is mathematically correct. By plugging all these numbers into the availability equation in Equation 1-1 and using a calculator, we get the two results, 0.9999700009 and 0.9999700017999. Now if we round these numbers, we get 0.99997 and 0.99997—the same. Figure 1-3 shows the work behind this.

Figure 1-3   *Comparing MTTF and MTBF for Availability*

$$\text{MTTF Availability} = \frac{\text{MTTF}}{\text{MTTF} + \text{MTTR}}$$

$$\text{Our MTBF Availability} = \frac{\text{MTBF}}{\text{MTBF} + \text{MTTR}}$$

$$\text{MTTF Availability} = \frac{200,000}{200,006}$$

$$= 0.9999700009$$

$$\text{Our MTBF Availability} = \frac{200,006}{200,012}$$

$$= 0.9999700017999$$

Both Equations Round to 0.99997

Relating the Percentage and DPM Methods

With MTBF and MTTR, it is possible to convert between the percentage and DPM methods. Since availability is a percentage and DPM is not, we need MTTR in order to do the conversion. MTBF will help because we use it to arrive at the percentage availability number. The best way to illustrate the conversion is through an example.

Assume that we have a network that is special because all the routers and switches in it have the exact same MTBF: 200,000 hours. Furthermore, assume that the MTTR for these devices is six hours because a support contract guarantees the replacement of any failed device in six or fewer hours. Using the availability equation, we can easily arrive at the same answer we got for these figures in the preceding section—an availability of 99.997 percent. Taking 99.997 percent and multiplying by the number of minutes in a year, we get the answer—15.78 minutes per year of downtime per device.

In order to predict annual downtime using the DPM method, we determine the total amount of downtime over one million hours and then convert that to annual downtime. First we divide 1,000,000 by 200,000 (MTBF) to get 5, which is the number of defects per million. Then we multiply that by the downtime (6 hours) to get the total downtime per million hours (30 hours). To convert to downtime per year, we simply calculate the ratio of "hours in a year" over one million hours, and multiply that by our 30 hour result. This produces .26 hours or 15.78 minutes, which matches our annual downtime result using the percentage method.

Although the conversion between percentage and DPM methods can be done, it usually is not. The DPM method is most often used to measure existing network performance. The percentage method is most often used to predict network performance based on a design. The reasoning for this is based on simplicity of use and the ease of getting the data to put into the equations.

For the percentage method, we simply take the MTBF provided by the manufacturer of the product or products in question. Then we estimate the MTTR based on the contract we sign with the provider of the network. From this we can estimate the predicted availability of the network or network device.

Figure 1-4 *Relating the Percentage and DPM Methods*

$$\text{MTBF} = 200{,}000 \text{ hours}$$

$$\text{MTTR} = 6 \text{ hours}$$

$$\text{Availability} = \frac{200{,}000}{200{,}006}$$

$$= 0.99997$$

$$\text{Annual Downtime} = (1 - 0.99997) * 525{,}960 \text{ minutes per year}$$

$$\boxed{\text{Annual Downtime} = 15.78 \text{ Minutes}}$$

$$\text{DPM} = \frac{1{,}000{,}000}{200{,}000}$$

$$= 5$$

$$\text{Downtime per Million Hours} = 5 * 6$$

$$= 30$$

$$\text{Failures per Year} = \frac{8766}{1{,}000{,}000}$$

$$= 0.008766$$

$$\text{Downtime per Year} = 0.008766 * 30$$

$$= .26 \text{ hours}$$

$$\boxed{\text{Annual Downtime} = 15.78 \text{ Minutes}}$$

For the DPM method, we accumulate millions of hours of run time (by machine or by use) and then note each failure that occurs.

Either way creates a scenario by which we can determine and compare performance over time or performance from one manufacturer to the other.

This book uses the percentage method because we are mainly concerned with answering the question: How available will this network be if we build it according to this design? Because the answer to this question is a prediction based on available information such as MTBF and suggested service contracts, the percentage method is the simplest way to provide the answer.

Additional Considerations in Measuring Availability

Although considering every possible scenario is beyond the scope of this book, some additional thoughts about measuring availability are in order. The following sections introduce the concepts of partial outages and process failures (that is, human error). Partial outages are mostly omitted from this book as they are an advanced availability subject and incredibly difficult to predict. The method for including human error-induced downtime is introduced here and described in more detail in Chapter 4, "Factors That Affect Availability."

Analyzing Time Spent in Network Outages

If you decide that you want to measure your network's availability after it is built, you might also decide that you want to know more than just the uptime and downtime. You might also want to know how much time is spent in partial outages. You can arrive at this data in several ways, but the following way is my favorite.

First you must know the type and quantity of devices on your network. You must also decide which you want to measure. Each time your network has an outage of any sort, you must log it and categorize it. You need to collect the following information for each outage:

- The device (including model, serial number, hardware version, software version, etc.)
- The nature of the outage (complete failure or partial outage)
- The time the outage began
- The time the outage was recognized
- The time the outage was diagnosed
- The time the solution was implemented
- The time the network was fully restored to normal operation

From this information, you can derive plenty of statistical information over time that will enable the reduction of downtime.

The first thing is to calculate DPM by counting the number of failures (of a particular device type) against the accumulated operating hours (of that particular device type). Next, take the average length of the outages (in hours) to determine the MTTR for that particular device type. This gives you the basic data that enables you to compare performance over time for your network. In Chapter 4, in the human error and standard processes section, we will perform an example that should clarify these ideas for you.

Next, compare the different devices and make sure that only those devices with the best performance are used in your network. If you find that some routers have a higher failure rate than other routers, then you should figure out why or possibly switch to the more reliable model. If a particular router is not as reliable as you would have expected, you should contact the manufacturer. Cisco Systems, for example, has improved the reliability of its routers through both hardware and software upgrades based on this type of feedback from customers.

Another way to improve availability is to improve your processes for handling network failures. Within a particular type of equipment and outage, analyze each of the time segments between the failure and the restoration. You are looking for the average and the range for each of the segments. If a particular segment shows a large range, consider it suspect. Compare the fast restoration cases (within this time segment) to the slow restoration cases to see why they were different. The reason for this difference is obvious.

Here is simple example. Say you notice that when routers fail, the average time to recognize the problem is five minutes, but sometimes it takes nearly an hour. This leads to further research. Every time a router fails between 8 a.m. and noon and between 1 p.m. and 5 p.m., the problem recognition time average is five minutes and the range is from three to seven minutes. Every time a router fails from noon to 1 p.m., the recognition time average is 35 minutes and the range is from four to 61 minutes. This should tell you that at least one person should remain in the network operations center during lunch hour.

This same method also works when a particular problem is difficult and some of your staff need more training to detect or solve the problem at the same speed as your senior staff. Finally, this method might point out a problem where the manufacturer could improve the troubleshooting capabilities of the product.

CHAPTER 2

The Basic Mathematics of High Availability

Calculating availability requires mathematics. As the depth of availability research increases, the mathematical equations get more complex. This book makes it possible for people unfamiliar with calculus to perform network availability analysis. This chapter is designed to introduce you to the equations we will be using in this book.

The equations in this book are as simple as possible, while still maintaining accuracy. Some more advanced availability experts might say that I have taken a few liberties that could make the results slightly skewed. However, I believe that the equations presented in this chapter will provide perfectly adequate results for comparing network versus network availability and estimating whether a particular design is better than another design.

Determining the Availability of Network Device Components

In order to calculate the availability of a network, you have to calculate the availability of the individual network devices comprising it. And in order to calculate the availability of a network device, you have to calculate the availability of its components. The calculation of the availability of the devices' components is the starting point of the mathematics of availability.

Cisco Systems uses what is called the *Telcordia* (formerly Bell Core) *Parts Count Method*. The Parts Count Method is described in Technical Reference document TR-332, "Reliability prediction procedure for Electronic Equipment" from December 1997.

NOTE   In order to avoid the complex mathematics that created the need for this simple book, this chapter summarizes the contents of TR-332. If you would like to get this document for further reading, you can purchase it from the Telcordia Web site at www.telcordia.com.

TR-332 describes the method used to determine the reliability of each component on a circuit board—capacitors, resistors, or other components. Each component is associated with a *FIT* (failures in 10^9), which represents the failures per billion hours of running time you can expect from that component. In other words, one FIT is one failure per one billion hours. TR-332 also includes factors by which you can influence the number of FITs for a particular component, based on things like temperature, environment, and quality control processes.

Cisco Systems uses a software product to do FIT calculations automatically. Cisco quality engineers feed the entire list of materials, called a *bill of materials* (BOM), that make up a circuit board into the program. Next, they tell the program any special adjustments that need to be made, such as running any particular components over their rated voltage or temperature. The program then returns the total FITs for BOM and the predicted MTBF for the circuit board.

Cisco MTBF Results

Over the past 15 years, Cisco Systems has found that the numbers produced by using Relex's (Telcordia TR-332 based) software are extremely conservative. In fact, Cisco uses a multiple of the results from the prediction software in an attempt to make the results more accurate. Even with this additional doubling of the MTBF, Cisco Systems products greatly outperform their predicted MTBFs. This is most likely a result of the software not accounting for conservatively engineered circuits and superior quality control of the components themselves.

A great example of these MTBF numbers is Cisco's 2500 line of products. Cisco has shipped more than a million 2500s to customers all over the world. When comparing the return rates to Cisco Systems repair and logistics organizations with the predicted MTBFs for the 2500s, it has been found that the product outperforms the estimates by a wide margin. In fact, 2500 routers on some networks have been running continuously, without a reboot or a glitch of any sort, for over eight years!

The MTBF numbers for Cisco products are analyzed and published internally for all Cisco employees. These numbers can be used to calculate MTBF for Cisco routers and switches at the request of customers. If you are a customer and you request an MTBF of a Cisco product, the person responding to your request will go into the MTBF database and get the MTBF for the components that make up your system. He or she will then either present you with the MTBF numbers from the database or use equations like those in this book to present the availability of the system to you.

NOTE   As you will see in Chapter 4, "Factors That Affect Availability," hardware is not the only thing that affects the availability of a network: methods are available to predict software MTBF as well as hardware MTBF.

Estimating MTTR of a Network

As you learned in Chapter 1, "Introduction to High Availability Networking," MTTR is another important component of availability. You can measure MTTR in an existing network by taking the average of the time the network is down for each failure. You can predict MTTR based on a variety of methods.

The method we will use in this book to predict MTTR is based on Cisco Systems service contracts. If a customer determines that high availability is required for a network, they could purchase a four-hour, on-site service contract. This contract would be somewhat expensive but would guarantee that a repair technician and parts would be on their site no more than four hours after they called Cisco for support. With this type of service contract, I would give that company an MTTR of four hours. If the company opted for a service contract of eight hours, I would give them an MTTR of about eight hours.

For our purposes in this book, the MTTR is arbitrary. The number you use should be based on the service contract you purchase from your service vendor. In this book, we will use a variety of MTTR values so that you can be sure to understand the impact of short and long MTTRs to network availability. You will also want to note, in Chapter 4, that software MTTR can often be much shorter than hardware if the software has self correcting capabilities.

The Availability Equation and Network Device Components

Chapter 1 includes a basic description of availability. In order to calculate availability, you must use the availability equation. The availability equation (shown again in Equation 2-1) describes how you use MTBF and MTTR to find a percentage result:

> The ratio of uptime to total time

In other words, the percentage availability is equal to the amount of uptime divided by the total time during some time period t. Time t will consist of both the running time and the non-running time for the box.

Equation 2-1   The Availability Equation

$$\text{Availability} = \frac{\text{MTBF}}{\text{MTBF} + \text{MTTR}}$$

As you can see, when you have MTBF and MTTR, you can calculate availability with a simple calculator.

Availability and Uptime/Downtime

When you have an availability percentage, you can calculate uptime and downtime. Conversely, if you have the uptime or the downtime you can calculate availability.

Because availability is a percentage that represents the uptime divided by the total time, you can multiply any time period by the availability number and get the amount of uptime over that period. Of course, the difference in the total time and the uptime is the downtime.

In most cases, you are going to want the downtime per year. You will do this by subtracting the availability from 1 and then multiplying the result by the number of minutes in a year.

If you have a device that is available 99.99 percent (or 0.99990), then you can expect 52.596 minutes per year of downtime as calculated in Figure 2-1.

Figure 2-1   *Getting Downtime from Availability*

1 year = 525,960 minutes*
Uptime = Availability * Time
Annual Uptime = Availability * 525,960
Annual Downtime = 525,960 – Annual Uptime

Availability = .9999
Annual Uptime = .9999 * 525,960
Annual Uptime = 525,907.4
Annual Downtime = 525,960 – 525,907.4
= 52.596

Downtime = (1 – Availability) * Time
Annual Downtime = (1 – .9999) * 525,960
= 52.596

*Adjusted for leap years

Determining the Availability of a Single Component

If you wanted to calculate the availability of a particular component, use the availability equation with the MTBF and MTTR for that component. If the component in question had an MTBF of 100,000 hours and an MTTR of 6 hours, then we could calculate the availability to be 0.99994. The resulting downtime would be about 31.5 minutes per year for that component as calculated in Figure 2-2.

Figure 2-2   *Finding the Downtime of a Single Component*

$$Availability = \frac{MTBF}{MTBF + MTTR}$$

$$MTBF = 100,000 \text{ hours}$$

$$MTTR = 6 \text{ hours}$$

$$Availability = \frac{100,000}{100,000 + 6}$$

$$Availability = \frac{100,000}{100,006}$$

$$Availability = 0.99994$$

$$Annual\ Downtime = (1 - .99994) * 525,960$$

$$= 31.5576 \text{ minutes}$$

Determining the Availability of Multiple Components

To calculate the availability of multiple components, you must understand more equations: the serial equation and the parallel availability equation. One important thing to remember is that components can be system components (such as circuit boards) or network components (such as routers or switches).

You will use the serial availability equation whenever all the parts must work for the system (or network) to work. Equation 2-2 shows the serial availability equation.

Equation 2-2   Serial Availability Equation

$$SerialAvailability = \prod_{i=1}^{n} ComponentAvailability_{(i)}$$

i represents the component number
n represents the number of components

In a serial system, if any component fails then the entire system fails. For example, if a product consists of a power supply and a circuit board, you have a serial system. If the power supply fails, then the system fails, and if the single circuit board fails, then the system fails.

Sometimes the components in a system are in parallel, or redundant. Although there are several different parallel designs, Equation 2-3 shows the basic parallel equation. This equation applies to the situation where two devices are in parallel with each other.

Equation 2-3   Parallel Availability Equation

$$ParallelAvailability = 1 - \left[\prod_{i=1}^{n} (1 - ComponentAvailability_{(i)}) \right]$$

i represents the component number
n represents the number of components

In a *parallel system,* two or more components are combined such that the system will work as long as any of the parallel components are still working. If you have two parallel components and one of them fails, the system continues (or at least should continue) to run without failure. Most systems that include parallel components also include serial components.

In order to calculate the availability of multiple components, you must understand the serial and parallel availability equations. The following sections describe these equations and how they relate to one another. First you will learn how to determine the availability of a serial system. Then you will learn how to combine parallel components to get their availability (that is, availability in parallel). Finally, we will discuss how to calculate the availability of a mixed serial/parallel system.

Serial Availability

In order to estimate the availability of a serial system, you multiply together the availability of the components. For example, in the system with a single circuit board and a power supply, you multiply the availability of the power supply by the availability of the circuit board. Figure 2-3 shows these calculations.

Figure 2-3   *Determining Serial Availability in a Two-Component System*

Power Supply = 99.999% availability
= 0.99999
Circuit Board = 99.994% availability
= 0.99994

System Availability = 0.99999 * 0.99994
= 0.99993

As you can see, two components with availability of 99.999 percent and 99.994 percent combined in a serial configuration provide 99.993 percent total system availability.

Because most systems contain more than two components, we need to use an equation that works for some number (*N*) of components. Although this equation contains a symbol that might be Greek to some of you (because it is), you can remember that all this equation does is multiply all the component availability's together, like the system in Figure 2-3. The symbol for multiplying *N* components together is a capital Greek letter Pi (Π). Figure 2-4 shows the equation and a short example.

Figure 2-4 *Determining Serial Availability in an N-Component System*

$$\text{System Availability} = \prod_{i=1}^{n} \text{availability}_{(i)}$$

Power Supply = 99.999%

Circuit Board 1 = 99.994%

Circuite Board 2 = 99.98%

$$\text{System Availability} = \prod_{i=1}^{n} \text{availability}_{(i)}$$

$$= .99999 * .99994 * .9998$$

$$= .99973$$

In English, you say, "For the components 'I' going from 1 to N (the number of components), multiply by availability$_{(i)}$." In programming this is a "for I equal 1 to N" loop, multiplying each availability by each other.

As you can see from Figure 2-4, the serial availability equation is simple to use even though is includes a Greek symbol.

Simple Parallel Availability

To find simple parallel availability, you first multiply the unavailability of each of the parallel parts. The result of the multiplication of the unavailabilities is subtracted from 1 to get the availability result. In the next section, we will talk about a more complex method of parallel calculation.

In Figure 2-5, you see a symbol with both I and N in it. As with the serial equation, this simply means to multiply each "unavailability of component (I)" by each other until *N* "unavailability of component (I)s" have been multiplied together.

Figure 2-5   *Determining Availability in a Parallel System*

$$\text{Parallel Availability} = 1 - \left[\prod_{i=1}^{n} (1 - \text{availability}_{(i)}) \right]$$

N = Number of Components in Parallel
I = The Component Number

To clarify the equation, let's look at a small example. Assume that you have a system and that inside the system are two components in parallel. For simplicity's sake, we'll say the two components are identical and both have an availability of 99.9 percent (that is, 0.999 availability). Figure 2-6 shows how we would combine these two components together to get their parallel availability.

Figure 2-6   *Determining Parallel Availability in a Two-Component System*

Component 1 = 99.9% availability

Component 2 = 99.9% availability

$$\text{Parallel Availability} = 1 - \left[\prod_{i=1}^{2} (1 - \text{availability}_{(i)}) \right]$$

$$= 1 - \left[(1 - .999) * (1 - .999) \right]$$

$$= 1 - \left[1 - .000001 \right]$$

$$= .999999$$

Percent Availability = .999999 * 100

Percent Availability = 99.9999%

It is important that we take note of a couple things about parallel availability. First, systems designed with parallel components usually have some method for moving work from the failed component to the remaining component. This feature is called a *fail-over mechanism*. Sometimes fail-over mechanisms themselves fail. We are going to exclude that probability in this book because we could continue exploring the depths of availability to no end if we went down that path. (You'll learn more about fail-over mechanisms in Chapter 4 in the network design section.) Next, we must note that simply combining a couple of items in parallel is not going to happen very often. In fact, most systems and networks include both parallel and serial components. The next section describes the method for calculating both parallel and serial scenarios.

Before we can move on to our next section on combining serial and parallel components, we need to introduce a more complex method of computing parallel availability.

N + 1 Parallel Availability

We have discussed how to calculate the availability when devices are in simple parallel arrangements. In other words, if we have any number of devices in parallel, we now know how to calculate the availability as long as any single device remains operational. This method is most often implemented in real life by having two devices when you need only one device.

In the real world, we might need more than one device for proper system or network functionality. An example is where we need at least two power supplies in our big router to supply enough power. In that situation, we might choose to have a single, backup power supply instead of two backup power supplies. This method of redundancy is called, *N + M redundancy.* N represents the number required and *M* represents the number installed.

Our coverage of N + M redundancy in this book is limited because we want to limit the mathematics required to simple equations as much as possible. However, in our examples in Chapter 7, "A Small ISP Network: An Availability Analysis," Chapter 8, "An Enterprise Network: An Availability Analysis," and Chapter 9, "A Large VoIP Network: An Availability Analysis," we will be using router and network examples which include the N + M and N + 1 redundancy methods.

Coverage of N + M is given to you by including the SHARC (System Hardware and Reliability Calculator) spreadsheet tool on the CD with this book. That tool can calculate N + M redundancy for you. The SHARC spreadsheet is introduced and used in Chapter 7. Appendix A describes the contents of the CD and the usage of the SHARC spreadsheet.

When you come across N + 1, calculate it using Equation 2-4.

Equation 2-4 The N + 1 Redundancy Equation

$$A = nA^{(n-1)} * (1 - A) + A^n$$

A = Total Availability
n = Number of devices

NOTE   We assume an equal availability for each component.

However, N + 1 and N + M redundancies are best done by the SHARC spreadsheet. We will not use this spreadsheet until the later chapters in order to make sure we have the basic equations memorized—before we start using the easy tools!

Serial/Parallel Availability

Most systems (and networks) contain both serial and parallel components. The method we use to calculate serial/parallel availability involves two steps:

Step 1 Calculate the parallel availability for all the parallel components.

Step 2 Combine the results of Step 1, along with all the serial components, using the serial availability method.

In order to perform these calculations, you need some knowledge about the system or network. You must understand the path through which the data will travel. You must understand which components are critical or redundant. The availability of a system or a network depends on the availability of the path between Points A and B between which data must flow. Chapter 3, "Network Topology Fundamentals," covers the basics of these considerations.

Because we know the parallel equation and the serial equation, we will now build those together into the serial/parallel equations and process. The best way to illustrate serial/parallel availability is by example, as shown in Figure 2-7. In this example, we consider a system that has a single circuit board and two redundant power supplies. The circuit board is 99.994 percent available, and each of the power supplies is 99.95 percent available.

Figure 2-7 *Determining Serial/Parallel Availability in a Three-Component Parallel Example*

Circuit Board = 99.994%
Power Supplies = 99.95%

Step 1: The parallel power supply component calculations

$$\text{Parallel Availability} = 1 - \left[\prod_{i=1}^{2} (1 - \text{availability}_{(i)}) \right]$$

$$= 1 - (1 - .9995) * (1 - .9995)$$

$$= .99999975$$

Step 2: The circuit board and redundant power in serial calculations

$$\text{Serial Availability} = \prod_{i=1}^{2} (\text{availability}_{(i)})$$

$$= .99994 * .99999975$$

As you can see, even though the power supplies are not all that reliable, combining two components in parallel greatly increases the availability of the overall system.

Determining Data Flow in a Network: Path Analysis

The most common situation that will occur in your studies of availability will be the combination of serial and parallel components in a large system. Furthermore, not all of these components will be required for data to flow in the scenario for which you are concerned. Many network devices connect a large number of networks together. If you are considering the availability of only the first two networks that the device joins, then you won't care if some component carrying traffic to the third network fails.

This consideration of the data flow is called *path analysis*. Path analysis makes it possible to use exactly the same equations that we have been using for calculating the availability of a system to calculate the availability of a network. In network availability calculations, we use the network devices, such as routers and switches, as components. In network computations, we might use path analysis to determine the data path through a Cisco 12000 router and use those components to analyze the availability of the Cisco 12000. Once that calculation is complete, we would use the result as a component in a network analysis.

Using Reliability Block Diagrams for Path Analysis

To perform a path analysis, creating an availability block diagram is often a good idea.

For now, we'll consider a very simple example of networking, using a large router with components that are not crucial to our calculations. We need to eliminate those from our calculations and perform the analysis of availability for something we care about. In Figure 2-8, a large network device is connected to three networks. We only want to know the availability from Network 1 to Network 2. Therefore, the hardware that supports the connection to Network 3 can be eliminated from our calculations.

Figure 2-8   *Analyzing the Path from Network 1 to Network 2*

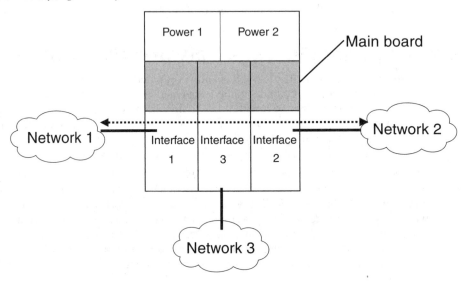

As you can see from Figure 2-8, our device includes two redundant power supplies called Power 1 and Power 2. Several steps are involved with calculating the availability of a device (or network) which has both parallel and serial components.

In this case our steps are

Step 1   Determine the availability of each component

Step 2   Compute the availability of the dual power supplies

Step 3   Multiply the availability of all components with the result from Step 2.

Figure 2-9 shows the availability analysis from Network 1 to Network 2.

Figure 2-9   *Path Analysis: Determining the Availability from Network 1 to Network 2*

Power Supplies = 99.9%
Motherboard = 99.994%
Interface Cards = 99.95%

Step 1: Parallel calculations

Power $= 1- [(1-.999) * (1-.999)]$
$= .999999$

Step 2: Serial calculations

Power = .999999
Motherboard = .99994
Interface 1 = .9995
Interface 2 = .9995

System Availability $= .999999 * .99994 * .9995 * .9995$
$= .998939$
$= 99.8939\%$

As you can tell from Figure 2-9, we used 99.9 percent for the power supplies, 99.994 percent for the motherboard, and 99.95 percent for each of the interface boards. After all the calculations were completed, the result of 99.8939 percent describes the availability from Network 1 to Network 2 via the device shown in the diagram. Note that interface 3 was not included in the calculations because it was not a required component. Using 525,960 minutes per year, and our standard method for calculation, we arrive at about 9.3 hours per year of downtime. Even with redundant power supplies, this system would cause a considerable amount of downtime in a network. As you proceed through this book, you will see many examples. Through these examples, you should learn a variety of ways to correct problems with too much annual downtime.

In Chapter 5, "Predicting End-to-End Network Availability: The Divide-and-Conquer Method," we are going to talk about the "divide-and-conquer" method of performing availability analysis. This will expand, greatly, on how one performs reliability block diagrams. What you should have learned here is that you need to consider which components to include in your calculations. After Chapter 5, you should know exactly how to perform the tasks.

CHAPTER 3

Network Topology Fundamentals

Network topology is crucial to the availability of a network. When I say "network topology" here, I am referring to both the arrangement of your networking devices and the failover methods you choose. Parallel topologies provide high availability because even if network devices fail, the network will still run. Serial topologies provide reduced availability compared to parallel topologies because the entire network depends on all the devices working, with little or no room for any failure. Of course keeping a network simple increases availability while at the same time limiting your ability to make all parts parallel.

Because of this complex balance between simplicity and redundancy, network design is nearly an art. All the mathematics in the world will show you that the parallel solution is more reliable. However, if the fail-over mechanism breaks because of some software bug or a misconfiguration, the parallel design basically created more things to break.

Although you are probably well versed in network design, this chapter is meant to be a quick refresher to tickle your memory and help you think about topology more specifically in terms of availability. Although topology can be a large subject, the basic building blocks for all networks are serial, parallel, and serial/parallel topologies. Limiting our studies to these three topologies will enable us to focus on our key goal of learning how to predict availability.

Serial Topology

Each device in a serial topology takes in some data from one direction and moves that data off to some other place. Although serial topologies often run switching or routing protocols, they are not usually used for healing the network when a network device fails. In a serial topology, the switching and routing protocols are run to segment the network traffic and make sure the right bits go to the right buckets.

Figure 3-1 shows a few network devices arranged in a serial topology. If any one of these devices fails, a major network outage would occur. Additionally, the devices are running a routing protocol to make sure that network traffic all goes to only the right place. Although a routing protocol is running, a failure will not result in another router taking over the traffic from the failed router.

Figure 3-1   *A Simple Serial Network Topology*

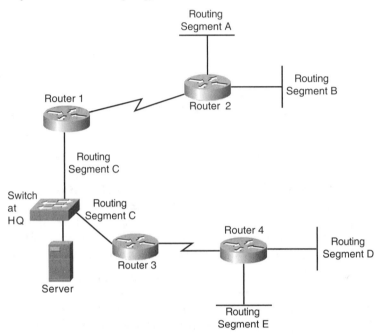

In Figure 3-1 you can see that any data that travels between Routing Segment A and any other location on the network would travel on exactly one path. Note that the routing segments in the diagram are IP segments (Layer 3 segments), and thus, the switch does not divide Routing Segment C into parts. As is convention, we will call these Routed Segments, Segments. To clarify the use of such a topology, we will assume some information and perform an availability study on the availability of the Server from Segment A.

Assume that Router 2 has an availability of 99.97 percent, Router 1 has an availability of 99.98 percent, and the switch has an availability of 99.99 percent. Figure 3-2 shows the computation of the availability between Segment A and the server.

Figure 3-2   *A Simple Serial Network Example*

$$\text{Serial Availability} = \prod_{i=1}^{n} \text{availability}_{(i)}$$

$$\text{Router 1} = .9997$$
$$\text{Router 2} = .9998$$
$$\text{Switch} = .9999$$

$$\text{Segment A to Server} = .9997 * .9998 * .9999$$

$$= .9994$$

The result—99.94 percent availability—shows that each of the three devices considered actually contributes some amount of downtime to the overall system.

NOTE   Remember that in this example we have not considered the server downtime or the downtime of anything in between the routers, such as the WAN between Routers 1 and 2. As we move forward, we will consider more and more of these types of things in our examples.

Parallel Topology

Unlike in serial topology, the fail-over mechanism is crucial to the operation of a parallel topology. Whether the fail-over mechanism is a bridging protocol, routing protocol, or some other method, you need to consider it carefully while performing availability calculations. This early in the book, we are going to assume that fail-over mechanisms work properly and instantly. Later, we are going to assume that the different fail-over mechanisms take a certain amount of time, and then we are going to add that time to our calculations.

In order to illustrate the parallel topology and its associated availability, we will use Figure 3-3 and Figure 3-4. Figure 3-3 shows a very simple parallel topology network. Figure 3-4 shows the calculations of the availability through the four routers in thenetwork.

Figure 3-3   *A Simple Parallel Network Topology*

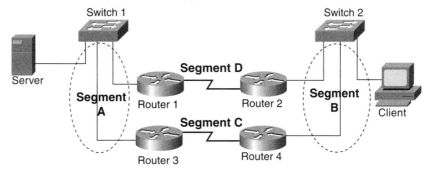

Figure 3-4   *A Simple Parallel Example*

Serial availability; Routers 1 & 2

Availability = .999 $*$ .999
            = .998

Parallel availability; Paths Through Routers 1 & 2 and 3 & 4

Availability = 1- [(1 - .998) $*$ (1- .998)]
            = .999996

As you can see from Figure 3-3, eliminating single points of failure and serial portions from a network is difficult. As a minimum, everyone will agree that eliminating all single points of failure is a financially expensive proposition. Notice the serial segments between Routers 1 and 2, and also notice that the switches at either end are single points of failure. To calculate the availability between Segment A and Segment B, we put the results of the two paths (Routers 1 and 2 and Routers 3 and 4) into our parallel availability equation.

For simplicity, assume that all four routers are the same and have availability equal to 99.9 percent. As you can see from Figure 3-4, the serial availability of a single path (Routers 1 and 2) is 99.8 percent. Running 99.8 percent in this topology through the parallel equation results in 99.9996 percent, which is an excellent result.

Of course, we didn't consider the downtime resulting from the non-parallel devices in this network such as Switches 1 and 2, the server, and the client. In calculations on a real-life network, you will want to include all the parts of the network. As we work through this chapter, we will add to Figure 3-3 in our discussion of the serial/parallel topology.

Serial/Parallel Topology

As you may have noticed in Figure 3-4, creating a network with all serial or all parallel topology is unlikely. I will even go out on a limb and say that nearly any highly available network will include both serial and parallel topologies. Even in the most redundant networks by large service providers, the last mile is rarely redundant. In order to calculate the availability of these networks, you need to combine serial availability results and put them into parallel equations. You will also need to combine parallel results and put those into serial equations. In large networks, you may find several levels of combined results going back and forth between serial and parallel before you are finished.

To clarify the notion of serial/parallel topology and path analysis, we will use Figure 3-3 to illustrate our network. Then we will use both the parallel and serial methods together to show the availability of the server from the perspective of the client. Once again our example is basic and leaves out some of the detailed calculations we will perform later in this book. However, we will begin this section by looking closer at the switches in our network.

As you can see in Figure 3-5, the switch itself includes parallel and serial components.

For the switch, assume the availabilities of these components are

- Power Supplies = 99.95%
- CPUs = 99.9%
- Interface Cards = 99.99%

Figure 3-5   *The Parallel and Serial Components of Switches 1 and 2*

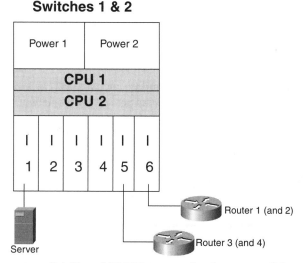

Assume an availability of 99.999 percent for the server of the network. The results from Figure 3-4 show that the four routers in the parallel configuration will supply 99.9996 percent availability between the two switches.

In order to perform the serial/parallel computations and finish the end-to-end calculations, perform the following steps:

Step 1   Compute the availability for each network component.

Step 2   Compute the availability of parallel components, which will be included in serial end-to-end calculations.

Step 3   Compute the end-to-end serial equations.

As you may have noted, Step 2 was completed at the network level when you computed the availability of the four routers. These steps were not done at the system level for the switch, and must be finished in order to move forward.

The switch is shown in Figure 3-5. Step 1 is assumed by the availability values listed previously—99.95, 99.9, and 99.99 percent for the various components. Step 2 requires computation of the parallel availability of power and CPU to prepare for switch end-to-end availability. Finally, Step 3 combines the results of Steps 1 and 2 into an end-to-end result for the switch. This is done in Figure 3-6.

NOTE   It is important to notice that only two interface cards were used in the end-to-end switch calculation. The reason for using two instead of three interface cards is that only two are required at any given time for connectivity. Another way to handle this is to include two interface cards in the router calculations and not in the switch calculations. At this point, learning the basics is the primary concern. That detail can be overlooked until the examples in Chapters 8 and 9.

As you can see in Figure 3-6, the switch calculations follow the same three-step process used for the serial/parallel network availability calculations. The switch result is 99.98 percent availability based on the components needed for the network to work properly.

Figure 3-6   *Network Availability Example – Serial/Parallel Switch Calculations*

Step 1: Calculate Individual Component Availabilities

Power Supply Availability   = 99.95
CPU Availability   = 99.9
Interface Card Availability   = 99.99

Step 2: Calculate Parallel Parts Availability

$$\text{Power Availability} = 1 - [\prod_{i=1}^{2} (1 - .9995)]$$

$$= .999999 \text{ (Truncated)}$$

$$\text{CPU Availability} = 1 - [\prod_{i=1}^{2} (1 - .9999)]$$

$$= .999999$$

Step 3: Switch End-to-End Availability

End-to-End = Power Avail * CPU Avail * Interface Avail * Inte Avail

$$= .99999975 * .999999 * .9999 * .9999$$

$$= .9998$$

With the switch results computed, the parallel routers results achieved and the server results assumed, you are ready to perform the end-to-end network calculations. Figure 3-7 summarizes the results and computes the end-to-end network availability for the serial/parallel example from the client computer's perspective.

As you can see, the results of the end-to-end calculation are based on the process of calculating the individual component availabilities, combining the parallel parts, and then combining those into the serial end-to-end results.

Figure 3-7   *Figure 3-7 Serial Parallel Example – End to end from the client perspective*

Step 1: Compute Network Component Availabilities:

Server Availability = .999999 (Assumed)
Router Availability = .999 (Assumed)
Switch Availability = .9998 (Calculated in Figure 3-6)

Step 2: Compute Parallel Portions of Network Availability
Redundant Routers Availability = 0.999996 (Computed in Figure 3-4)

Step 3: End-to-End Computations
Network End-to-End Availability = Switch * Routing * Switch * Server

= .9998 * .999996 * .9998 * .99999

= .99959 (Rounded)

Summary

In order to compute serial/parallel system or network availability, you need to follow a process. The example in this chapter was a simple version of a process called the divide-and-conquer process, which will be covered in Chapter 5. The two key concepts that you should take away from this chapter are that availability analysis requires careful consideration about how the serial and parallel equations are applied to networks. Each system or network segment requires the application of the equations to be broken into logical steps.

Predicting Availability

Chapter 4   Factors That Affect Availability

Chapter 5   Predicting End-to-End Network Availability: The Divide-and-Conquer
Method

Factors That Affect Availability

Many misconceptions exist regarding what things need to be considered when designing a highly available network. Many network designers consider only the hardware availability when designing their networks. Over-simplified methodology is often supported by a lack of information provided by the manufacturers of internetworking equipment. It is difficult to remember that software will cause downtime when the product manufacturers clearly state MTBF predictions for the product, but completely omit any reference to software availability. It is even more difficult to consider the proposition that good and documented processes for installing, maintaining, and upgrading a network will have a critical effect on network availability.

This chapter discusses the five major factors that cause networks to have downtime. Because the study of availability is really the study of when your network is *not down*, you must make sure you are aware of the major contributors to downtime. Without considering at least these five key contributors to downtime, your estimates may be less accurate than desired:

- Hardware
- Software
- Environmental considerations
- Network operations and human error
- Network design

If you account for each of these factors in your estimates when you plan your network, the results will be accurate enough for all but the most critical networks. The principles used in this book apply to any network and should give you a great background to apply your knowledge to other considerations not specifically included.

The hardware contribution to network downtime is the easiest factor to grasp because anyone who has ever considered network availability has considered hardware failure. It is both the most commonly calculated contributor to network downtime and the easiest to predict.

Anyone thinking about designing a highly available network knows that software always includes bugs. Assuming that some downtime will result is only logical. The difficult part of estimating software availability is determining what actually constitutes downtime and what does not.

Catastrophic failures are when a router crashes as a result of a software problem and has to be rebooted in order to recover. These types of failures are the most noticeable in a network because, when they occur, network management stations will have green icons turn yellow or red and network operators will be scrambling because a router just went away. Also these types of failures cause all the traffic through that router to stop; whereas, a partial failure might only stop traffic of a particular nature.

Partial failures are much harder to detect than catastrophic failures. Sometimes a bug in software can cause certain types of data to fail or slow down. Users might think the network is congested even though only a few users are actually using the network. Everyone using that particular type of data would lose productivity.

Service outages are another type of software failure. It is possible that a network may continue to run at full speed with respect to throughput of data, but some control process, such as a security feature, fails. This could appear as a working network as long as you don't log off and then attempt to log back on! Once off and unable to get back onto the network, you might be convinced of the apparent downtime.

Network design includes selection of topology and protocols for self-healing. In designing a network, you can consider how various routing protocols and hot standby protocols affect availability of the network and then choose the most appropriate ones.

Topology is a crucial design consideration that affects the availability of a network. Assuming that two routers are placed in parallel, doubling the 9s is theoretically possible. However, in real life, the effectiveness will be limited by the probability that the fail-over mechanism will actually work properly. The speed at which the routing protocol works will also be a factor when one of the routers fails. If the routing protocol doesn't work, having routers in parallel is pointless.

For example, in a strictly data network, you might select OSPF because it is an industry standard and usually works fine even when all the switches and routers do not come from one supplier. On the other hand, if your network is carrying voice traffic, OSPF might be too slow to move traffic from a failed router to a working router for your needs.

When it comes to the ways that the environment can wreak havoc, the possibilities seem limitless. We could discuss earthquakes, floods, volcanic activity, and a whole bunch of other things. Furthermore, we could consider things as simple as temperature and humidity. In order to limit the scope of the environmental considerations, we will simply focus on loss of power to devices.

Because loss of power is something you can plan for, we can discuss methods of increasing availability by implementing solutions such as battery backup and generators.

Although network operations and human error are discussed last in this chapter, both are definitely very important considerations. In fact, human error may arguably be the largest contributor to network downtime in many large networks.

As we dive deeper into the five things that cause network downtime, you should make sure that you understand how to account for these things in network availability calculations. By the time you get to the end of this chapter, they should start feeling easy and familiar.

A Chronic Human Error Problem

In the mid-1990s I performed support services for a large financial corporation in California. During two years, I repeatedly solved the same problem over and over. This problem caused network downtime and productivity losses each and every time it occurred. Specifically, this particular company had decided that DHCP was not acceptable for its IP addressing scheme and it wanted each and every workstation on the network to have a fixed address. Since fixed addresses had to be programmed into the individual workstations and since the network was growing rapidly, the technicians that did the programming of the addresses into the workstations made mistakes occasionally.

The problem was that the occasional mistake at the workstation installation level was a monthly hit to the network in the form of duplicate IP addresses. If you were not careful in those days, it was easy to reverse the default gateway address with the IP address when installing an Apple Macintosh. Inputting the addresses in the wrong way would bring down the entire segment because the Macintosh would respond to every PC on that segment trying to get off the segment. Each time this occurred, the customer would think the problem was with the router at the segment-to-backbone intersection and would call to tell me that the router wasn't working. Each time I would use a protocol analyzer to find the duplicate address and tell them the MAC address of the offending workstation.

If I knew then what I know today about network availability, I know could have convinced the management to change the workstation installation procedure to eliminate this problem.

While this example certainly shows how network operations policies affect availability, do not limit your thoughts to this type of example. Network operations provides hundreds of opportunities to reduce (or increase) you network's availability.

In thinking about predicting the availability of a network, it becomes obvious that human error could likely contribute to network downtime. As you go through each of the five sections in this chapter, your goal should be to learn how to mathematically account for the five major contributors to network downtime. Human error and network operations will simply become one other calculation to make.

Predicting Hardware Availability

Although hardware is very likely to contribute to your network's outages, it may or may not be the largest contributor. The fact that I cover hardware first is because it is easiest, not because it is the most important factor to consider in network availability.

Nearly everyone that gets involved with estimating network reliability or availability will first begin by making estimates about the hardware. Only a small percentage actually move on to include the other things covered in this book. This small percentage is most likely a result of the relative ease of obtaining hardware reliability estimates and the difficulty in obtaining information on the other factors. Because most network designers have at least some idea about hardware availability, presenting that first and then building up from there makes sense.

An interesting thing for you to do is to check out some of the products you are currently running, find out what the MTBF is for these products and then find out what the MTBF includes. In most cases, you will find that the number reflects only the hardware. As we introduce the methods for computing hardware availability, we will start with smaller ideas and build outward. You might visualize this as moving outwards in concentric circles.

In order to start simple and build, I will quickly describe how MTBF and MTTR are learned just so you have a flavor for background purposes. Then we quickly move on to examples that are more mundane to network availability. We begin with a small system and grow to larger systems and finally a small network.

MTBF and MTTR

It is important when predicting availability of a particular device to understand how the MTBF and MTTR were determined. This knowledge will enable you to determine the appropriate confidence in your results. After all, you cannot get good results unless the numbers entered into the equations are valid in the first place. Without specific statements about how the MTBF and MTTR numbers were derived, I would be wary of any network availability study.

The telecommunications industry standard method for determining MTBF is the Telcordia (Previously Bellcore) Parts Count Method. The component count method is described in Bellcore TR-332. Another widely used standard for predicting MTBF is the standard Mil-Hdbk-217, which is used by the electronics industry. Cisco Systems uses the Telcordia Parts Count Method to compute its MTBFs.

Bellcore TR-332 is a technical document available for purchase at

telecom-info.telcordia.com/site-cgi/ido/index.html.

Complete coverage of this method is beyond the scope of this book, but this chapter explains the basics.

Computing MTBF: The Telcordia (TR-332) Method

When counting devices to determine the MTBF of a circuit board, it is assumed that if any single component (for example, IC, fuse, capacitor, resistor) fails then the entire circuit board (device) will fail. The environment for the components that make up the device must also be considered. The following factors are considered:

- Temperature
- Electrical Stress
- Quality
- Environment

Bellcore TR-332 spells out how to include each of these factors. With these assumptions and considerations taken into account, the process of performing the component count method is very simple.

For each component on the circuit board, a FIT number is determined. A FIT is a failure per ten billion hours of operating time. A device might have a number like "3" for its FIT which would mean that, on average, it would be likely to have three failures per ten billion hours of operating time. This scenario does of course assume that we replace or repair the device after it fails.

Once we have the FIT number for each of the components on the circuit board, we simply add them all up to get a total number of FITs. Calculating the MTBF becomes a simple matter of arithmetic.

The important thing to remember about this section is that most telecommunications companies use the Bellcore method to calculate hardware MTBF for their products. However, because so many electronics companies use the Mil-Hdbk-217 specification, it is also acceptable. You should simply verify that MTBF estimates you get are based on one of these two standards.

Computing MTTR

You have a variety of ways to calculate MTTR. In this book, I am going to show a very simple way that is accurate enough for our purposes. In this chapter, in the section on process and human error, you will also see a way to improve on the basic method we see here. However, note that the enhanced method really applies to operating network as opposed to proposed networks.

Let us make two assumptions:

- The actual time to replace a failed network device is very short.
- The time to get someone into the right room, with the right part to actually perform the replacement, is the time consuming part of fixing failed devices.

For example, if you had a slide in card fail on a router, the four hours it takes to get the replacement is far longer than the five minutes it takes to perform the swap. Therefore, we will assume the MTTR for each device on a network is equal to the time it takes to have a spare part and a knowledgeable person arrive to make the repair. So if you have purchased a four-hour on-site service contract, you could use four hours as the MTTR for each product covered under the contract.

In some cases, you might want to add a couple hours if you anticipate that the repair itself might take long enough to be considered. Or if you have a "next day" type of service contract, you might want to consider failures that occur involving a weekend.

Predicting MTTR is mainly an exercise in common sense. You can feel free to add or subtract hours from your base assumption as you see fit. The key to accomplishing the goals in this book is to be consistent. If you predict an MTTR of four hours when looking at the availability of one proposed network design, you should use that same number for an alternate design. Naturally very different devices could create very different MTTR results. As with MTBF, MTTR figures are averages. Averages also include mean and variance.

Calculating the Availability of a Simple Network Device

For our first example calculation, we will use a very simple device. Let us assume a router with a WAN port and a LAN port, which is used to connect a small network to another remote network. The router's major components include a motherboard, a power supply, and a plastic enclosure. For this simple case, Figure 4-1 shows you what this product might look like.

Figure 4-1   *A Simple Network Device*

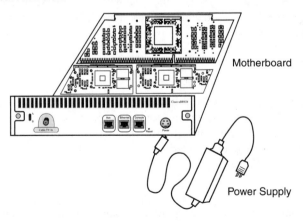

Motherboard

Power Supply

We assume that the enclosure will not fail and that we are going to do calculations for the power supply and the circuit board. In this case, the circuit board and the power supply are considered serial because if either of them fails then the entire system fails.

Equation 4-1 shows the availability equation introduced in Chapter 1, "Introduction to High Availability Networking," and Chapter 2, "The Basic Mathematics of High Availability."

Equation 4-1 The Availability Equation

$$\text{Availability} = \frac{\text{MTBF}}{\text{MTBF} + \text{MTTR}}$$

Equation 4-2 shows the availability equation for serial devices.

Equation 4-2 The Serial Availability Equation

$$\text{SerialSystemAvailability} = \prod_{i=1}^{n} \text{PartAvailability}_{(i)}$$

n=number of parts

First, we need to determine the MTBF of the power supply and motherboard. Although MTBF numbers are not currently public information for most companies, you can usually get them by asking your sales representative. Their response will likely take a couple days while they find the information for you. Any company that cannot provide at least hardware MTBFs for you is unlikely to have reliable products appropriate for a highly available network.

For this example, assume the MTBF of the power supply is 500,000 hours and the MTBF for the router motherboard is 250,000 hours. For MTTR, we are going to assume 32 hours for both devices, based on a typical service contract for an average small network. This assumes a 24-hour service contract and adds some time to account for weekends. Remember, if a service contract is for "next business day service" and the failure happens Friday afternoon, the response time will not be under 24 hours.

The motherboard result, whose derivation is shown in Figure 4-2, could be greatly improved with a better service contract involving four-hour on site service.

Figure 4-2   *Finding the Availability of the Motherboard*

Motherboard Availability

$$\text{Availability} = \frac{250,000}{250,000 + 32}$$

$$= \frac{250,000}{250,032}$$

$$= 0.9998720$$

Figure 4-3 shows the calculation of the availability of the power supply.

Figure 4-3   *Determining Power Supply Availability*

Power Supply Availability

$$\text{Availability} = \frac{500,000}{500,000 + 32}$$

$$= \frac{500,000}{500,032}$$

$$= 0.9999360$$

Using our method for combining parts in serial, we calculate the system availability for this product in Figure 4-4.

Figure 4-4   *Calculating the Availability of a Small System*

System Availability

$$\text{Availability} = \prod_{i=1}^{n} \text{Part Availability}_{(i)}$$

$$= 0.999872 * 0.999936$$

$$= 0.999808$$

As you can see from Figure 4-4, this system would have an availability of 0.999808, which we might call "three 9s, almost four" if we were talking about the hardware availability in layman's terms.

Experimenting with MTTR for Better System/Network Availability

I have always found it interesting to mess around with the numbers when doing these calculations to see if there is a cheap, easy way to get better availability out of a system or network. If we decide this network is important enough to make sure we always get things fixed in less than eight hours (perhaps by purchasing a high end support contract), then we get a quick win as shown in Figure 4-5.

Figure 4-5   *Experimenting with Decreasing MTTR*

<u>Same System With 8 Hour MTTR</u>

$$\text{Availability (1)} = \frac{250{,}000}{2500{,}008}$$

$$= 0.999968$$

$$\text{Availability (2)} = \frac{500{,}000}{500{,}008}$$

$$= 0.999984$$

$$\text{System Availability} = 0.999968 * 0.999984$$

$$= 0.999952$$

This small increase in the servicing of the device increases the availability from "three 9s, almost four" to "four and a half 9s." This may not seem like a whole bunch, but if you do the math, it equals a reduction from about 100 minutes per year of downtime to about 25 minutes per year.

Calculating the Availability of a Redundant Single System

In this example, we will account for redundant components within a single device. This router is modular in design and has some parts that are redundant and some parts that are single points of failure. Figure 4-6 shows a chassis (with a backplane), two I/O cards, two load-balancing redundant CPUs, and two load-sharing redundant power supplies. We will assume that the purpose of this device is to move traffic from I/O Card 1 (Card 1) to I/O Card 2 (Card 2), and anything stopping that flow of data will constitute downtime.

Figure 4-6   *Redundant Components Within a Single Device*

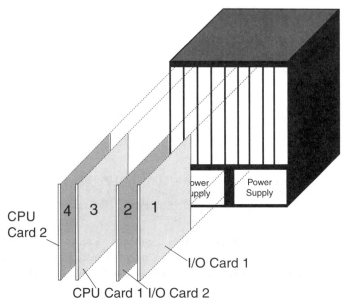

In order for the data to flow, both I/O cards, the chassis, at least one power supply, and one CPU (Cards 3 and 4) must be working properly. It is possible that one CPU (cards 3 and 4) and one power supply could fail and no noticeable downtime would result. As you might remember from Chapter 2, this is called a parallel/serial model.

The calculations for the system will be serial in that we will calculate the availability of the serial components and then multiply them together. However, two of the components will themselves be parallel components. Equation 4-3 shows the availability equations needed for this example.

Equation 4-3   Three Availability Equations

$$\text{Availability} = \frac{\text{MTBF}}{\text{MTBF} + \text{MTTR}}$$

$$\text{SerialPartsAvailability} = \prod_{i=1}^{n} \text{PartAvailability}_{(i)}$$

$$\text{ParallelPartsAvailability} = 1 - \left[\prod_{i=1}^{n} (1 - \text{PartAvailability}_{(i)}) \right]$$

First, we need to calculate the availability for each of the parts in our system as done in Figure 4-7.

Figure 4-7   *Calculating Component Availability*

<u>Individual Parts Availability</u>

$$\text{Chassis Availability} = \frac{400{,}000}{400{,}000 + 4}$$

$$= 0.99999$$

$$\text{I/O Card Availability} = \frac{200{,}000}{200{,}000 + 2}$$

$$= 0.99999$$

$$\text{Power Supply Availability} = \frac{500{,}000}{500{,}000 + 2}$$

$$= 0.999996$$

$$\text{CPU Availability} = \frac{100{,}000}{100{,}000 + 2}$$

$$= 0.99998$$

Once you have the availability for each of the parts, it is time to combine those parts that are in parallel as calculated in Figure 4-8.

Figure 4-8   *Determining Parallel Component Availability*

<u>Parrallel Parts Availability</u>

$$\text{Parallel CPU Parts Availability} = 1 - \prod_{i=1}^{2} (1 - 0.99998)$$

$$\text{Parallel CPU Parts Availability} = 1 - ((1 - 0.99998) \star (1 - 0.99998))$$

$$\text{Parallel CPU Parts Availability} = 0.9999999996$$

$$\text{Power Supply Availability} = 1 - \prod_{i=1}^{2} (1 - 0.999996)$$

$$\text{Power Supply Availability} = 1 - ((1 - 0.999996) \star (1 - 0.999996))$$

$$\text{Power Supply Availability} = 0.999999999984$$

The final step is to combine all the parts, including the parallel results, into the final system availability as calculated in Figure 4-9.

Figure 4-9   *Calculating the Availability of a Redundant Single System*

System Availability

Chassis Availability = 0.99999

Parallel CPU Parts Availability = 0.9999999996

Power Supply Availability = 0.999999999984

I/O Card Availability = 0.99999

I/O Card Availability = 0.99999

$$\text{Serial Parts Availability} = \prod_{i=1}^{n} \text{ComponentAvailability}_{(i)}$$

Serial Parts Availability = 0.99999
0.99999
0.99999
0.9999999996
*   0.999999999984
0.999969999884

As you can see, we have performed a variety of different steps in order to arrive at our final availability figure. Routers with redundant components provide considerably higher availability than a similar router without redundant components. One obvious thought to leave you with is the likely increased cost of such a design.

Although we skipped this step in the preceding example, a refresher to reliability block diagrams (RBDs) is a good idea here. As you will remember from our introduction in Chapter 2, RBDs are a good way to make sure you are performing the combining of serial and parallel parts as appropriate. Figure 4-10 shows the RBD for this system.

Figure 4-10   *The Block Diagram of a Simple Redundant System*

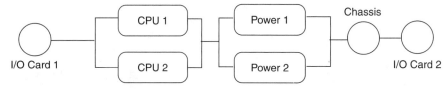

As we move forward in the book and begin to cover more complex systems or networks, you will see RBDs used more often. In real life, you will find that is what you must do to perform your calculations. For simple systems, you can go directly to the math. For complex situations, you will want to draw the RBDs to make sure you are doing the right math.

Calculating the Availability of a Network Segment

Now let us work on a networking example. We will use the two pieces of hardware whose availability we have already calculated to build a small network segment. Then we will perform the availability analysis on that small network.

NOTE   Do not forget that we are still only looking at the hardware part of the availability picture so far.

For this example, we are going to assume that the small simple router is at some remote site and that the more complex and redundant router is at some central site (see Figure 4-11). The two ports on the small router will be one each of a WAN and a LAN port. The two I/O cards on the central router will be WAN aggregation and LAN back-haul. We will assume that what we want to measure is the availability of a resource on the central router's LAN side from the perspective of a PC at the remote site.

Figure 4-11 *A Small Network Segment Availability Model*

Notice that nothing is redundant in the network. That will come later. For now, let us just work up to a couple routers in serial. After we get through the basics, we will start making things more complex.

The first step in analyzing the availability of a network is to make sure we know the data path. In this example, that is intuitively obvious. Once we understand the data path, we can create our reliability block diagram as in Figure 4-12. As you can see, we have two devices that will be likely to cause downtime between A and B.

Figure 4-12 *The RBD for the Network Segment*

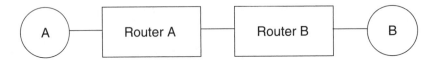

Simple Network Reliability Block Diagram

Recall that serial availability is calculated as shown earlier in the chapter in Equation 4-2.

Because we have already done the availability calculations for the two devices in this example, we can take those results and go directly to the solution for this simple network segment as illustrated by Figure 4-13.

Figure 4-13 *Network Segment Availability*

Network Segment Availability

Availability Router A = 0.999808

Availability Router B = 0.99997 (rounded)

Network Segment Availability = 0.999808 * 0.99997

Network Segment Availability = 0.999778 (rounded)

To figure out what this translates to in annual downtime, we can simply subtract this result from one and multiply the result by the number of minutes in a year, as shown in Figure 4-14.

Figure 4-14 *The Actual Downtime of the Network Segment*

Network Segment Downtime

Network Segment Availability = 0.999778

Minutes/Year = 525,960

Annual Downtime = (1 − 0.999778) * 525,960

Annual Downtime = 116.76 Minutes

As you can see from the results, we are looking at a little under two hours of downtime per year on this network segment when considering the perspective from the PC to the host resources. This still considers only the downtime caused by hardware failures. As we move forward, we start including other factors. Our next section begins this process with a discussion of how one could consider software in their availability predictions.

Predicting Software Availability

To predict the availability of a network or a device in a network, you need to consider the software contribution to downtime. We are now going to explore the software contribution to downtime. We are going to talk a little bit about how MTBF and MTTR is determined for software and then we are going to use those results in some examples. By the end of this section, you should be able to include software downtime in your availability calculations.

The hardest part about considering software in availability calculations is determining what MTBF to use. Many methods are available for calculating reliability of software, and they are mostly very difficult to perform or are not very accurate. The best of the simple ways to derive an accurate MTBF for software is to make field measurements. Companies developing software should perform these measurements in concert with their customers and then provide the results to all of their customers. That way their customers will have a mechanism for performing availability calculations with the software contribution included.

We are going to look at two ways to measure software MTBF. The first method introduces the subject, is easy to perform, but it is not perfectly accurate. The second method is more accurate, requires more effort, and takes a longer time to perform. The idea here is not for you to learn how to perform the calculation of software MTBF yourself, but simply to introduce you to how companies might do this on your behalf. Again, your goal is to understand how to include the results in your availability predictions.

Calculating Software MTBF

There are currently two ways that the Cisco IOS Software has been measured in the field to determine its MTBF.

The first method was developed by a co-worker and I because we needed to get some idea about Cisco IOS Software availability over time. The fact that this first method had some minor inaccuracies in it didn't really matter because we wanted to compare version to version performance and didn't really need any absolute measurement. We mitigated any inaccuracies inherent in the method by looking at large numbers of routers and making sure our results reflected what we observed.

The second version was proposed by Scott Cherf of Cisco Systems. He spent a lot of time during 1998 and 1999 looking at data from Cisco's internal network and measuring actual failures on our network. Scott showed his work to several of us in 1999, and we not only liked it, but considered it to be a great new way of performing availability measurements on the Cisco IOS Software. Because he was using Cisco's internal network, however, the sample size was limited to a single very large enterprise network.

In the future, Scott's methods of calculation along with my method of assessing large numbers of routers will be used to measure the availability of several large customer networks. With a large sample size and excellent methods, the IOS MTBF measurements should be the most accurate in the industry.

In this book, I will write about both methods and the results at the time of writing. This will definitely give you the tools you need to include some basic software MTBF figures in your calculations. You might want to check with Cisco Systems to find out the most up to date MTBF measurements of Cisco IOS Software. If you are not using Cisco IOS Software, you may want to find out what the current MTBF measurements are for whatever software you are using. I would advise you to ask what method was used to determine any software MTBF and MTTR numbers provided before using them in your calculations.

MTBF Calculation Method I: The Survival Method

In the battle between large internetworking companies, high availability has become a key factor of success. Because availability is easily calculated from MTBF and MTTR, searching for software availability quickly becomes a search for MTBF and MTTR. If one were to make an assumption about MTTR, then the remaining variable in calculating availability (MTBF) would be the only variable that must be measured.

MTBF Calculation Method I: Assuming an MTTR for Cisco IOS Software

Before actually deriving MTBF, one can assume an MTTR for calculations using the follow logic:

1 MTTR represents the time between failure and resumption.

2 If a router fails due to hardware, it is not a software problem.

3 In an operating network, software failures take the form of a temporary problem most often involving the router rebooting.

4 The average router running Cisco IOS Software takes about six minutes to resume normal operation after a software forced crash or failure.

Note   It takes only a couple minutes for most Cisco routers to reboot. However, some additional time has been added because it also takes a few more minutes for the router to compute all its routes and to begin forwarding traffic. This six-minute figure is an estimate based on observation. It is an average of all Cisco routers, from the smallest to the largest. Smaller routers will probably reboot faster. Larger routers with more routes might take slightly longer.

---

5 Therefore, we assume an average MTTR of six minutes for software that is configured to automatically reboot on any software error that causes a complete failure.

This logic leaves out the possibilities of partial crashes, crashes that fail to recover, and other situations. However, this assumption is reasonable based on the observations performed over a five-year period of looking at problems with Cisco routers.

Because this logic allows us to assume one of the two variables in the availability equation (refer to Equation 4-1), we need only derive MTBF in order to determine availability.

MTBF Calculation Method I: Average Life Measurements

The **show version** command in the Cisco IOS Software includes information such as how long the router has been running and why it last rebooted. Noticing this leads one to believe there might be a way to derive MTBF if you could simultaneously execute this command on large numbers of routers. By looking at a large number of routers totaling up all their operating times and dividing by the number that had last rebooted due to a software error, we might have an approximation of MTBF.

Mathematically, this method involves the summation of the running times of a large number of routers along with the summation of the routers in the measured group that were last rebooted due to a software forced error. This method involves the following logic process:

1 MTBF of a large number of routers will end up being the average time between failures as opposed to the actual time for any one router.

2 MTBF relative to software involves only those routers that have had a software failure.

3 Power applied to a router does not count as a software failure.

4 A software forced crash definitely counts as a software problem.

5 The summation of the time a group of routers has been operational since their last failure is an extremely conservative measure of the time they might run between failures.

6 The summation of the routers that were last started after a software forced crash/reboot can be used to represent those routers that failed due to a software problem.

Equation 4-4 describes the equation proposed for our first method of calculating software MTBF for Cisco IOS Software.

Equation 4-4   Proposed Availability Equation for Cisco IOS Software

$$
MTBF = \frac{\displaystyle\sum_{i=1}^{N} RouterRunningTimeAccumulated_{N}}{\displaystyle\sum_{i=1}^{N} RoutersLastRebootedWithSWError_{N}}
$$

In the medical industry, methods similar to this method are called "mean survival time" studies.

Looking for large numbers of routers where access to run the **show version** command could be gained was the next step in verifying this theory. As it turned out, Cisco has a high end support organization that performs this operation regularly as they monitor the health of customer networks via a tool they call NATKIT.

NATKIT was used to get a dump of a network with 543 routers. This particular network was that of a service provider running a large Frame Relay network using mostly Cisco 2500 series routers.

Using method one, the MTBF of the IOS running on their network was about 45,000 hours. Finding out that IOS was performing so well was exciting. One must remember that this is a large service provider network running GD (General Deployment) software. Obviously, this would make the results higher than what most customers should expect. This particular company is excellent at running their network and has strict control policies to ensure the best availability possible for any given hardware and software.

Given the results from the first experience of testing the theory out in a real world situation, further data was accumulated. NATKIT output for a half dozen of our largest customers' networks was gathered and studied using method one. As the information was gathered, the method was criticized as being too liberal. As a result, a considerably more conservative method was considered that involved simply dividing the running time by the number of routers.

Table 4-1 represents results obtained by simply averaging the running time divided by the number of routers measured. A variety of topologies, equipment, and business use of the networks is included.

Table 4-1   *Cisco IOS Software MTBF Field Measurements by Router Class*

Product Type	Cisco IOS Software Release 10.3	Cisco IOS Software Release 11.0	Cisco IOS Software Release 11.1	Cisco IOS Software Release 11.2	Cisco IOS Software Release 11.3	Cisco IOS Software Release 12.0
1XXX	N/A	N/A	1268	N/A	N/A	537
25XX	4754	6349	9794	3777	2887	N/A
26XX,36XX	N/A	N/A	6264	4036	1494	N/A
4X00,5X00	N/A	4078	4760	1746	N/A	N/A
RP, RSP, 7X00	N/A	4696	4467	1877	N/A	N/A

All Cisco IOS Software MTBF Field Measurements are in hour units.

While these MTBF's are extremely conservative, they are still very good. For example, with an MTTR of 0.1 hours (time to reboot the router) the 6349-hour MTBF for 25XX routers running Cisco IOS Software Release 11.0 produces an availability of 99.9984 percent, which is nearly five 9s. It is intuitive that Cisco IOS Software is capable of delivering very high availability once it has been in a network long enough to stabilize.

The lowest MTBF figure of 537 hours has 99.98 percent availability. This result is one of using newly released software on devices that are likely to be rebooted inadvertently, which would result in artificially low results. The higher numbers represent more mature versions of the software. This is precisely what one would expect: newer software has more problems than older software.

In Table 4-2, Cisco IOS Software MTBF results are divided up by network type instead of router class. As before, this is calculated from the data gathered from about 4800 routers on six different networks. Also, two methods are used to perform the computation and then an average is taken in the right-hand most column.

Table 4-2   *Cisco IOS Software MTBF Field Measurements by Network Type*

Customer Profile	Total Hours / Number Routers		Total Hours / SW Errors		Average of Two Methods
Enterprise	$\dfrac{770,711}{402}$	= 1917	$\dfrac{770,711}{17}$	= 45,335	23,626
Service Provider	$\dfrac{6,706,765}{1079}$	= 6216	$\dfrac{6,706,765}{37}$	= 181,264	93,740
Enterprise	$\dfrac{6,710,017}{1940}$	= 3,459	$\dfrac{6,710,017}{36}$	= 186,389	94,924
Service Provider	$\dfrac{1,968,592}{544}$	= 3619	$\dfrac{1,968,592}{43}$	= 45,781	26,510
Service Provider	$\dfrac{7,066,474}{899}$	= 7860	$\dfrac{7,066,474}{23}$	= 307,238	157,549
Total Enterprise	$\dfrac{7,480,729}{2342}$	= 3194	$\dfrac{7,480,729}{53}$	= 141,145	72,170
Total Service Provider	$\dfrac{15,741,831}{2522}$	= 6242	$\dfrac{15,741,831}{103}$	= 152,833	79,538
Grand Total	$\dfrac{23,222,560}{4864}$	= 4774	$\dfrac{23,222,560}{156}$	= 148,862	76,818

By taking the average of both an extremely conservative method and a more liberal method, the results appear to be somewhat realistic. At the very least, one can get a worst case and best case set of MTBF's using this method.

The result of this method is that you can use a Cisco IOS Software MTBF of 72,170 for an enterprise type network and 79,538 for a Service Provider type network. These numbers reflect actual measurements of six real life large networks. Of course, these are very well run, mature networks, which should be taken into account in your calculations.

MTBF Calculation Method II: Interfailure Method

In September of 1998, the Cisco internal IS network was instrumented to collect software execution time and failure events from the EMAN network management system, a precursor to the Cisco Resource Manager product. Polling devices on the network collected the execution time every 24 hours. Failures were collected using the SNMP Trap mechanism, which notifies a management station each time a device is reloaded. The data used in this report were taken between September 1998 and October 1999.

NOTE   I want to thank Scott Cherf of Cisco Systems again for his efforts and for sharing his work on Cisco IOS Software availability. Without Scott's efforts, this section on computing IOS MTBF would not have been possible.

For the purpose of these estimates, only reloads resulting from software forced crashes or bus errors were counted as failures. The measurement approach used is referred to as a "Failure Terminated Test Case." Each failure interval (interfailure time) measured is bounded at both its start and end by a failure event with the exception of the first interval, which may be bounded at the start by either a failure or a cold load.

Time was measured as machine execution time (in seconds) for a specific software version so the individual lifetimes measured in this report represent software versions rather than network devices. Execution time accumulated between the last observed failure of a version and the end of the test is excluded from these estimates by convention. Excluding the time between the last observed failure of a system and the end of the test is called censoring. Censoring is a method commonly used in studies that try to estimate the mean lifetime of subjects in medical trials. If a subject is still alive at the time the study ends, we can't know what his or her true lifetime was, so we exclude that subject from the calculation and call it a censored observation.

The IS network is typical of the environment found in many of Cisco's enterprise customer installations, both operationally and topologically. For this reason, we refer to measurements taken from it as representative of an Enterprise Operational Profile. The measures should reflect those we'd see in similar customer environments—that is other Enterprise configurations.

Caution should be used when applying the measures to environments other than enterprise operational profiles. Your confidence in the applicability of these measurements and estimates should be related to the degree of similarity between Cisco's internal IS environment and your own. Therefore, your confidence should increase proportional to the degree of similarity between these environments.

The software's performance in significantly different environments may be higher or lower than the estimates given in this document. Due to the high level of configuration volatility in the Cisco IS network coupled with the large number of heterogeneous versions and the presence of experimental software, these estimates are believed to be very conservative when compared with those that would be found in a more stable and homogeneous environment. Although we at Cisco know a lot about running networks, we tend to allow a fair bit of experimentation on our own. We are constantly pushing the bleeding edge on our network in order to test things in the real world before our customers.

Figure 4-15 shows the distribution of the natural logarithm of 472 interfailure times observed for Cisco's 11 series software. This group includes all minor versions running on the IS network from the 11.0, 11.1, 11.2, and 11.3 releases.

Figure 4-15 *The Scatter Diagram For Cisco IOS Software Release 11.x*

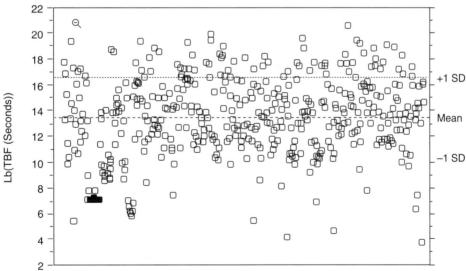

Figure 4-16 shows a histogram of the data in Figure 4-15 plotted under a normal curve.

Figure 4-16 *Fitting the Curve*

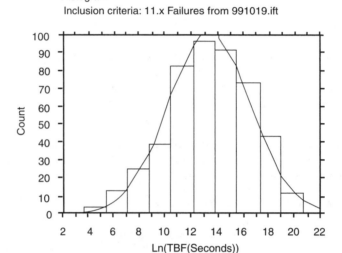

Although assuming an exponential distribution for hardware failures is common, both theory and experience indicate that the lognormal distribution is more appropriate for software rates. It's clear from Figure 4-16 that the data does in fact fit the lognormal curve very nicely.

Although the particular curve here, "lognormal," is a bit of a stretch for most folks' math, reliability experts use these terms and even more complex terms all the time. For the layman, you can simply assume lognormal to be the name for the shape of this curve. Again, one of the key points of this book is to shield its readers from this type of terminology as best possible. So please just take note that the data measured fits this curve very nicely. Because the data does fit the curve so nicely, we are then able to use a bunch of equations associated with that curve as we proceed through this method of measuring the IOS availability.

Table 4-3 gives summary statistics for the entire 11.x series observations.

Table 4-3 *Cisco IOS Software 11.x Summary Statistics*

11.x Failures 991019	Ln(TBF(Seconds))
Mean	13.395
Standard Deviation	3.143
Count	472
Minimum	3.689
Maximum	20.646
Variance	9.879

Using the equations described in Dimitri Kececioglu's *Reliability Engineering Handbook*, we can calculate MTBF using the mean of the log interfailure times in conjunction with the variance as shown by Figure 4-17.

Figure 4-17 *MTBF from Mean and Variance*

$$\text{MTBF} = \exp(\text{Mean} + \tfrac{1}{2}(\text{Variance}))$$
$$= \exp(13.395 + \tfrac{1}{2}(9879))$$
$$= 91{,}742{,}839.7 \text{ seconds}$$
$$= 25{,}484.1221 \text{ hours}$$

Figure 4-18 provides the availability of the Cisco IOS Software 11.x series.

Figure 4-18 *Interfailure Method Availability*

$$\text{Availability} = \frac{\text{MTBF}}{\text{MTBF} + \text{MTTR}}$$
$$= \frac{25{,}484.1}{25{,}484.1 + .1}$$
$$= 0.999996076$$
$$= 99.9996076\% \text{ Availability}$$

The MTTR for Cisco IOS Software is estimated as six minutes (.1 hour) in this calculation and is based on observation of average router reload times.

NOTE Remember that we are using major crash/reboot figures in this book in order to simplify the math.

As you can tell from Figure 4-18, 99.999 percent availability is the result for all of the 11.x software measured on the Cisco network. If we reduce our results to measuring only Cisco IOS Software that has achieved the stability called GD, then the results change.

Table 4-4 shows the estimation parameters for Cisco's GD level software. Of the four minor releases in the 11.x series, Cisco IOS Software Release 11.2(13) was the most recent version to be qualified GD at the time of writing.

Table 4-4   *Cisco IOS Software 11.2 Statistics*

GD 11.X Failures	Ln(TBF(Seconds))
Mean	17.18
Standard Deviation	2.093
Count	7
Minimum	14.66
Maximum 19.96	19.96
Variance	Variance 4.379

As we did for the entire Cisco IOS Software 11.x software set, we repeat the calculations for the IOS 11.x GD software in Figures 4-19 and 4-20.

Figure 4-19   *Interfailure MTBF for GD Cisco IOS Software*

$$MTBF = \exp(\text{Mean} + \tfrac{1}{2}(\text{Variance}))$$
$$= \exp(17.18 + \tfrac{1}{2}(4.379))$$
$$= 258{,}265{,}840 \text{ seconds}$$
$$= 71{,}740 \text{ hours}$$

Figure 4-20   *Interfailure Availability for GD Cisco IOS Software*

$$\text{Availability} = \frac{MTBF}{MTBF + MTTR}$$
$$= \frac{71{,}740.51}{71{,}740.51 + 0.1}$$
$$= 0.9999986$$
$$= 99.99986 \text{ Percent}$$

As you can see, the 71,740.51-hour MTBF achieved for GD Cisco IOS Software Release 11.x is very close to what we get using the other method for measuring Cisco IOS Software MTBF. Confirmation of like results by different methods gives us considerably more confidence in our estimates of Cisco IOS Software MTBF measurements.

You have now been introduced into the methods used to derive MTBF and MTTR for software. You are ready to get to the part where we use this information to perform availability predictions. The following procedures for calculating availability and including software contribution to downtime are the most important part of this software section.

Using Cisco IOS Software MTBF Results

You have seen the two ways that we have derived an MTBF for Cisco IOS Software. Because the measurement work is ongoing, I am going to use two numbers for including IOS in this book. First, I will use 10,000 hours of MTBF with a 0.1-minute MTTR for Cisco IOS Software on any product that has new features. For products that have are mature and stable, I will use 30,000 hours of MTBF and a 0.1 MTTR. Based on the measurements to date, these are extremely conservative numbers. If you use these numbers, the results you will get will be as accurate as possible for predicting availability based on the data we have gathered so far. All else being equal, your network should perform better than any estimates completed using these numbers. With that in mind, it is time to move on to performing some examples.

Examples of Including Software Availability

The next sections show a couple of examples on how to include software MTBF in an availability calculation. The first example is the simplest possible of accounting for software in a system availability study. Moving on, the examples get more complex and more realistic while showing the method for incorporating software in the calculations of system or network availability.

NOTE   Keep in mind that we are still not considering three key factors in network downtime. These examples consider hardware and software only.

Determining Availability of a Simple Network Device with Mature Cisco IOS Software

For our first example, we will use a very simple device. In fact, we will use a device we used earlier in the chapter so we do not have to start from the beginning. Because we already did all the hardware calculations, we can start with those results and add the software availability component. Refer to Figure 4-1 to refresh your memory about the router in question. You may want to go over that earlier example to refresh your memory of the hardware calculations.

What we need to do now is to start with the hardware system availability and add in the software component. Before we can combine hardware and software availability into system availability, we must calculate the software availability. Because we are assuming mature software, we will use the 30,000-hour MTBF and the 0.1-minute MTTR for the calculation as demonstrated in Figure 4-21.

Figure 4-21 *Availability of the Software*

Software Availability

SW Availability = $\dfrac{30,000}{30,000 + 0.1}$

SW Availability = 0.9999967

Because the entire system will fail if the software fails, we are going to add software in the same way that we would any other component in a serial system. Equation 4-5 shows the calculations.

Equation 4-5 *System Availability Including Hardware and Software*

System Availability

$$\text{Availability} = \prod_{i=1}^{n} \text{PartAvailability}_{(i)}$$

HardwareAvailability = 0.999808

SoftwareAvailability = 0.9999967

System Hardware and Software Availability = 0.999805

Determining Availability of a Redundant Single System

Again, we will start from where we left off in our example from the previous hardware section. Figure 4-6 shows the redundant router we analyzed for hardware availability. In this example, we again need to add the software contributions to the existing calculations previously performed. As you remember, we performed several steps to determine the hardware availability for the somewhat redundant system. The two steps that must be revisited here are the step where we calculated the availability of the parallel components and the step where we combined all of the components in serial. You can refer back to Figures 4-9 and 4-10 to refresh your memory.

Now in adding software considerations to these calculations, what we have to do is think about what is required for data to flow through the system and how software might affect this. Software runs on CPU cards, and there are two redundant CPUs in this system. Therefore, we are going to have to add the software calculations to the CPU cards and roll that up into the system level calculations. If we only had a single CPU (on the motherboard) then we could simply multiply the result from Figure 4-9 by the IOS availability and go straight to solution. This system, however, incorporates two copies of the IOS running in parallel on two parallel CPUs.

From Figure 4-8, we see that the parallel CPU cards were calculated to have availability of 0.99998 each and combined together to provide 0.99999 in total. Because each card actually runs its own Cisco IOS Software in this system, we need to combine the 0.99998 availability of each card with the Cisco IOS Software availability. We can then recombine the CPU cards together and then finally combine them into the entire system as done in Figure 4-22.

Figure 4-22   *Availability of a Redundant System; HW and SW Only*

System Availability

$$\text{CPU Hardware Availability} = \frac{100,000}{100,000 + 2}$$

$$= 0.99998$$

$$\text{CPU SW Availability} = \frac{30,000}{30,000 + 0.1}$$

$$= 0.9999967$$

$$\text{CPU Hardware and SW Availability} = 0.99998 * 0.9999967$$

$$= 0.999976$$

$$\text{Parallel CPU (HW/SW) Availability} = [1 - (1 - .999976) * (1 - .999976)]$$

$$\text{Parallel CPU (HW/SW) Availability} = 0.9999999994$$

$$
\text{Serial Parts Availability} =
\begin{array}{r}
0.99999 \\
0.99999 \\
0.99999 \\
0.9999999994 \\
* \ 0.999999999984 \\
\hline
0.999969999684
\end{array}
$$

As you can see from Figure 4-22, the availability of this system is not affected very much by Cisco IOS Software. With redundant CPUs and thus redundant Cisco IOS Software in this particular box, the overall downtime due to software problems would be greatly reduced. Reliable software running in redundancy contributes very little to system downtime.

Consider that there is an underlying assumption here—if the actual cause of failure in this particular system were the Cisco IOS Software, there is some chance that this problem would affect both CPUs. Because failure of the redundancy system is beyond the scope of this book, we don't measure it here. For our purposes, the results achieved without these advanced considerations should suffice.

Predicting Availability Considering the Environment

In some networks, considering the environment's affect on downtime might be too much work. For example, if a power outage were a happy break time for a large percentage of the employees, then including environmental considerations in your availability calculations would be a waste of time. Power failures are not that common and can be ignored if everyone appreciates them as a good excuse to take a break.

For telephone and financial companies where downtime is measured in minutes and each minute can have significant financial or other cost, environmental considerations are crucial. If the power goes out in your house and you need to call 911, you probably do not care whether your telephone is running from a battery or a diesel generator—what you care about is getting a dial tone when you pick up the telephone.

The environment has many ways of causing network downtime. Floods, earthquakes, wind, and other things can all cause problems for your network. The most common problem these things cause is loss of electrical power to your devices. Things like flooding happen occasionally as well, but most folks don't expect a network to work when it is underwater. Let us assume that whenever the environment affects your network's availability, it will be in the form of a loss of power. This simplifies our calculations to a reasonable scope.

Our method will be to first show some methods for getting MTBF and MTTR, plus availability. Once we have availability, we can include it in our calculations along with the rest of the components in a network.

One tangent we need to explore will be some discussion on how to mitigate power loss at your network site. Whether you use generators or batteries, highly available networks will need some form of mitigation for lost power. After a little coverage on mitigation of lost power, we can describe by example the method for including power loss in your availability predictions.

As when we did system calculations, incorporating another availability figure into our predictions is simply a matter of determining the right way. By the end of this section you should be able to incorporate downtime contributions from power outages into your availability predictions.

MTBF and MTTR for Electrical Power

As with predicting MTBF and MTTR for hardware and software, deriving MTBF and MTTR for electrical power is also best left to experts. However, we present some basics here in order to give you the background for including them in your calculations. Understanding where the MTBF and MTTR numbers come from will help you in understanding how to include them in your availability predictions.

Most telephone companies have an expert in predicting the availability of electricity for a particular geographic region. This person will use information from sources such as the public utilities commission in their area, the local electric company, and other related organizations. One such organization is called the North American Electric Reliability Council (NERC), which was formed after a blackout on November 9, 1965, left 30 million people without electricity across the northeastern United States and Ontario, Canada. NERC was formed by electric power companies to promote reliable electricity supply in North America.

NOTE   NERC's web site, www.nerc.com, provides some examples of power failures by year in their databases. They have a group named "Disturbances Analysis Working Group," which has documented major power outages over time. The link to their data is www.nerc.com/dawg/database.html.

We can look at NERC's 1999 data to see that a major electrical power outage occurred on the United State's west coast for 29 minutes as a result of a failure of a power station. Because 29 minutes was the annual downtime in this case and because that was the only outage in that region for 1999, we can also estimate availability as shown in Figure 4-23.

Figure 4-23 *Direct Computation of Power Availability*

Calculating Power Availability

Availability = 1 – Unavailability

1 Year = 525,960 Minutes

Unavailability = 29 Minutes

$$\frac{29}{525,960} = 0.0000475 \text{ Unavailability}$$

1 – Unavailability = .999945 Availability

In addition to calculating availability, you could calculate the MTBF and MTTR given 29 minutes of downtime in a year as done in Figure 4-24.

Figure 4-24 *Computing MTBF, MTTR, and Thus Availability*

Calculating Power MTBF/MTTR

1 Year = 525,960 Minutes

Unavailability = 29 Minutes

MTTR = 29 Minutes

MTBF = 525,960 − 29

$$\text{Availability} = \frac{525,931}{525,931 + 29}$$

Availability = .999945

Although this oversimplified example not only represents a single sample and is unlikely to be very realistic, it does give you a flavor for how these types of calculations might be performed. For this book, we needed a number to use for our calculations. Twenty-nine minutes per year works out to be over four 9s availability for electrical power. This will work fine for our purposes of learning how to use the data.

Before we move on to some examples, we need to cover a quick concept on how one might mitigate downtime due to power losses.

Mitigating Power Loss

Now that we have an availability number we can use to perform network availability studies while considering power loss (environmental considerations), we should think about mitigating the downtime. To telephone companies, 29 minutes of annual downtime is too much. Four 9s due only to one of the contributors of unavailability would definitely make it difficult to run a highly available network.

Given that 29 minutes per year of downtime due to power loss is too much, mitigation via the use of either a generator or battery backup begins to make sense even at considerable cost. In fact while I have used telephone companies for many of the examples in this book, many non-telephone companies put considerable expenditures into making sure they do not lose power to their critical business networks and computing equipment.

Cisco Uses Power Generators

Cisco Systems is an example of a company that has put considerable money into making sure their network stays up in case of a power outage.

In June 1997, there was a power outage at the San Jose site. Although Cisco had a generator that was supposed to keep things up and running, it failed to do the job correctly and the technical support department ended up being offline for a while.

Cisco's Customer Advocacy management was irate that the backup generator failed to do its job. If customer satisfaction is as important to you as it is to Cisco, then this type of outage will likely drive you to consider mitigating power loss as well.

Shortly after this outage, an entire building and generator complex had been completely replaced at a cost of several million dollars, guaranteeing that should the power fail in the future Cisco Support will continue working without interruption.

The new generator is tested from time to time just to make sure it will work in the event of a real power outage.

The forms that mitigation of power loss can take are normally some sort of battery backup, some sort of generator, or both.

The battery backup method usually involves purchasing enough batteries to provide power for your network for the length of time anticipated for any single power outage. In between outages, the batteries can be recharged and made ready for the next outage. This method is fairly simple and reliable. In the event power is lost for longer than anticipated, however, your network will be down for the balance.

The generator method involves having gas or diesel powered generators that automatically start running in the event regular power is lost. Assuming a large tank for fuel, you could run your network throughout a very long power outage. However, engines take time to start and you are likely to suffer some downtime while you switch from regular power to generated power.

The combination of both battery and generator backup enables some companies to withstand power outages to such an extent that they are likely to be without power only under extreme circumstances. With both generator and battery backup, the power can be constantly supplied to the network without downtime during the switchover, and the generators can be used to extend the operating time. This method is obviously the most expensive method but may be considered the best method for critical networks.

As we move forward, we will show how to incorporate the downtime due to power loss in your availability predictions. As with other contributors to downtime, we start simple and get more complex as we move through our examples.

Battery Backup

In performing research about battery requirements for network devices that pass voice traffic, a figure of eight hours has come up several times. Many large telephone companies use that number as the average requirement for battery backup for their typical power loss scenario.

Given the 29 minutes of downtime in California in 1999, eight hours might appear to be too much. If we looked at other areas such as a storm ridden East Coast, we might consider it very risky to have only eight hours of battery backup.

At any rate, we are going to do our battery backup example assuming the batteries are designed to create eight hours of battery backup.

It is possible for a battery backup system to fail. We give our battery backup an availability of 99.9 percent (.999). In Figure 4-25, we depict a network segment with battery backup. What we want to do is to compute the availability, in this case, from the perspective of the home user. We will calculate the availability of the Internet from this household.

Figure 4-25 *Simple Battery Backup Topology*

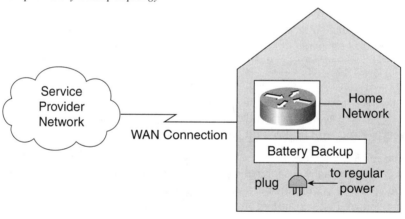

In Figure 4-25, assume that the service provider has an availability of .99999. Additionally, assume the router in the home has an availability of .9999. We also assume .999945 availability of power to this household as we calculated earlier in this section based on 29 minutes per year of downtime. We should do a RBD to make sure we understand how to perform our calculations. Figure 4-26 shows the RBD for this example.

Figure 4-26 *Battery Backup RBD*

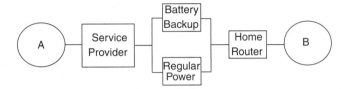

Note that our parallel construction of the power availability depends on never exceeding eight hours of outage for the regular power component is important. In that event, downtime would need to be increased by adding that excess amount directly to the bottom line of our downtime result.

Table 4-5 shows the various network component availability figures.

Table 4-5   *Battery Backup Example Availability Figures*

Item	Description	Value/Result
Service Provider	Total availability provided by the service provider to the Internet.	.99999
Home Router	The availability of the home router and its power supply.	.9999
Power Company	Power from the power company at 29 minutes per year of downtime is 525931÷525960.	.999945
Batter Backup	The availability of the battery backup device.	.999

With the availability figures for each component in our network and the RBD, we are ready to perform the availability calculations. Figure 4-27 depicts the calculations for this example.

Figure 4-27 *The Battery Backup Example Availability Calculations*

Step 1: Parallel Power Computations

Power Company   = .999945
Battery Backup   = .999
Power Availability = 1 − [(1 − .999) (1 − .999945)]
                          = .999999 (truncated digits)

Step 2: Total Availability

Power   = .999999
Service Provider = .99999
Home Router   = .9999
Total Availability = 999999 ∗ .99999 ∗ .9999
                            = .999889
Average Annual Downtime = 525,960 (1 - .999889)
                            = 58.38 minutes

As you can see in the calculations, the result of having a battery backup device in this situation results in about 58 minutes per year of downtime. The power loss of 29 minutes per year is mitigated greatly by this battery backup.

One thing that is important to note is that the construction we used for this is that of a parallel set of components for our battery and power company. In reality, the battery backup is most likely to fail during a power loss. Even if it failed some other time, we probably wouldn't notice until we lost power. To correct the simple parallel calculations, you could multiply the unavailability (1 − .999) of the battery backup by the time it will be needed (four hours). This would result in an additional 15 seconds, converted from hours, of annual downtime.

Without the battery backup, the 58 minutes of downtime each year would work out to be approximately 87 minutes per year.

Generator Backup

For situations where network availability is even more critical, generator backup might be required. Generator backup is often used in conjunction with batteries inside large telephone company facilities. When the power fails, power is switched over to battery. If the power remains off for any length of time and the batteries begin to run down, then the generator will start and keep the batteries charged.

In order to illustrate how one might calculate this, we will take the previous example and change the annual expected power outage from 29 minutes to 12 hours. Remember that we have a battery capable of providing 8 hours of battery backup. If we had a power outage of 12 hours, then our additional downtime would be 4 hours—the difference between what the battery can mitigate and the outage. Our total annual downtime for this example would be approximately 5 hours per year (58 minutes plus 4 hours) without a generator to mitigate the additional 4 hours of downtime.

The generator would provide another parallel method of providing power to our CPE router. Because this new network device affects the availability, we need a new RBD to account for the generator. Figure 4-28 shows the revised RBD to include the generator.

Figure 4-28 *The Generator Example RBD*

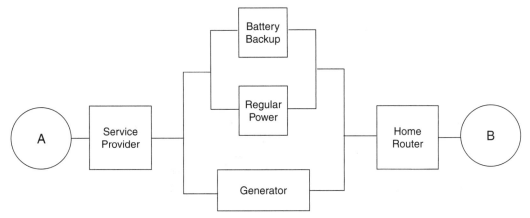

The RBD could be drawn in a variety of different ways. However, the results will be the same because we are really putting three devices in parallel. The grouping shown here allows us to use the results from our previous example.

In order to perform the availability calculations, we need an availability figure for the generator. For this example, let us assume a generator availability of 99 percent or .99. Figure 4-29 depicts the calculations for the scenario where we have 12 hours without power and no generator available. As you see in the diagram, the parallel power solution creates an extremely high availability for power, which results in identical calculations for the end to end between this and the previous example.

Figure 4-29 *The Generator Example Availability Calculations*

Step 1: Parallel Generator

Previous Power Availability = .999999

Generator Power Availability = .99

New Power Availability   = $1 - [(1 - .999999)(1 - .99)]$

$\qquad\qquad$ = .999999 (truncated digits)

Step 2: Total Availability

Power   = .999999

Service Provider = .99999

Home Router   = .9999

Total Availability = .999999 * .99999 * .9999

$\qquad\qquad$ = .999889

Average Annual Downtime = 525,960 (1 − .999889)

$\qquad\qquad$ = 58.38 minutes

However, the parallel construction shown in the calculations is not perfect. As with the battery, the generator is most likely to fail (or be recognized as down) during the four-hour period we are without power because that is the only time it is used. If we multiply the unavailability of the generator (1 − .99) by four hours, the result is an additional 2.4 minutes of downtime. Although small, relative to a four-hour power loss, this result does show that you might want to get a generator with .999 availability to reduce your downtime to seconds.

The difference between a full solution to power failure and a partial solution makes a huge difference. In this example, we went from about five hours to about one hour of downtime for our network by using battery-and-generator power-loss mitigation.

Power Loss Summary

The key to incorporating power loss into your availability calculations is to use the expected annual power outage for your area. Starting with that and then mitigating it makes the work easy. Each item you use to mitigate power loss will have its own availability number and thus some additional contribution to network downtime.

If you calculate the mitigation to power by using a parallel construction, you are technically correct because the availability equation takes into account that devices may or may not fail at the same time. We all know that in real life, however, power-mitigating devices are more likely to fail when they are in use than when they are inactive.

As long as you take into account the amount of power loss you can expect and then consider the availability of the things you use to back up your power, you will have a reasonable prediction. Make sure you are consistent in your methods if you are using this to decide between two different methods of power loss mitigation.

Including Human Error and Process in Availability Calculations

One of the more difficult concepts to include in availability predictions is the human error contribution to network downtime. This concept is not difficult to believe. It is not even particularly difficult to measure when it does happen. The difficulty arises when we attempt to predict these mistakes in advance. Of course, human error normally occurs when standard operations processes allow it to happen. A company process that mitigates human errors is a mainstay for highly available networks.

In this section, we are going to discuss the contribution of downtime due to human error and standard processes in a slightly different way from our previous methods. In the previous chapters, we focused on quantitative analysis. In this chapter, we must depart from strictly quantitative analysis and include more qualitative analysis. There will be some quantitative analysis but that will be limited. At the time of writing, there is a shortage of available information for quantitative analysis of process impact on network downtime.

The first section will outline some historical examples of downtime that were at least partly due to operations processes not mitigating the possibility of human error. We will use this section to establish a qualitative look at how network downtime is caused by human error. Only a minor amount of quantitative data will be presented.

In the second section we will discuss how you might determine the impact or scope of particular human errors by examining in a slightly different method the two examples used in the first section.

After a single short quantitative analysis of how to include any available process downtime data into your calculations, we will move onto a qualitative section.

We are going to look a process you might use to put into motion a method of constantly improving the availability of a network (or reducing the human error). This will include a repeated process involving prediction, measurement, gapanalysis, and change management.

Historical Downtime Due to Human Error and Process

In order to estimate downtime due to human error, we first go back and observe downtime caused by human errors. By looking at historical examples, we will be able to make some assumptions about processes that cause network downtime and processes that mitigate downtime.

During 1997, there was a large network in the United States down for over 24 hours. This particular outage was partially caused by the network equipment, but definitely enhanced by human error. At the heart of this network, two very large switches carried large amounts of traffic and talked to virtually every other major device on this network. Because the administrators wanted to perform a software upgrade of these two devices with a minimum amount of scheduled downtime, they upgraded them both simultaneously. They did not have a working plan on how they would go back to the previous version of software on those switches if the upgrade failed to perform properly. When the upgrade was applied and the switches were rebooted, they did not function properly. The network went down. It took over 24 hours for everything to get back to normal. Had the administrators performed the upgrade one at a time, there might have been little or no outage. With a smooth rollback plan, the outage might have been limited to as little as two hours. This example details how company processes allow human error to create downtime.

It is reasonable to assume that the actual downtime encountered in this instance represents the MTTR. We can make an estimate of the MTBF if we decide that the last downtime incurred because of human error was 18 months prior to this event. In Figure 4-30, you can see how we might relate a particular process (or lack thereof) and estimate the impact it would have on network availability.

Figure 4-30 *Estimating Process Downtime Contributions - Example 1*

$$\text{MTTR} = 24 \text{ hours (the actual measured downtime)}$$

$$\text{MTBF} = 18 \text{ months} = 13{,}149 \text{ hours}$$

$$\text{Availability} = \frac{13{,}149}{13{,}149 + 24}$$

$$= .998178$$

$$\text{Annual downtime} = 525{,}960 * (1 - .998178)$$

$$= 958.3 \text{ minutes}$$

$$= \sim 16 \text{ hours}$$

As you can see from these basic calculations, an error such as this creates a large amount of average annual downtime. Very few companies will allow this to happen more than once, so our estimates of future downtime are likely to be somewhat overzealous. For a company building a network that has not been in the networking world before and that did not implement planning and rollback processes for upgrades, this is the type of downtime I would predict for them.

During 1994 and 1995, there was a medium-sized enterprise network in the U.S. that incurred repeated downtime due to a single repeated problem. As the company hired more employees and put them onto the network with a new personal computer, duplicate IP addresses were being programmed into the PCs occasionally. Once that PC came online, it would cause some of the other PCs to try to talk to it instead of the router servicing that network segment. In other words, instead of sending packets to a router for forwarding, all the other PCs would send packets to the new PC where they would be discarded. This situation was an obvious case of a process causing downtime. This company had a problem in their process of IP address allocation, and thus, they had repeated downtime of a couple hours. The frequency of this problem was about one time each quarter. The actual downtime per event was about 90 minutes. Figure 4-31 shows how we take this problem and put it into numerical format.

Figure 4-31 *Estimating Process Downtime Contributions - Example 2*

$$MTTR = 90 \text{ minutes}$$

$$MTBF = \frac{525,960}{4}$$

$$= 131,149 \text{ minutes}$$

$$\text{Availability} = \frac{131,490}{131,490 + 90}$$

$$= .99932$$

$$\text{Annual downtime} = 525,960 * (1 - .99932)$$

$$= 359.75 \text{ minutes}$$

$$= \text{~6 hours}$$

As you can see, this company would likely suffer approximately six hours of downtime per year until they created a process to exclude this possibility. Most companies today don't have this downtime because they use DHCP to dynamically assign IP address in a way that precludes this particular error.

Creating a Map of Downtimes Caused by Process Issues

As anyone that has worked in an internetworking technical support role can tell you, humans will configure things improperly that unfortunately will cause downtime. This happens most often when companies attempt to grow their network and break a rule that causes previously working portions of the network to stop working. One humorous note is that the person making the mistake rarely realizes the problem is not with the new component, but rather with what they have done to their network by attempting to install the new component improperly. For this reason, we will include several components in our table involving the things that occur regularly as network engineers and technicians attempt to grow their network.

Table 4-6 includes the two previous results performed in Figures 4-12 and 4-13 as well as several other assumed examples.

Table 4-6   *Sample Downtime Contributions from Human Error and Process Issues*

Process Issue	Availability	Annual Downtime
Lack of Rollback Planning process for large upgrades.	0.998178	16 hours
Lack of process for controlling IP addresses for new PCs.	.99932	6 hours
Lack of test process before introducing new products into a production network.	.999	8 3/4 hours
Lack of password control process—security breaches	.995	44 hours
Allowing changes to routers without considerable process and testing.	.999	8 3/4 hours

There are certainly a lot more examples of processes that cause problems in networks and processes that mitigate network problems. For now, let us stick to this small amount of information in order to proceed with the next section where we will go over including these types of figures in our availability predictions.

Incorporating Process Issues in Network Availability Predictions

In the first section, we showed how one could derive an availability number from examples in process errors. Then we saw how we might form a table of typical process problems and their associated impact on network downtimes. In this section, we will use the generated table to perform a sample calculation of availability including human error and process contributions to overall downtime.

The first thing we must do is to create a RBD of our scenario. Do this to associate the error with the scope of the downtime. From the scope, we can determine how to apply the downtime. A smaller scope will generate downtime on only a portion of the network. A large scope will cause downtime to be applied to the entire network.

To keep things simple, we will use a simple network diagram depicting two home sites connected to the Internet via a service provider. In order to clarify setting scope, we will perform the calculations for an error made by the home user which only affects their network and then perform the calculations when the mistake takes down the service provider's network. Figure 4-32 shows the simplified network diagram.

Table 4-7 includes the data needed to perform the calculations of network downtime on an annual basis as a result of the errors observed.

Figure 4-32 *The Network Diagram for Human Error Examples*

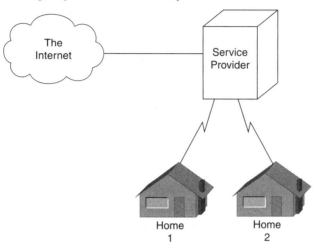

Table 4-7   *The Availability Numbers for Human Error Examples*

Network Component	Availability or Frequency	Annual Downtime
The Service Provider Network	.99999	5.2 minutes
Home Networks 1 and 2	.9999	52 minutes
The Internet	.999999	.86 minute
Error in Service Provider Network	35,064 hours	60 minutes
Error in Home Network 1	12,000 hours	120 minutes

For our calculations, let's assume two different errors resulting in two different sets of calculations. The first error will occur when the user in Home Network 1 does something that make their network unable to connect to the service provider network for two hours. Let us assume this error happens one time per 12,000 hours. Because this error does not affect a network other than the small home network where the user made the error, the impact to Home Network 2 is zero. In our RBD in Figure 4-33, you can see how we draw this concept.

Figure 4-33 *The RBD for Human Error Examples*

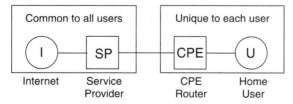

For the home user in Home Network 1 depicted in Figure 4-32, this outage does count, and we can perform the calculations as shown in Figure 4-34.

Figure 4-34 *Home User Human Error Calculations*

Base Internet Availability for User 1

Internet * SP * CPE1 = .999999 * .99999 * .9999

$$= .999889$$

Annual Downtime = [525,960 * (1 − .999889)]

$$= 58.4 \text{ minutes}$$

Downtime for Human Error

$$MTBF = 12,000 \text{ hours}$$

$$MTTR = 2 \text{ hours}$$

$$\text{Availability H.E.} = \frac{12,000}{12,000 + 2}$$

$$= .99983$$

Annual Downtime = [525,960 * (1 − .99983)]

$$= 87.6 \text{ minutes}$$

Total Availability = Base Availability * Human Error Availability

Total Availability = 0.999889 * 0.99982

Total Availability = 0.9971

Total Annual Downtime = 525,960 * (1 − .9972)

$$= 147 \text{ Minutes}$$

As you can see from Figure 4-34, the total downtime a user is likely to have will be 147 minutes on average. Imagine if 10,000 users each made this change affecting the entire network: the network would hardly ever be operational.

The second error will be a mistake made by the service provider. The service provider mistake will take all of the customers out of service for one hour. This mistake will happen one time every four years as shown in Table 4-7.

Figure 4-35 shows the calculations for the downtime caused by this mistake.

Figure 4-35 *Service Provider Human Error Calculations*

$$\text{Best Downtime from Figure 4-34} = 147 \text{ minutes}$$

$$\text{Availability} = \frac{(525,960 - 147)}{525,960}$$

$$= .99972$$

Availability as a Result of SP Mistake:

$$\text{Availability} = \frac{35,064}{35,064 + 1}$$

$$= .99997$$

$$\text{Total Availability} = .99997 * .99972$$

$$= .99969$$

$$\text{Total Downtime} = [525,960 * (1 - .99969)]$$

$$= 163 \text{ minutes}$$

Because we have used our standard method of computing serial availability results, our end result does not simply add 30 minutes to 147 minutes. In fact, a possibility exists that the two outages will happen at the same time. Thus, the theoretical average downtime per year is 163 minutes instead of 177 minutes. There are some truncation and rounding errors, but please note the process as opposed to the actual values.

Now that we know how to include human errors into our predictions, I think a short discussion about operations processes is in order.

Mitigating Human Error Through Operations Process

The goal of predicting, measuring, and generally doing all this availability work is to make highly available networks. Because a large amount of data on human error contribution to network downtime does not exist, I feel it is appropriate to put together a simple process by which you might establish your own data over time.

This section discusses a simple process by which you might determine the contribution of human error to your network downtime, predict future contribution, and then mitigate that contribution.

The Algorithm to Improve Network Availability

The algorithm we will use to constantly improve network availability will include four key steps. Each of those steps should be atomic in nature. That is to say, each step should be performed on its own. While the data from the other steps may be used in a subsequent step, intermixing the data will invalidate the results and break the process.

Figure 4-36 shows a high level diagram of the process for improving network availability via operational processes.

Figure 4-36 *Operations Process to Increase Availability*

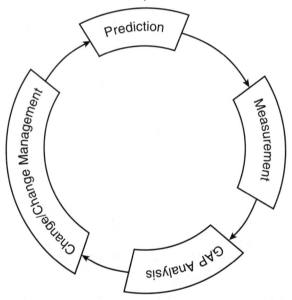

The four steps can be listed as follows:

Step 1 Prediction

Step 2 Measurement

Step 3 Gap Analysis

Step 4 Change/Change Management

The rest of this section will be spent explaining each of these sections in more detail.

Prediction

The prediction phase is the easiest to explain. Prediction is done using all of the tools we have been covering so far in this book. You should predict the availability of the network as best you can with the information you have. As you will see in Chapter 5, "Predicting End-to-End Network Availability: The Divide-and-Conquer Method," predicting the network availability may be compounded by different perspectives.

At a high level, establishing percentage availabilities for any particular portion of the network that you want to measure must be done at this stage of the process.

Once these availability figures have been calculated, they should be archived until they are required for Step 3 in this process, which is the gap analysis step.

You will need to use the advanced divide-and-conquer techniques from Chapter 5 in order to accomplish this step completely. For the explanation of this process, you need simply understand that you will be producing percentage availability predictions for your network and storing them for future use.

Measurement

The measurement phase of the process differs somewhat from what he have done so far in the book. Instead of predicting the availability of a network, you will actually be measuring the availability of the network. Additionally, in this phase we will also be using the failures per million operating hours method as we introduced in Chapter 1.

To produce the numbers required to successfully complete the gap analysis done in Step 3 of our process, you will need to collect a variety of data about your network over time. Basically, you need to keep track of the total operating time, the number of failures, and the downtime of your network. The downtime will require further details.

The operating time of your network should be the total number of hours of operation. This includes both uptime and downtime. This number should be multiplied by the average number of users serviced by the network during that time. This will eventually become our denominator in our failures per million hours equations.

The downtime hours will need to be accounted for by keeping accurate track of each failure. For each failure, keep track of the time to restore the network to working order, which we will average to generate the MTTR. Additionally, several other times involved with the restoration of the network in each failure should be recorded. Figure 4-37 indicates the various times that need to be measured in order to successfully complete the accurate measurement of network availability.

Figure 4-37 *Data to Collect for Each Failure*

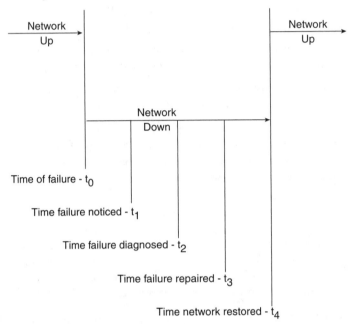

As you collect the data shown in Figure 4-37, the data should be entered into either a spreadsheet or a database because we are going to want to perform a variety of calculations on the data. When collecting this information, you will need to collect both the date and the time for each item in the timeline.

In the gap analysis phase of operating our network, we will be performing a variety of calculations using the information captured during the measurement phase.

One interesting point to make at this time is that you can select how long the measurement phase lasts in order to make the math easier. For example, if you had about 1000 users on your network, you could end the data collection phase every 1000 hours. One thousand hours translates to about six weeks, which could be a convenient frequency for evaluating the health of your network and performing any changes.

Gap Analysis

In this phase of our operation process, we perform all the calculations to turn our data collected in the measurement phase into meaningful reports. Additionally, we will convert some of that data into percentage availability figures so that we can compare the measurements with the predictions. If the measurements do not match the predictions, we can begin more detailed investigation, make changes, or otherwise decide what action to take towards improving our network's availability.

The first calculations most folks make are to simply calculate the number of failures per million hours and the average time to repair each failure. As you will see, we don't really have to wait one million hours in order to get failures per million hours. We can use multipliers such as numbers of users to get one million hours much faster than 114 years! As we've learned earlier in this book, MTTR is generated by taking the total hours of downtime and dividing it by the number of failures to get the average amount of downtime per failure. An example will clarify these points.

Let us assume that our network supports 1000 users. Let us also assume that our network is very simple and every failure has affected all of the users. Assume that during the last 5.95 weeks (1000 hours) we have had five failures. Table 4-8 lists the data that we collected from the five failures.

Table 4-8   *Data Collected over 1,000,000 Operating Hours*

Failure	Time(0) Failure	Time(1) Noticed	Time(2) Diagnosed	Time(3) Repaired	Time(4) Restored
One	1345	1400	1430	1445	1500
Two	1330	1345	1415	1430	1445
Three	0300	0500	0530	0545	0600
Four	0200	0430	0500	0515	0545
Five	1000	1015	1045	1100	1115

Figure 4-38 outlines our first simple calculations.

Figure 4-38 *Basic Failures Per Million Hours Calculations*

Hours of Operation = 1000

Users Serviced = 1000

Total Operating Hours = 1,000,000

Number of Failures = 5

Defects per Million = 5

Total Hours of Downtime = 15:00 – 13:45
14:45 – 13:30
06:00 – 03:00
05:45 – 02:00
11:15 – 10:00

Total Hours of Downtime = 1.25 hours
1.25 hours
3.00 hours
3.75 hours
+1.25 hours

Total = 10.5 hours

Average $= \dfrac{10.5}{5}$

MTTR = 2.1 hours

As you can see, we have five defects per million hours of operating time with an MTTR of 2.1 hours. To know whether or not that is a good result, we would probably want to compare this with our availability predictions made when we designed our network. To do that, we must convert our five defects per million hours and MTTR of 2.1 hours into percentage availability. Because percentage availability is the ratio of uptime over total time, we need only subtract our downtime from our total time of one million hours and divide that result by one million hours. Figure 4-39 shows this calculation.

Figure 4-39 *Converting Defects per Million to Percentage Availability*

5 failures * 2.1 hours/failure = 10.5 hours

$$\text{Availability} = \frac{1,000,000 - 10.5}{1,000,000}$$

$$= .9999895$$

As you can see from the calculations, we achieved a result of four, nearly five, 9s availability during the period. In order to continue with this example and to explore some of the other data available in our example, we will proceed under the assumption that our target and predicted availability was .99999 or five 9s exactly.

The next thing we will do in our analysis of the data that we measured is to look for any opportunities for improvement. Achieving our goal of five 9s may be possible with changes that may be obvious by looking at our data. Some of you may have noticed that the time to notice a network problem was considerably longer if the problem occurred in the middle of the night. What we want to do next is to show how we find these types of things using reports that can be generated from the data we gathered.

Our next set of calculations is to calculate the average for each of the time periods we measured and the range. Those that have the math skills may also want to calculate the standard deviation, but that is not absolutely required to make sense of the data. Table 4-9 shows the results of plugging all the data into a calculator capable of calculating mean, range, and standard deviation. Range and standard deviation are mathematics I am trying to shield you from having to fully understand. What they do is to tell us a little extra information about the average, or mean, in the first column. These two figures tell us when a lot of the results are not close to the mean. They also tell us when the amount of time to notice a problem is inconsistent.

Table 4-9   *MTTR Interval Computations*

Phase	Mean Time	Range	Standard Deviation
Time to notice problem	1.05 hours	2.25 hours	1.11 hours
Time to diagnose problem	.5 hour	0 hour	0 hour
Time to fix or solve problem	.25 hour	0 hour	0 hour
Time for network to return to normal operation	.3 hour	.25 hour	1.12 hours

As you can see in the phase where someone has to notice that the network has a problem, the range and standard deviation is much larger than in the rest of the phases.

NOTE   In most cases, it won't be quite this obvious. But I am trying to make a point here.

In many cases if we see a raise in range or standard deviation, we may have found an opportunity for improvement. If you do find a phase that looks suspicious, perform a post mortem on each of the failures and try to figure out why the phase is less consistent than the other phases. In this case, we look at the time to notice the problem for each of the five cases and we learn that problems in the middle of the night take too long to discover. Presumably we would then put a corrective action into place such as making sure our night shift operators don't sleep on the job.

Assuming we were able to reduce our time of problem discovery to 15 minutes during the two failures that occurred during the night, we would reduce our network downtime by four hours. This reduction in downtime would allow us to make our five 9s.

Change/Change Management

The change management phase is the time when we make changes to our network or operational procedures. If we made the changes described in the previous section, out of cycle, we would have no way of knowing if our changes were doing good or bad for our network.

In the previous section, you saw that we were able to track down a process problem by using the measurements and calculations done in the appropriate phases. The process should continue such that we make any changes during the change/change management phase, document those changes, update our availability predictions if necessary, and then proceed with the measurement phase. This repetitive process will make increases in availability highly likely.

Human Error and Operation Process Summary

As with the other contributors to downtime in a network, human error and standard process can be accounted for. In the absence of large amounts of data to use for prediction, we have to establish a process for gathering data that can help us determine downtime related to human error or process issues.

As with the other sections in this chapter, you should also understand how to include any human error or process information you have into your predictions for network availability.

Network Design

Our final area of consideration in causes of downtime is that of fail-over mechanisms. Routing protocols, hot standby protocols, and bridging protocols are all examples of fail-over mechanisms. We should think about two considerations when predicting the availability of a network or segment running a particular fail-over mechanism. First, we must account for the time it takes to perform the fail-over. Second, we should account for the possibility that the fail-over mechanism itself fails. Because this is an introductory level book, however, our coverage will assume that fail-over mechanisms work. We will only discuss inclusion of the time it takes for a fail-over to occur and the associated downtime.

For our introductory level purposes, we will not go into the details of the various fail-over mechanisms. However, a brief description of the highlights is appropriate. Therefore, we will start this section with a quick discussion on the two major groupings for fail-over mechanisms: load sharing and standby. Following that brief discussion, we will perform some examples of including fail-over mechanism considerations in your predictions of network availability.

Load Sharing Redundant Fail-over Mechanisms

The key feature of load sharing redundancy is that two or more systems will be constantly loaded with no more than 50 percent of the total load. Should one of the devices fail, the remaining device or devices would be able to pick up the load with little or no interruption of services. The most common load sharing products you will see in the internetworking industry are power supplies. Nearly every product with redundant power supplies works in a load sharing redundant mechanism. If a large router requires 100 watts of power, there would likely be two power supplies each capable of 110 watts of power in the router. Normal operation would have each of the two power supplies running at about 45 percent of its total capacity. In the event of a failure, the remaining power supply would be able to continue providing power for the entire system. The failed power supply could be replaced at a convenient moment.

Standby Redundant Fail-over Mechanisms

The key feature of standby fail-over mechanisms is that at least one device will be idle, waiting for a primary device to fail. Once the primary device fails, the standby, or backup device, takes over the primary devices job. The most common devices you will see that are put into a primary/backup or active/standby configuration are entire routers running a non-load sharing routing configuration. Many Cisco routers can be configured using what is called the Hot Standby Routing Protocol (HSRP). In that situation, a backup router is standing by, monitoring the primary router. In the event of a failure, the standby router can begin passing traffic in as little as five seconds.

Examples of Fail-over Mechanism Calculations

In this section we work through some examples that include fail-over mechanisms in availability predictions. By working through these examples, you should learn how to perform this analysis on your own. At the end of this section, you should be able to determine if a fail-over mechanism must be included in your calculations. You should also understand how to include the fail-over in your calculations if warranted. Within the examples, appropriate tutorial text will be included to help you achieve your goals.

Fail-over Calculations: OSPF in a Data Only Network

In this example, we will use a network with a topology that generates the RBD included in Figure 4-40. I leave it up to you to determine what that network might include.

Figure 4-40 *Failover Calculations: RBD for an OSPF Data Only Network*

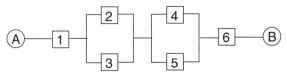

In our RBD, you can observe six different routers in a serial/parallel configuration. We assume that all the routers are running the OSPF routing protocol and that all of the routers have .999 available. This .999 was derived from an MTBF of 8757.234 hours and an MTTR of 8.766 hours. Further, we are going to assume that OSPF is able to notice a router failure, fix that failure, and resume normal operation in 35 seconds per failure. This network is used for passing IP data only and carries no voice or video traffic.

Figure 4-41 provides the calculations for determining the availability from A to B in the RBD.

In the calculations depicted in Figure 4-41, we begin by estimating the downtime of the network based on zero time for fail-over. As with previous examples, we calculate the availability of the parallel parts and then perform the end-to-end serial calculations. With base availability calculated, we need to know the number of router failures to expect each year. We calculate that for a single router and multiply that by two so we that know how many times each year OSPF will be required to fail-over. This is then included in the redundant router pair calculations. Because of the distributed property of multiplication, we could add it later, but this example clearly shows where and how OSPF will contribute to downtime.

Figure 4-41 *Failover Calculations - OSPF Data Only Calculations*

Parallel Parts

Router Pairs 2, 3 and 4, 5 = [1 − (1 − .999) * (1 − .999)]

= .999999

Without OSPF

Router 1	.999
Routers 2, 3	.999999
Routers 4, 5	.999999
Router 6 *	.999
End to End	.998

Base Downtime = 525,960 * (1 − .998)

= 1051.92

Failures/Year

MTBF = 8756.234

MTTR = 8.766

Hours/Year = 8766

$$\frac{MTBF + MTTR}{Hours\ in\ year} = \frac{1\ Failure\ per\ year}{per\ router}$$

OSPF Fail-overtime = 35 second

= .58 minutes

Router Pair Base Availability = .999999

OSPF Downtime = 1.16 minutes

OSPF Availability $= \dfrac{525,960 − 1.16}{525,960}$

= .99998

Router Pair Availability = .999998 * .999999

= .999997

End-to-End = .999 * .999997 * .99999 * .999

= .99799

Downtime w/OSPF = 525,960 (1 − .99799)

= 1057.2 minutes

Note that there are rounding and truncating errors in these calculations. Our results end up a little bit off, but in order to be more accurate, we would need to show eight and nine digits worth of 9's in these diagrams—which is very difficult to read.

Failover Calculations: OSPF in a Voice Network

For this example, let's use the same basic network as in the previous example. To have some semblance of acceptability, however, increase the availability of each router from .999 to .99999. The MTBF for each router will be 8765.91 hours and the MTTR will be .08766 hour. This really means each router will fail one time each year and be down for five and a quarter minutes each time.

Our RBD is the same as in Figure 4-40, but our calculations for the network's availability will be different as indicated in Figure 4-42.

As you can see from the calculations, this network would have just short of 14 minutes per year of downtime including the fail-over protocol. Because this is a voice network and our target for voice networks might be five 9s, the additional time spent failing-over is not particularly good. We will look at an alternate fail-over mechanism in our third and final example.

Failover Calculations: Static Routes and Hot Standby in a Voice Network

For this third and final example of how to include fail-over mechanisms in availability predictions, we will again use the same network and the same routers. However, this time we will not be running OSPF for our fail-over protocol. Furthermore, on the routers that are not redundant, there will be no fail-over protocol at all because that would accomplish nothing. For all the routers in this network, we will run static routes and export static. Routers 2 and 3 and routers 4 and 5 we will be paired for the purpose of running the HSRP protocol, which we will assume can fail-over in five seconds in this network. Figure 4-43 shows the calculations.

Figure 4-42 *Failover Calculations - An OSPF Voice Network*

Parallel Parts

Routers 2, 3 and 4, 5 = [1 – (1 – .99999)(1 – .99999)]

= .9999999999

Without OSPF

Router 1	.99999
Routers 2, 3	.9999999999
Routers 4, 5	.9999999999
Router 6	* .99999
End to End	.99998

Annual Downtime = 525,960 * (1 – .99998)

= 10.52 minutes

Failures/Year

MTBF = 8765.91

MTTR = .08766

Hours/Year = 8766

$$\frac{MTBF + MTTR}{Hours\ in\ year} = 1\ Failure\ per\ year$$ per router

OSPF Failure = 35 seconds

= .58 minutes

Considering OSPF

Routers 1,6 not affected
Pairs 2, 3, and 4, 5 equally affected 2 times per year
Paired Routers Availability

= .999999 (truncated)

2 Routers, 2 Failures = 1.16 minutes

OSPF Availability = $\frac{525,960 - 1.16}{525,960}$

Router Pair Availability = .999998 (rounded)

= .999998 * .999999

= .999997

End-to-End = .999999 * .999997 * .999997 * .99999

= .999974

Downtime = 525,960 (1 – .999974)

= 13.7 minutes

As you can see from the calculations, this network would have just short of 14 minutes per year of downtime including the fail-over protocol. Because this is a voice network and our target for voice networks might be five 9s, the additional time spent failing-over is not particularly good. We will look at an alternate fail-over mechanism in our third and final example.

Figure 4-43 *Fail-over Calculations: With HSRP Voice Network*

Parallel Parts

Routers 2, 3 and 4, 5 availability = .9999999999

Serial Parts

End-to-End = .99998

Annual Downtime = 10.52 minutes

Failures per Year = 4

4 Failures Cause Fail-over = 20 seconds

= .333 minutes

Total Downtime per Year = 10.858 minutes

$$\text{High Availability} = \frac{525{,}960 - .333}{525{,}960}$$

= .999999

End-to-End = .999999 * .99998

= .999979

Downtime = 525,960 (1 − .999979)

= 11 minutes

As you can see in the calculations using HSRP, we are able to reduce our network downtime by using a faster fail-over protocol. The new result of 11 minutes is getting closer to our desired result of 5.26 minutes per year. As you can see from our three examples on considering fail-over protocols in your calculations, the math is easy. What is not so easy is to figure out exactly how to make the results better.

Summary

For each of the five major contributors to network downtime, we have performed calculations to include them into our availability predictions. Armed with these tools, you should now be ready to proceed to the next chapter where we learn about how to take a large network and divide it up into smaller parts that we can study more easily. As we move forward in the book, you will find that we do not spend time on all five contributors in every example. If you do not feel comfortable with your ability to account for each of the five factors, you may want to make sure you add those you feel comfortable with wherever they are not done for you.

References Used in This Chapter

Garg, S., von Moorsel, A., Trivedi, K., Vaidyanathan, K. *A Methodology for Detection and Estimation of Software Aging*. Proceedings of the 9th International Symposium on Software Reliability Engineering. California: IEEE Press, 1998. pp. 283-292.

Juhlin, B.D. *Software Reliability Engineering in the System Test Process*. Presentations at the 10th International Conference on Testing Computer Software, 1993, Washington D.C. pp. 97-115.

Kececioglu, Dimitri. *Reliability Engineering Handbook*, Volume 1. New Jersey: Prentice-Hall, 1991. pp. 238-240.

Lyu. M. (ed.). *Handbook of Software Reliability Engineering*. California: McGraw-Hill, 1996.

Musa, John D. *Software Reliability Engineered Testing*. New York: McGraw-Hill Professional Publishing, 1998. pp. 97-135.

Mullen, R. *The Lognormal Distribution of Software Failure Rates: Origin and Evidence*. Proceedings of the 9th International Symposium on Software Reliability Engineering. California: IEEE Press, 1998. pp. 124-134.

Predicting End-to-End Network Availability: The Divide-and-Conquer Method

We often hear network designers and their management say things like, "We want to build a five 9s network," or "We want our network to be five 9s." This terminology is a very loose way of saying, "I want my customers to experience no more than five minutes per year of downtime." To reach these types of goals, you should predict the availability of your network before you actually build it. Because networks that require these types of goals are complex and often include several layers of redundancy, having a simple way to look at the availability of a complex network is a good idea.

In this chapter, we will describe a process by which we divide a network into reasonable scenarios and create reliability block diagrams (RBD) for each scenario. Once we understand how to predict the availability of a network by scenario, we can take a look at how you might go about improving the design of the network in order to increase the availability.

Before we move into the actual steps of the divide and conquer process and examples, I want to note something. In this chapter, we are only considering availability of systems and their associated hardware and software. I am intentionally omitting the other contributors to network downtime in order to make understanding the divide and conquer process easier. In Part III, "Examples of Analyzing Real-World Availability," we will resume considering the additional factors of availability.

The Divide-and-Conquer Steps

When we begin to study the availability inherent in a complex network, we quickly notice that there are various different scenarios. Voice over IP (VoIP) networks have scenarios that are easy to see. A person making a telephone call to the house next door will utilize a completely different network than a person making a telephone call across the country.

The first step to using the divide-and-conquer method is to recognize that more than one scenario exists on the network in question. Once you have decided that there are multiple scenarios, you are ready to begin using the divide-and-conquer algorithm.

The divide-and-conquer algorithm is represented by the following steps:

Step 1 Determine the scenarios and create RBDs for each scenario to be analyzed. Make sure to include redundancies.

Step 2 Perform calculations for each network component in the RBD.

Step 3 For each scenario

— Perform calculations on serial sections, contained within parallel sections, to determine an availability figure for the section.

— Perform calculations on parallel sections into an availability figure for the parallel section.

— Repeat as required until the end-to-end result can be achieved via a single serial end-to-end calculation.

Step 4 For each scenario, multiply all sections (including results from Step 3) into the end-to-end availability result.

In the following sections, you will be shown a network followed by an example of how each step is performed. For the entire rest of the book, the examples will use these methods. Each example will determine the path through a network or a device (scenario determination), create the RBD, and divide the RBD into manageable sections as required. Finally, the calculations will be performed.

A VoIP Network Example

The first step in any availability analysis of a network is to look at a network diagram. We must understand what the network looks like. We must also understand what each of the components in the network are and how they are all connected together. We must understand how redundancy is designed into the network and where these redundancies exist.

Figure 5-1 shows a VoIP network that would deliver voice services to people in two office buildings. In the diagram, you can see devices that control the network and devices that allow calls to go into the public switched telephone network (PSTN). As you can guess, not all devices are used for every telephone call. One or more different scenarios will exist based on who is making a call and where it's going.

Figure 5-1   *A Simple Two-Building VoIP Network Example*

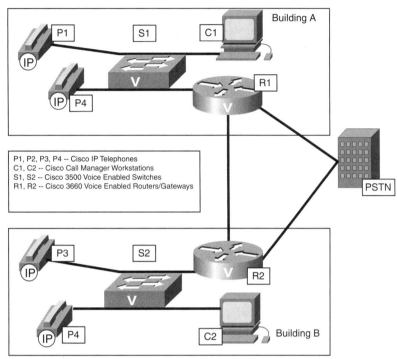

In Figure 5-1, a person in Building A calling another person within Building A would utilize two IP telephones, the switch, and the call control center (labeled as "C1" in the diagram). A person in Building A calling someone in Building B would use everything in Figure 5-1 except the connections that go out to the PSTN.

NOTE

In real life, we often call other buildings by dialing an extension. For example, I can call folks in other buildings at my company by dialing a five-digit extension. In some cases, that doesn't work. Often when the five-digit extension doesn't work, I can dial 9 to get an outside line and then dial their full telephone number and get them on the line.

This provides an exception to our example. In this case, a building to building telephone call is using the PSTN.

Obviously, we need to determine exactly what we mean when we ask about the "availability" of this network. That question is best answered by creating scenarios. Scenario determination represents the first step in our divide-and-conquer method and the following section provides an example of how we do this.

Step 1: Determine Scenarios and RBDs

To explain how to establish a scenario, we'll walk through an example. This scenario creation will use the VoIP network we just described.

Figure 5-2 shows an RBD for a telephone call made from one phone in Building A to another phone in Building A. We would use a very similar diagram to show the same scenario for a call within Building B.

Figure 5-2 *An Availability Block Diagram of a Simple, In-Building Voice Scenario*

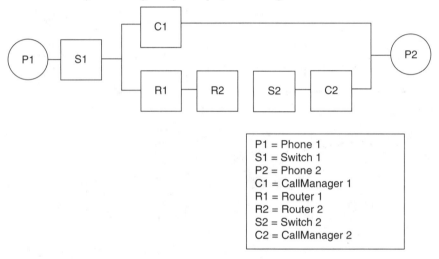

P1 = Phone 1
S1 = Switch 1
P2 = Phone 2
C1 = CallManager 1
R1 = Router 1
R2 = Router 2
S2 = Switch 2
C2 = CallManager 2

Although in the network diagram both telephones connect to the switch (labeled S1) in our RBD, other components are required for the telephone call to operate. In Figure 5-2, you can see that we have accounted for the concept that if the call control center (C1) fails, there is an alternate call control center (labeled C2) available. However, that parallel construct creates a need for additional equipment as depicted in the lower parallel path.

Before we perform calculations, we need to create an RBD for any scenarios for which we want results. We are going to look at two more scenarios.

The next scenario we will illustrate is a call from a telephone in Building A to a telephone in Building B. Figure 5-3 shows the RBD for this scenario.

Figure 5-3   *An Availability Block Diagram of a Simple, Building-to-Building Voice Scenario*

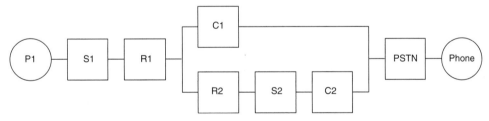

P1 = Phone 1
S1 = Switch 1
C1 = CallManager 1
R1 = Router 1
PSTN = Public Switched Telephone Network
R2 = Router 2
C2 = CallManager 2
S2 = Switch 2
P3 = Phone 3

* In this book, we assume that cables never fail.

In this scenario, we have chosen to use the PSTN as a backup to the wire that would run between the buildings. In this case, we really wouldn't be able to consider the call control centers (C1 and C2) as redundant because both would have to be working in order for the redundancy of building to building connection to work.

Our final scenario for this network will be that of a telephone call from inside Building A to some site that is outside the network on the PSTN. Figure 5-4 depicts the availability block diagram for this scenario.

Figure 5-4   *An Availability Block Diagram of a Simple, On-Net-to-Off-Net Voice Scenario*

P1 = Phone 1
S1 = Switch 1
R1 = Router 1
C1 = CallManager 1
R2 = Router 2
S2 = Switch 2
C2 = CallManager 2
PSTN = Public Switched Telephone Network
Phone = Some phone on the PSTN

In the figure, you can see that we have shown parallel call control centers, using the building to building connection. Again, we see that different scenarios can create different RBDs. This will definitely affect the method by which we perform our calculations.

Step 2: Calculate the Availability of the Network Components

Now that we have explored the data flows required for our various scenarios and created our RBDs, we are ready to begin performing network component availability calculations. We need to look at the RBDs and make a list of the devices we must include in our availability calculations.

Because we are calculating the availability for all three scenarios, we are going to include all the devices in the network and block availability diagrams. If we only wanted to calculate the availability for the first scenario, without CallManager redundancy, we would not have to compute availability for Switch 2 or the PSTN. This would reduce our workload in this step if we didn't have to perform the other scenario calculations.

Table 5-1 describes the system availability for each of the devices used in our scenarios. We have assumed the availability for the devices in order to simplify the explanation of the divide-and-conquer method.

Table 5-1 *The Availability of the System-Level Components in a Simple VoIP Network*

System	Availability
Cisco IP telephone	0.99995
Cisco Catalyst 3500 voice-enabled switch	0.99980
Cisco 3660 voice-enabled router/gateway	0.99985
Cisco CallManager workstation-clustered/redundant	0.99999
PSTN	0.9997

Step 3: Scenario-by-Scenario Redundancy Computations

In this section, we are going to perform the calculations done in Step 3 of our divide-and-conquer algorithm. For each scenario, we are going to combine the availability of network devices in serial and parallel subsections until we are ready to perform end-to-end calculations for our scenarios.

The Scenario 1 Redundancy Section Computations

Scenario 1 has redundancy in that the call control center C2 backs up the call control center C1. If you look at the RBD in Figure 5-2, you can see that the path to call control center C2 spans several devices. In order for C2 to be available for this scenario, a serial set of equipment including two routers and a switch must also be operational.

Step 3 of our algorithm requires first computing the availability of Router 1 (R1), Router 2 (R2), Switch 2 (S2), and CallManager (C2). This is the serial subsection of the parallel call control section. Once that result is obtained, we combine that result with the availability of call control center 1 (C1) in order to obtain a result for the entire parallel section in our network. That result is used in Step 4 of our process when we perform the end-to-end network availability calculations.

Figure 5-5 depicts the calculations for the serial and the parallel components within Scenario 1 of our VoIP example.

Figure 5-5   *The Redundancy Component Calculations for Scenario 1 (In-Building: Figure 5-2)*

Serial Subsection Calculations

R1 Availability = .99985
R2 Availability = .99985
S2 Availability = .99980
C2 Availability = $*$.99999
Subsection Availaility = .99949

Parallel Section Calculation

C1 Availability = .99999
C2 Backup Subsection Availability = .99949
Parallel Availability = 1 − [(1 − .99999) * (1 − .99949)]
Total Parallel Section Availability = .999999*

* Truncated to 6 digits

As you can see from the calculations, the redundant call control centers improve the availability of call management from five 9s to so many 9s we just call it six! When we perform the end-to-end calculations, the call control portion of the network will not be the place that causes any significant downtime.

The Scenario 2 Redundancy Section Computations

Scenario 2 also includes a section with redundancy. Looking at the RBD in Figure 5-3, we can see that two paths exist from building to building. The voice call could go between the buildings via the cable from R1 to R2 (routers 1 and 2) or it could (if required) get to the remote building by traversing the PSTN.

In this case the cable itself is so reliable, we are assuming near perfection. In reality, we would have to have a partial failure of one of the routers in order to see that path drop. When considering that the PSTN connection between the two buildings is also very available, we are going to assume six 9s for this parallel section without even performing the calculations.

The key point that you should derive here is that a parallel section in our RBD was created. This parallel section needs to be analyzed before we include the parallel section in the end-to-end results. In this case, we assumed .999999 as the result to use in our end-to-end Scenario 2 calculations.

The Scenario 3 Redundancy Section Computations

Scenario 3 provides another example of parallel redundancy with serial subcomponents. Again, the redundancy is with respect to the call control centers. The RBD shown in Figure 5-4 shows the redundancy here. However, this time the additional devices required to support the connection to C2 is reduced from Scenario 1. In Scenario 1, we would never use R1 unless C2 were required. In this scenario, we will use R1 regardless. The additional devices are R2, S2, and C2 as shown in the RBD (refer to Figure 5-4).

The calculations we will perform are very similar to those we performed for Scenario 1. We first compute the availability of the three serial devices that represent half of our parallel component. Then we multiply that result with the other half of our parallel component—C1. Figure 5-6 shows the calculations for this.

Figure 5-6   *The Redundancy Component Calculations for Scenario 2 (On-Net-To-Off-Net: Figure 5-4)*

Serial Subsection Calculations

R2 Availability =   .99985
S2 Availability =   .99980
C2 Availability = $*$ .99999
                _____
            =   .99964

Parallel Section Availability

C1 = .99999

C2 Backup = .99964

Parallel = $1 - [(1 - .99999)(1 - .99964)]$

= .999999*

* Truncated to 6 digits

Again, the results for the parallel section are nearly perfect and we will use six 9s of availability when we perform our end-to-end calculations for Scenario 3.

Summary of Step 3: Redundancy Calculations by Scenario

In each of the three scenarios, we have determined the availability for the redundant section of the network. As it turns out in this example, they are all six 9s of availability due to truncating. If you perform the calculations yourself on your calculator, however, you can see that there are actually slight differences. You could assume 1.0 as the availability for the wire between the two buildings.

Another possibility would be to include the network modules in the two routers as part of the wire in Scenario 2 and omit them in the calculations of the routers themselves. As you perform calculations in real life, you must determine these considerations for yourself based on your understanding of how the network functions. The process of dividing and conquering our network into its parallel and serial components remains the same.

Step 4: End-to-End Availability Calculations for Each Scenario

We now enter our fourth and final step in the divide-and-conquer process. We have created our RBDs, calculated the availability for each of our network components, and determined the availability of the redundant sections of our network.

All that remains is to perform the end-to-end calculations for each scenario using the serial availability equation.

Scenario 1 End-to-End Network Availability Computations

Scenario 1, as depicted in Figure 5-2, includes redundant call control centers. The availability of that section of the network is .999999. Figure 5-7 includes that result with the rest of the component availability figures from Table 5-1 in the end-to-end calculations for Scenario 1.

Figure 5-7   *The End-to-End Availability Calculations for Scenario 1*

$$
\begin{array}{rl}
\text{Switch 1 Availability} = & .99980 \\
\text{Call Control Center Availability} = {} * & \underline{.999999} \\
\text{Scenario 1 Availability} = & .999799
\end{array}
$$

As you can see, the result of the calculations is nearly entirely based on the availability of the switch (S1). The switch S1 provides only three 9s of availability in this simple network. After we finish our end-to-end calculations for our scenarios, we can look into improving our results.

The Scenario 2 End-to-End Network Availability Computations

Scenario 2, as depicted in Figure 5-3, includes building to building connections via a wire and the PSTN. The availability of that section of the network is .999999 but we are going to use the 1.0 in order to show that section as virtually perfect. Figure 5-8 includes that result with the rest of the component availability figures from Table 5-1 in the end-to-end calculations for Scenario 2.

Figure 5-8   *The End-to-End Availability Calculations for Scenario 2*

$$
\begin{aligned}
\text{S1 Availability} &= .99980 \\
\text{C1 Availability} &= .99999 \\
\text{R1 Availability} &= .99985 \\
\text{Connection} &= 1.0 \\
\text{R2 Availability} &= .99985 \\
\text{C2 Availability} &= .99999 \\
\text{S2 Availability} &= {}_* .99980 \\
\hline
\text{Scenario 2 Availability} &= .99928
\end{aligned}
$$

As you can see, the result of the calculations is .99928. Three 9s of availability is very low for a network that carries voice traffic. Again, you can see there are several devices in serial with low availabilities.

The Scenario 3 End-to-End Network Availability Computations

Scenario 3, as depicted in Figure 5-3, includes redundant call control centers again. The availability of that redundant section is .999999. Figure 5-9 includes that result with the rest of the component availability figures from Table 5-1 in the end-to-end calculations for scenario 2 below.

Figure 5-9   *The End-to-End Availability Calculations for Scenario 3*

$$
\begin{aligned}
\text{Switch 1} &= .99980 \\
\text{Router 1} &= .99985 \\
\text{Call Control} &= .999999 \\
\text{PSTN} &= {}_* .9997 \\
\hline
\text{End-to-End Availability} &= .999349
\end{aligned}
$$

As you can see, the result of the calculations is .999349. Again we have been limited to a result of only three nines by a couple of serial devices with only three nines of availability.

Section Summary: The End-to-End Network Availability Results

After computing the end-to-end results for our example network using the divide-and-conquer method, we have learned two things. First, we learned that the divide-and-conquer method is easy to use. Second, we learned that this particular network has some availability results we might want to improve.

Because one of the key goals of performing availability predictions is to enable a network designer to improve the design before actually building the network, I am including the following section on Designing Networks for Availability Goals. If you are only interested in predicting availability of networks without redesigning them yourself, you could skip this section and move to the next chapter.

Designing Networks for Availability Goals

We have taken a fairly simple network, divided it into manageable scenarios, and performed the availability calculations for the different scenarios. The next problem is to take a look at those results and determine some methods for improving the availability of the network by making specific changes. To do this we must make a list of our goals. In Table 5-2, we describe the availability for our scenarios. The first column depicts the results of our network as specified. The second column includes the likely availability results one might get if they used a traditional method of purchasing a phone line for every phone in the building. The final column represents a goal we might set for our network using new-world technology, taking into consideration the cost savings of the new technologies.

Table 5-2   *Table of Availability Results and Goals*

Scenarios	Current Network Design	Traditional Telephone Network Results	Goals for Our Network
In-building calls	.999799	.9999	.9998
Building-to-building calls	.99928	.9997	.9994
Building-to-PSTN calls	.999349	.9997	.9996

Interestingly enough, our network has performed reasonably well based on Table 5-2. We nearly equal traditional technologies for in building calls. Our building-to-building and building-to-PSTN scenarios could use some work. Here are our preliminary conclusions:

- The in-building results are close enough. If we wanted to improve the availability of .999799 to .9998, the first thing I would do is to see if we could put a more highly available part into the switch. Perhaps we could change to a more stable version of the software or add a redundant power supply.

- Building-to-building calls suffer considerably by using the new-world model compared with the traditional model. We will need to examine this scenario more carefully. We definitely would like to improve the results for this scenario.

- Calls from the building onto the PSTN are below our goals. This is partly caused by the PSTN. However, we will want to make our network as available as possible if we want to sell any of them to customers wanting high availability.

Overall we have two cases where availability is a little lower than we would like.

If we look at the RBDs for Scenarios 2 and 3 (refer to Figures 5-3 and 5-4 respectively), we might see opportunity for improvement. In both diagrams, we see that the Switch S1 is in serial configuration and has the lowest availability.

In order to improve the availability of our two scenarios, we might decide to dual-home switches S1 and S2 with redundant switches S3 and S4. This would create a situation where the switches would be in parallel instead of serial configuration. We are actually going to perform the steps of the divide-and-conquer process for Scenario 2 relative to our redesign.

To examine this concept, we need a network diagram that depicts the proposed new design. Figure 5-10 depicts our network if there were a way to make the switches redundant.

Figure 5-10 *A Revised VoIP Network with Improved Design*

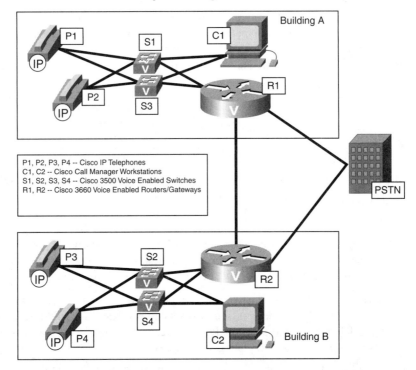

If you look carefully, you can see that there are now four switches instead of two and that the phones, call control centers, and the routers are all connected to two switches instead of only one. With this new network design, we need to redo our RBDs for our scenario.

Figure 5-11 shows the RBD for Scenario 2 following the rules of the new, improved network design.

As you can see in the RBD, there are now two additional redundant sections of our network that need to be calculated before we can redo our end-to-end calculations. After that, we can determine the actual improvement we get by adding redundancy to our network. Because we already performed the analysis of the individual components, you are reminded that we performed Step 1 of our process by redoing our RBD. We performed Step 2 previously.

We are now ready to perform the calculations to determine the availability of our switches when they are in parallel, as in Figure 5-12.

Figure 5-11 *Scenario 2 Revised RBD*

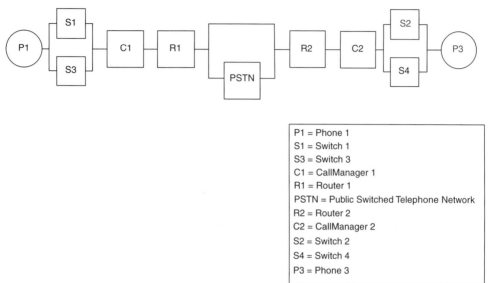

```
P1 = Phone 1
S1 = Switch 1
S3 = Switch 3
C1 = CallManager 1
R1 = Router 1
PSTN = Public Switched Telephone Network
R2 = Router 2
C2 = CallManager 2
S2 = Switch 2
S4 = Switch 4
P3 = Phone 3
```

Figure 5-12 *The Revised Redundancy Component Calculations*

$$S1, S2, S3, S4 = .99980$$
$$S1, S3 \text{ and } S2, S4 \text{ in Parallel} = 1 - ((1 - .9998)(1 - .9998))$$
$$= .999999 \text{ truncated}$$

The new availability of .999999 for the area of the network that provides our switching service should provide a big improvement when compared with the previous value of .9998 for that area.

We are now ready to perform our final step in analyzing the availability of our new improved network. Figure 5-13 shows the end-to-end calculations for our improved VoIP network.

Figure 5-13 *The Improved Scenario 2 End-to-End Calculations*

$$\begin{aligned}
S1 \text{ and } S3 \text{ Switch Availability} &= .999999 \\
C1 \text{ Availability} &= .999999 \\
R1 \text{ Availability} &= .99985 \\
\text{Connection} &= 1.0 \\
R2 \text{ Availability} &= .99985 \\
C2 \text{ Availability} &= .99999 \\
S2 \text{ and } S4 \text{ Switch Availability} &= *\ \underline{.999999} \\
&\ .999678
\end{aligned}$$

Our new calculations for Scenario 2 come in at .999678. By putting the lowest performing device in our network (relative to availability) in a redundant topology, we have considerably improved our availability. In fact, our new availability achieves the goal that we had determined to be reasonable for the scenario in Table 5-2.

A fun exercise that you might want to try would be to calculate the new availability that we would get if we redid the divide-and-conquer steps for Scenario 3. The final answer for those that would like to do the work is .999548.

Summary

The divide-and-conquer method makes it easy to figure out the availability of a network. Once a network is analyzed, alternative scenarios can be analyzed. Regardless of the size or complexity of the network, the divide-and-conquer method should make performing availability calculations much easier.

Examples of Analyzing Real-World Availability

Chapter 6   Three Cisco Products: An Availability Analysis

Chapter 7   A Small ISP Network: An Availability Analysis

Chapter 8   An Enterprise Network: An Availability Analysis

Chapter 9   A Large VoIP Network: An Availability Analysis

Three Cisco Products:
An Availability Analysis

This chapter provides a foundation for determining the availability of real-world internetworking switches and routers. As you know, any network availability prediction must include the prediction of availability for each of its components. This chapter walks through three examples that will be highly valuable:

- The Cisco uBR 924 is a small network device that connects cable company customers to their network.

- The Cisco uBR 7246 is a device with some redundancy built in that resides at a cable company's central site.

- The Cisco 12000 is a highly reliable and redundant system that is used in many backbone network situations.

Once you have read each of the examples in this chapter and understand the process, you should be able to perform similar availability calculations on any system. With minor modifications, the examples in this chapter should be applicable to just about any switch or router.

Cisco uBR 924 Availability Calculations

The Cisco uBR 924 is a simple cable router (often called a cable modem) and is called *customer premises equipment* (CPE). Cable routers are generally used to connect household networks to the Internet. This particular router includes a cable port, two telephone ports, and four Ethernet ports. This enables a WAN connection to the Internet over the cable port. The household data networking is serviced by the four Ethernet ports. The two telephone ports make it possible for two normal household telephones (or fax machines, modems, and so on) to be connected and used over the cable network.

Because this device might be used to provide telephone service, its availability must be calculated and explained to customers so that they can confidently deploy the device in their network. The companies purchasing this product from Cisco Systems are likely to be large cable companies that want to provide telephone services over their cable network infrastructure. These companies will then rent or lease the uBR 924 to their customers.

The uBR 924, shown in Figure 6-1, is a relatively simple device to analyze for availability as you need to analyze only two major components and an operating system.

Figure 6-1   *The Cisco uBR 924 Cable Router*

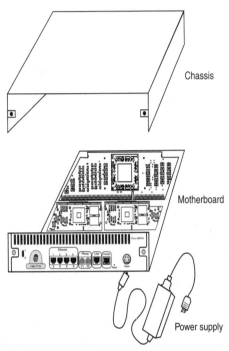

The MTBF calculated using the Telcordia (formerly Bellcore) parts count method of the uBR 924 cable router is 135,182 hours. The power supply was included in those calculations since it is always present and is serially attached to the motherboard. The uBR 924 is a relatively new product. Because the Cisco IOS Software that runs on this product is new and is still having new features added regularly, we are going to use 10,000 hours for the MTBF of the Cisco IOS Software.

The MTTR for this device is going to be estimated at 12 hours for the hardware and 0.1 hour for the software. In most cases, the hardware will be replaced the same day or the next morning if it fails. If the software crashes, the router should reboot in less than six minutes.

Although this device is simple, we will go ahead and show a block diagram of the product's operational parts in order to make sure that we understand any parallel, serial, or serial/ parallel paths for the data. This enables us to arrange our calculations properly and with consideration for redundancy. As you can see from Figure 6-2, the block diagram for this product is very simple. In this particular case, the reliability engineer that provided the MTBF for the hardware included the power supply MTBF as part of the motherboard MTBF. This leads to a single MTBF for both parts. This is a good example of why you should know what your MTBF numbers are based on.

Figure 6-2   *The uBR 924 Reliability Block Diagram*

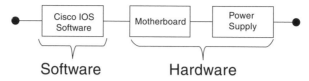

If we were including this device in a network, then we would have some idea of where the device might be located and, thus, some idea of the potential losses in power that could contribute to annual downtime. Without a full network and customer profile, however, we are unable to analyze downtime due to any of the other factors that might come up.

Figure 6-3 shows the availability of the Cisco uBR 924 cable router based on hardware and software analysis. In the final steps, the number of downtime minutes each year is calculated.

Figure 6-3   *The Availability Calculations for the Cisco uBR 924 Cable Router*

Step 1: Motherboard and Cisco IOS Software MTBF and MTTR

	MTBF	MTTR
Motherboard	135,182 hours	12 hours
Cisco IOS Software	10,000 hours	0.1 hours

Step 2: Motherboard and Cisco IOS Software Availability

$$\text{Motherboard Availability} = \frac{135,182}{135,182 + 12}$$

$$= 0.99991$$

$$\text{Cisco IOS Software Availability} = \frac{10,000}{10,000 + 0.1}$$

$$= 0.99999$$

Step 3: System Availability

$$\text{System Availability} = .99991 * .99999$$

$$= .9999$$

Step 4: Downtime per Year

525,960 minutes per year $*$ (1 − .9999) = 52.6 minutes per year of downtime

As you can see from the calculations, the overall downtime for the uBR 924 is 52.6 minutes per year. Although this is a little bit high if we are planning to use this device in a telephone network, it is an acceptable data product.

Later in Chapter 9, "A Large VoIP Network: An Availability Analysis," we look at a cable network that includes a device similar to the uBR 924. At that time, you will see how several minutes of downtime affects an end-to-end network calculation for a voice over cable network. Additionally, you will see how to account for losses of availability due to other factors besides hardware and software.

Cisco uBR 7246 Availability Calculations

The Cisco uBR 7246 cable head end router is the head end that a uBR 924 would connect to via a cable company's "cable plant." For our purposes, we will consider the cable plant to be a simple coax cable between the uBR 7246 and the uBR 924. However, this is definitely not true in the real world, and in Chapter 9 you will see that we account for downtime (and explain additional detail) of the cable plant in our network calculations.

Figure 6-4 shows a diagram of the uBR 7246 router. On the front side of the router, the key features are the four slots on the lower half that allow insertion of up to four adapter cards for cable ports. The recessed upper half includes three slots for the insertion of CPU cards and LAN back-haul port adapters. On the back side of the router (not shown), the notable features are the two bays for accepting the dual redundant power supplies.

Figure 6-4 *The Cisco uBR 7246 Router*

The uBR 7246 is a partially redundant router. It has dual redundant power supplies. If two power supplies are installed and operational and one fails, the router will continue operating without any problem. The failed power supply can be replaced, and the uBR 7246 can continue to run with redundant power. The redundant power supplies for the uBR 7246 are predicted to have an MTBF of 746,269 hours each.

The uBR 7246 can accept one or more cable cards that connect to the cable plant. These are single points of failure for the data in and out of the router. There are several models of "cable network interface modules" for the uBR 7246. We are going to use the uBR-MC16C, which has a predicted MTBF of 275,046 hours.

The uBR 7246 does not use redundant processors. A variety of different CPUs are available. We will use the NPE225, which has an estimated MTBF of 269,800 hours.

The final non-redundant parts required to finish off the design of our uBR 7246 are the base chassis and the LAN back-haul port. For these MTBFs we use the 232,948 hours for the chassis and 360,383 for the I/O controller with built-in Fast Ethernet.

We need a block diagram showing the major parts required for this system to be available. Figure 6-5 shows both the serial and the parallel portions of the system. As you can see, there are two parallel components, which will need to be counted as a subsystem in the end-to-end serial calculations.

Figure 6-5   *The uBR 7246 Reliability Block Diagram*

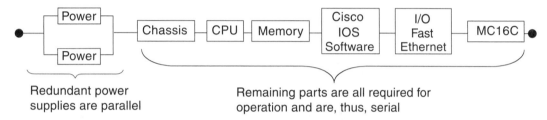

Because this particular device normally resides inside a cable company's central location, it is possible to service this box very fast. In some cases, with the parts on hand, the box can be serviced in well under two hours should anything fail. In nearly all cases, four hours is a conservative estimate for MTTR of the hardware devices. With that in mind we have decided to perform out calculations based on a four-hour MTTR for all hardware parts and a .1-hour MTTR for the Cisco IOS Software.

Because the software for the uBR 7246 has been available for over a year, it is possible to select a stable version. With this in mind, we will estimate 30,000 hours for our software MTBF. As you saw in Chapter 4, "Factors That Affect Availability," in the section on calculating software MTBF, this is a conservative number for stable versions of Cisco IOS Software.

Table 6-1 lists all the parts in this router and their associated MTBF and MTTR assumptions.

Table 6-1   *uBR 7246 Router Component MTBF and MTTR Values*

Part	Description	MTBF	MTTR
uBR 7246	Universal broadband router chassis	232,948	4
uBR-7200-I/O-FE	uBR I/O process with Fast Ethernet	360,383	4
MEM-I/O-FLD48M	20 MB Flash memory	333,166	4
NPE-225	CPU for uBR 7246	269,800	4
uBR-MC16C	MC16C cable module	275,046	4
PWR-uBR-7200-AC	Power supply	746,269	4
SU7M3-12.0.7SC	Cisco IOS Software	30,000	0.1

With each of the components of the system described for MTBF and MTTR, we are ready to proceed to the calculations for availability. In the set of calculations shown in Figure 6-6, you will find an extra step compared to the previous uBR 924 example. That is a result of the redundant power supplies and the calculations required to include them in our calculations.

Figure 6-6   *The uBR 7246 Availability Calculations*

Step 1: Component Availability

uBR 7245	$= \dfrac{232,948}{232,948 + 4}$
	$= 0.9999828$
uBR-7200-I/O-FE	$= \dfrac{360,383}{360,383 + 4}$
	$= 0.9999889$
MEM-I/O-FLD48M	$= \dfrac{333,166}{333,166 + 4}$
	$= 0.9999880$
NPE225	$= \dfrac{269,800}{269,800 + 4}$
	$= 0.9999852$
uBR-MC16C	$= \dfrac{275,046}{275,046 + 4}$
	$= 0.9999854$
PWR-VBR7200-AC	$= \dfrac{746,269}{746,269 + 4}$
	$= 0.9999946$
SU7M3-12.0.7SC	$= \dfrac{30,000}{30,000 + .1}$
	$= 0.9999967$

Step 2: Redundant Components

Power availability $= [1-\{(1 - .9999946) * (1 - .9999946)\}]$
$= 0.999999999971$

Step 3: System Availability

Part	Availability
uBR 7245	0.9999828
uBR-7200-I/O-FE	0.9999889
MEM-I/O-FLD48M	0.9999880
NPE225	0.9999852
uBR-MC16C	0.9999854
PWR-VBR7200-AC	0.999999999971
SU7M3-12.0.7SC	$*$ 0.9999967

System availability $= .999927$ (Hardware and software only)

Step 4: Annual Downtime

Annual Downtime $= 525,960 (1 - .999927)$
$= 38.4$ minutes

As you can see from our calculations, the uBR 7246 availability is very good. When two uBR 7246 routers are used in parallel, they provide a highly available solution appropriate for use in voice networks. Chapter 9 includes the uBR 7246 as a key component in a voice network.

Cisco 12000 Availability Calculations

The Cisco 12000 router, normally used in data centers, provides a connection point powerful enough to connect several large networks. This particular router includes several redundant components and is, thus, the perfect candidate to depict a highly redundant system example. Figure 6-7 shows the front side of the Cisco 12000, including the various slots for different components.

Figure 6-7   *The Cisco 12000 Router*

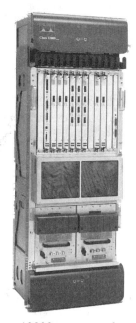

The Cisco 12000 router can be configured in a variety of different ways. There are several redundant items. As a result of the complexity of this product, you will find that the chassis is actually divided up into several serviceable components as listed in Table 6-2.

Table 6-2   *Cisco 12000 Router Components*

Part Number	Description	MTBF	MTTR
GSR12012	GSR12 backplane	620,367	6
GSR12-BLOWER	Blower assembly	570,288	4
PWR-GSR12-AC	AC power supply	316,456	4

continues

Table 6-2   *Cisco 12000 Router Components (Continued)*

Part Number	Description	MTBF	MTTR
GSR12-CSC	Scheduler fabric	272,584	4
GSR12-SFC	Switching fabric	422,115	4
GRP-B	Route processor	87,070	4
4OC3/ATM-IR-SC	4 port ATM card	108,304	4
S120Z-12.0.10S	Cisco IOS Software	30,000	.2
MEM-GRP-FL20	20 MB Flash memory	333,166	4
MEM-DFT-GRP/LC-64	Program/route memory	1,984,827	4

Because the Cisco 12000 router will reside in a central site that is staffed, we are going to give each of the hardware devices a four-hour MTTR. We make an exception and add two hours for the back plane because it would be a difficult replacement involving removal of all of the sub-components. The Cisco IOS Software is going to get a .2 hour MTTR. Although we normally use .1 hour, this is a box that is likely to have very large routing tables and could, thus, take some extra time to boot and begin forwarding packets after a software crash.

With MTBF and MTTR numbers for all of the components in the system, the next step is to create a reliability block diagram (see Figure 6-8) showing the parallel and serial components.

Figure 6-8   *Cisco 12000 Reliability Block Diagram*

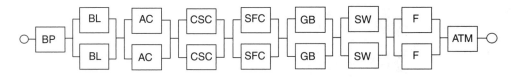

```
BP  = Back Plane
BL  = Blower
AC  = AC Power
CSC = Scheduler Fabric
SFC = Switch Fabric
GB  = Route Processor
SW  = Cisco IOS Software on GRP-B
F   = Flash Memory on GRP-B
ATM = ATM Card
```

As you can see from Figure 6-8, the Cisco 12000 power supplies, route processors, and switch fabrics run in parallel. The chassis and the ATM module are serial components. The two-step process for calculating the availability of the 12000 is to calculate the availability of the parallel subsystems and then to use those results in the calculations of the entire system using the serial availability equation. The actual calculations are done for you in Figures 6-9 through 6-11.

Figure 6-9   *The Cisco 12000 Availability Calculations: Step 1*

Component Calculations

Availability of:

GSR12012-Backplane $= \dfrac{620,367}{620,367 + 6}$

$= .999992$

GSR12-Blower $= \dfrac{570,288}{570,288 + 4}$

$= .999993$

PWR-GSRR-AC $= \dfrac{316,456}{316,456 + 4}$

$= .999987$

GSR12-CSC $= \dfrac{272,584}{272,584 + 4}$

$= .999985$

GSR12-SFC $= \dfrac{422,115}{422,115 + 4}$

$= .999990$

GRP-B $= \dfrac{87,070}{87,070 + 4}$

$= .999954$

40C3/ATM-JR-SC $= \dfrac{108,304}{108,304 + 4}$

$= .999963$

S1207-12.0.IOS $= \dfrac{30,000}{30,000 + .2}$

$= .999993$

MEM-GRP-FL20 $= \dfrac{333,166}{333,166 + 4}$

$= .999988$

MEM-DFT-GRP/LC-64 $= \dfrac{1,984,827}{1,984,827 + 4}$

$= .999998$

Figure 6-10 *The Cisco 12000 Availability Calculations: Step 2*

Sub-System Assemblies

Serial Assemblies

Processor Board and its memory items

$$
\begin{array}{rcl}
\text{GRP-B} &=& .999954 \\
\text{MEM-GRP-FL20} &=& .999988 \\
\text{MEM-DFT-GFT/LC-64} &=& .999998 \\
\text{S1207-12.0.105} &=& *\ \underline{.999993} \\
&& .999933
\end{array}
$$

Parallel Assemblies

$$
\begin{aligned}
\text{Processors} &= [1 - 1(1 - .999933)(1 - .999933)] \\
&= .9999999955 \\
\text{Switch Fabric} &= [1 - 1(1 - .99999)(1 - .99999)] \\
&= .9999999999 \\
\text{Scheduler Fabric} &= [1 - 1(1 - .999985)(1 - .999985)] \\
&= .9999999775 \\
\text{Power} &= [1 - 1(1 - .999987)(1 - .999987)] \\
&= .9999999998 \\
\text{Blowers} &= [1 - 1(1 - .999993)(1 - .999993)] \\
&= .9999999995
\end{aligned}
$$

Figure 6-11 *The Cisco 12000 System Availability Calculations: Steps 3 and 4*

Step 3: System Availability

Backplane	=	.999992
ATM	=	.999963
Processors	=	.999999995
Switch Fabric	=	.999999999
Scheduler Fabric	=	.999999999775
Power	=	.9999999998
Blowers	=	* .999999995
System	=	.99995

Step 4: Annual Downtime

$$= [525,960 * (1 - .99995)]$$
$$= 23.67 \text{ minutes/year}$$

As you can see from the calculations, this large system generates 24 minutes per year of downtime. While this may seem like a lot of downtime for a system that supports such large networks, it is not. These systems are almost always used in parallel, which creates a network design that has a high availability. The network calculations for two 12000s in parallel will be done in the service provider network example in Chapter 9.

CHAPTER 7

A Small ISP Network: An Availability Analysis

In this chapter, we are going to go through the process of predicting the availability for a small Internet service provider. We will do this by using all of the techniques we have learned as we have gone through the book. We are also going to begin using some tools to do our work, rather than doing all of the computations by hand. As you work through the chapter, you will notice the inclusion of some screenshots from a spreadsheet. These screenshots are from a Microsoft Excel spreadsheet that we call SHARC, System Hardware Availability and Reliability Calculator.

The SHARC spreadsheet is included on the CD-ROM that accompanies this book. SHARC is included for educational purposes only, and there are some licensing rules regarding this Cisco Systems software on the CD. The rules are if you want to use SHARC for your own network or for educational purposes, then you are free to do so. Using SHARC as a tool to sell networking equipment or services requires additional licensing from Cisco Systems.

SHARC enables us to perform system level availability calculations considerably faster than if we had to do them all by hand. If you are not comfortable with system level calculations, you should take some time to verify the SHARC results by hand.

Given that we are going to use SHARC, we still need to perform our calculations using the processes and equations you have learned throughout this book. Our first set of tasks will be to define the network, make various assumptions, and determine our scenarios. From there, we will move into the calculations for the individual systems in the network. Finally, we will combine the individual systems and compute the availability for our scenarios.

The Small Internet Service Provider Network

The focus of the chapter is to perform the tasks involved with predicting availability figures for a small Internet service provider network. As you have seen, this will require several steps. In this section, we will define the network, make our assumptions, and determine the scenarios we want to analyze.

The network on which we are going to perform our calculations resembles a small service provider for modem and ISDN dialup customers. The equipment used is a little bit more than would be required for this particular network but would enable a lot of growth. End customers use either a modem or an ISDN router to dial up the ISP. Their calls are routed via twisted pair into their local PSTN. The calls are then forwarded to the ISP machinery via T1 lines.

Once the end user traffic has been delivered to the ISP machinery, it is aggregated in access servers and then back-hauled into the backbone network for the service provider. This traffic can be delivered on the ISP network or it can be sent to the Internet. The Internet connection is done via a connection to the local Network Access Point (NAP) of the Internet. Before the calls can be connected, they must be authenticated by the ISP. Redundant UNIX computers at the ISP site perform this connection.

Figure 7-1 depicts the network diagram for this small service provider.

Figure 7-1   *A Small ISP Network Diagram*

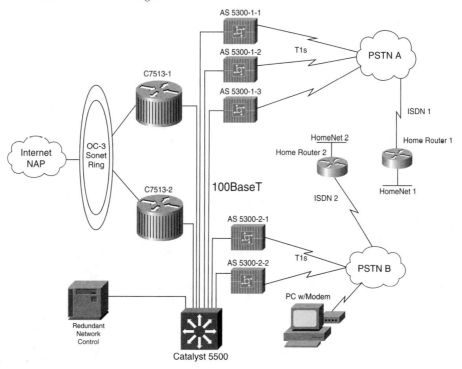

As you can see in the diagram, two Cisco 7513 routers carry the ISP's backbone traffic. Access aggregation is performed by Cisco AS5300 routers. The AS5300s are connected to the 7513s via a Catalyst 5500 switch. Network control will be provided by a pair of UNIX workstations running DHCP, RADIUS, and other processes. If the customer is using a modem, they will own it themselves. If the customer is using an ISDN router, it is likely they will be using the Cisco 800 ISDN-to-Ethernet router. The control computers are shown attached to the Catalyst 5500 in the ISP network.

We are primarily concerned with the availability of the network from the customer's perspective. Because customers on this network are mainly attempting to access the Internet instead of each other, our data flow will be from the customers to the Internet and back. There are two major categories of customers and that creates two scenarios for us to analyze for each ingress point in our network. Because there are two ingress points, we have four scenarios. However, we are going to look at only two scenarios. The first is a modem dialing into the ingress point of three AS5300s (PSTN A equipment in Figure 7-1). The second is where there is an ISDN router attached to the ingress point of two AS5300 routers (PSTN B equipment in Figure 7-1). You might wish to use the intermediate results from these two scenarios and perform the calculations for the others on your own for additional practice.

The first scenario describes the access to the Internet for customers that are using a modem. The second scenario is for customers that are using an ISDN router. The largest difference in the scenarios will be downtime at the customer premises. There may be other differences as well because certain equipment at the ISP site may not be used in all cases.

Because modems are usually purchased by consumers who own their PC, the ISP is not normally responsible for downtime when that part of the network fails. Additionally for these customers, if they have no dial tone then that's unlikely to be attributed to their ISP. Dial tone is the responsibility of the customer's telephone company. In the modem dialup scenario, the ISP is responsible for the access aggregation point and further into the network as depicted in the reliability block diagram (RBD) in Figure 7-2.

Figure 7-2   *The RBD for Scenario 1 of the Small ISP*

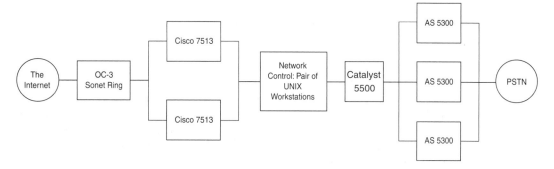

As you can see, the RBD shows three AS5300 access routers configured in parallel. However, that is not strictly true. If a customer dials into AS5300-1-1 (from Figure 7-1) and it fails, then they will be disconnected. They should be able to immediately dial back and get connected to AS5300-1-2 or AS5300-1-3, but the fact that they were disconnected and had to call back is going to cause them to have a couple minutes of downtime. The fail-over mechanism for the AS5300 ingress ports (T1 ports) is that the PSTN switch will recognize a down port and route the calls to one of the ports that is available.

As you may have noticed, three AS5300 routers are attached to the PSTN represented as A. Relative to our studies so far, this setup represents a new redundancy construction. Instead of having two devices in parallel, this is an example of having three devices in parallel. It could be possible to have this configured for either one backup and two primary devices or one primary and two backup devices. In this case, we are going to assume two primary devices and one backup device.

NOTE   Although we have not previously specifically mentioned the case where backup devices are not related to primary devices in a one-to-one relationship, they do exist in the real world. This scenario is called *N + 1 redundancy*. It is also possible to have a situation where you might have some number *N* primary devices with some number *X* in standby.

The mathematics representing these situations are a little bit more complex. We overcome that issue by using the software on the CD included with the book. The CD has the capability of performing these types of calculations. We simply put in the total number of devices in parallel and the number of devices required for success and it will do the calculations for us.

The general equation for N − 1 of N (sometimes this is called N + 1 by network designers) redundancy is:

$$A = nA^{(n-1)} * (1 - A) + A^n$$

Where A = Availability and n is the number of devices.

Although complete coverage of N − 1 of or N − 2 of N redundancy schemes is beyond the scope of this book, the spreadsheets included make short work of these types of calculations. We'll simply call these N + 1 designs and let the spreadsheet do the work for us.

The Cisco 7513s, network control computers, and the A5300s are part of an OSPF routed network over the 100BaseT network provided by the Catalyst 5500. The connection to the Internet is over an OC-3 connection, which is via static routes in the 7513s that route any non-local traffic into the Internet for further processing. The NAP sends appropriate traffic to the ISP for the addresses it supports.

Figure 7-3 shows the RBD for Scenario 2. Scenario 2 includes more equipment. Customers using an ISDN connection to the Internet will perceive downtime if their computer is working and they still can't gain access to the Internet. Access requires both the PSTN and the home router to be added to the RBD.

Figure 7-3   *The RBD for Scenario 2 of the Small ISP*

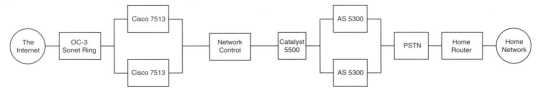

The PSTN network is relatively transparent to a small ISP. We will simply use numbers for MTBF and MTTR likely to be provided by the telephone company for that section of the network. The home router will be included as well and that will be the Cisco 800 router figures. The rest of the Scenario 2 devices will be almost exactly the same as in Scenario 1. We will have only two AS5300s in this scenario. The N + 1 redundancy calculations will be *simple parallel*.

Scenario 1 of The Small ISP Example

With an idea of the data flow through our network, we have been able to determine a few scenarios. As we learned in Chapter 5, "Predicting End-to-End Network Availability: The Divide-and-Conquer Method," we will use the divide-and-conquer method. We will divide the scenario into smaller parts. Then we will combine the results of those parts together.

When we finish with this scenario, you will see that many of the results will be used in Scenario 2.

System Level Calculations for Scenario 1

Now that we know how the devices are connected together as depicted in the RBD in Figure 7-2, we can perform the system level calculations for Scenario 1. Because there are a variety of ways these types of systems can be configured, it was important to have the scenario information before we start the system level calculations. In most cases, the system level calculations from Scenario 1 will work in Scenario 2.

In this section, we will start at the furthest extremity of our network and work our way into the Internet. Each system will require analysis for hardware and software contribution to network downtime. Some additional downtime should be calculated for environmental considerations. In the next section, when we begin calculating the end-to-end network availability, we will perform the calculations for the human error and network design contributions to network downtime.

For the PSTN and other components of our network not under our control, we will simply assume reasonable availability figures. If you are a system administrator or are responsible for these types of calculations, you should be able to get real figures from your service provider or telephone company.

The Cisco AS5300 System Availability Calculations for Scenario 1

The AS5300 router is complex enough that calculating the availability will require some extra thought. The design of the product includes a redundant power supply, but this power supply is not hot-swappable. Therefore, we will treat the device as a single component regarding MTBF but will reduce the MTTR to one hour because we will be able to order the part on failure and swap it out at our convenience. The router will not be down as a result of the typical failure but will simply be in need of the one hour maintenance downtime.

There will be 17 digital modem cards, which is one more than we actually need to cover our four T1 ports worth of traffic. The single carrier card will be a single point of failure.

At some point in the future, each of the AS5300 routers could switch the four-T1 card to an eight-T1 card and add another carrier card full of modems. For now, we are creating a small ISP with room for growth. Figure 7-4 shows the AS5300 router in order to give you an idea of what this router looks like. Because the design of the AS5300 includes cards that can be easily spared and swapped, we are going to assume a variety of MTTR times for the different components.

Figure 7-4   *The Cisco 5300 Router*

In determining the RBD for the AS5300 system, we assume an N + 1 configuration of the modems and a serial configuration for each of the other devices in the router. The redundant power supply is not shown in Figure 7-5 because we have included the redundancy in the power supply MTBF. One final notation is that when we calculate the availability for the AS5300 for ISDN termination as opposed to modem termination, the calculations will change. It might be fun for you to guess what we will do for Scenario 2 before we get there.

Figure 7-5   *The Cisco 5300 RBD for Scenario 1*

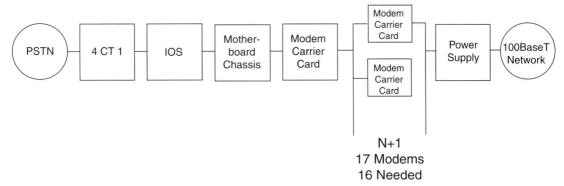

With the RBD completed and an understanding of how the device functions, we are ready to begin our calculations. However, we first need to list out the MTBF and MTTR numbers for each component as done in Table 7-1.

Table 7-1   *The Cisco 5300 MTBF and MTTR Assumptions*

System Component	MTBF (Hours)	MTTR (Hours)
AS5300 chassis and motherboard	45,218	4.0
AS5300 4 CT1 module	211,152	4.0
AS5300 Modem Carrier Card	290,930	4.0
AS5300 Mica Modem module	1,102,292	4.0
AS5300 redundant power supply	500,000	1.0
Cisco 5300 IOS	10,000*	0.1

* Although the Cisco IOS performs at 10,000 MTBF in most situations, the assumption of 10,000 hours for the AS5300 may be somewhat optimistic considering the complexity of the device. However, the actual number does not really matter for the purpose of learning how to perform the analysis.

As you can see in Table 7-1, the MTBF and MTTR numbers reflect our ideas about replacing components in the time it takes to get the parts. We have also made a couple other assumptions. First, we assume that the Mica modem MTBF figures include the Mica modem firmware. Second, we have assumed a 500,000-hour MTBF on the power supply, which might be a little bit optimistic because this particular supply sets new records in power per cubic inch.

Regardless of the actual MTBF numbers, the calculations remain the same for hardware and software as shown in Figure 7-6.

Figure 7-6 *The Cisco 5300 Availability HW/SW Computations*

Cisco Systems, Inc.

© 1998 Cisco Systems, Inc.

System Hardware Availability and Reliability Calculation Worksheet
For Series-Parallel Configurations

System Description: The Cisco 5300 Series Router

Prepared by: Chris Oggerino
Date: 30-Jan-01

System Availability % = 99.98668583% The fraction of time the system is operational.
System Unavailability % = 0.01331417% Equal to 1-Avail., and is the fraction of time the system is non-operational.
Annual Downtime (Min.) = 70.0 Equal to System Unavailability times 525,960 minutes per year.

System MTBF (Hrs.) = 7,559 The mean time to go from an operational to a non-operational state.
System MTBPR (Hrs.) = 6,770 The mean time between any part restoration (including the time to repair).
System MTTR (Hrs.) = 1.0 The mean time to repair the system, or the mean time to go from a non-operational to an operational state.

Move to far right for scientific notation →

Part Description	n (QTY)	m (No. Req.)	Part MTBF (hrs.)	Part MTTR (hrs.)	Part Availability	Combined Part Availability	Combined Part MTTR	Combined Part MTBF
Chassis/Motherboard	1	1	45,218	4	99.99115475%	99.99115475%	4.0	45,218
Carrier Card	1	1	290,930	4	99.99862512%	99.99862512%	4.0	290,930
6 Modem Module	17	16	1,102,292	4	99.99637712%	99.99999982%	2.0	1,116,840,633
Power Supply	1	1	500,000	1	99.99980000%	99.99980000%	1.0	500,000
4 T1 Card	1	1	211,152	4	99.99810567%	99.99810567%	4.0	211,152
Cisco IOS Software	1	1	10,000	0.100	99.99900001%	99.99900001%	0.1	10,000

NOTE   If you round off the figures created in the SHARC spreadsheet and use them to compute the minutes per year of downtime, the rounding will cause you to arrive at slightly different numbers than the spreadsheet.

The resulting .99987 (rounded) availability for the AS5300 will lead to approximately 70 minutes of downtime each year due to hardware and software for this device. Because this device resides at the central ISP site, we are not going to perform the other calculations for power, human error, or network design at this time. Those calculations will be done when we aggregate this device with the other devices in our network calculations in the final section of this chapter. The numbers from the spreadsheet will be used in the network computations, and the other three items will be applied to all of the devices at the ISP site.

One final note about the AS5300 results is that we will be performing a slightly different calculation for Scenario 2 because we do not need modems for ISDN connections.

The Catalyst 5500 System Availability Calculations for Scenario 1

Although the Catalyst 5500 system is providing basic switching for our ISP network, it is a key component in this network. The Catalyst 5500 is currently designed as a single point of failure. The Catalyst 5500 switch is intended to be a reliable device and has several redundant components. Figure 7-7 shows you a picture of a Catalyst 5500.

Figure 7-7   *The Catalyst 5500 Router*

In thinking about the operation of this device, we determine that the motherboard and the 24 port 100BaseT switch card are single points of failure, but the SUP II CPU card and the dual power supplies are redundant. Figure 7-8 shows the RBD for the Catalyst 5500.

Figure 7-8 *The Cisco Catalyst 5500 RBD*

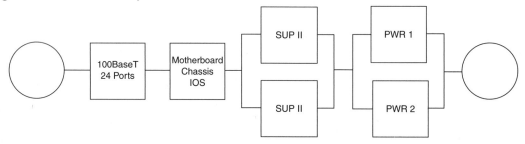

To perform the calculations for the Catalyst 5500 switch we need to list out the MTBF and MTTR for each of the components as done in Table 7-2.

Table 7-2 *The Cisco C5500 MTBF and MTTR Assumptions*

System Component	MTBF (Hours)	MTTR (Hours)
C5500 chassis and motherboard	182,207	4.0
C5500 24 100BaseT module	195,240	4.0
C5500 Dual SUP II cards	94,252	4.0
C5500 redundant power supply	746,269	4.0
Cisco C5500 IOS software	10,000*	0.1

* The Catalyst 5500 IOS Software MTBF is a rough estimate based on similar devices. For the purposes of this text, the actual number does not matter.

With the RBD and the MTBF/MTTR numbers, we are ready once again to use the SHARC spreadsheet to derive the system availability and annual downtime for the Cisco Catalyst 5500 router. Because our switch has redundant CPUs (SUP II cards) and each of those will run the operating system, we need to do a two step process as we have done before when capturing the availability of parallel components. Figure 7-9 shows the calculations for combining the operating system availability with the CPU hardware.

By including the software contribution to downtime on CPU, we can include the CPU in a redundant configuration in our system level calculations as shown in Figure 7-10. Figure 7-10 includes the results from Figure 7-9 that show the SUP II with software to have an MTBF of 9041 hours and an MTTR of .5 hour. This does include the concept of four-hour MTTR for the hardware and 0.1-hour MTTR for the software.

Figure 7-9   *The Cisco C5500 Availability: CPU HW and IOS Results*

System Hardware Availability and Reliability Calculation Worksheet
For Series-Parallel Configurations

© 1998 Cisco Systems, Inc.

Prepared by: Chris Oggerino
Date: 30-Jan-01

System Description: The Cisco C5500 SUP II and IOS Calculation

System Availability % =	**99.99475629%** The fraction of time the system is operational.
System Unavailability % =	**0.00524371%** Equal to 1-Avail., and is the fraction of time the system is non-operational.
***Annual* Downtime (Min.) =**	**27.6** Equal to System Unavailability times 525,960 minutes per year.
System MTBF (Hrs.) =	**9,041** The mean time to go from an operational to a non-operational state.
System MTBPR (Hrs.) =	**9,041** The mean time between any part restoration (including the time to repair).
System MTTR (Hrs.) =	**0.5** The mean time to repair the system, or the mean time to go from a non-operational to an operational state.

Move to far right for scientific notation →

	Part Description	n (QTY)	m (No. Req.)	Part MTBF (hrs.)	Part MTTR (hrs.)	Part Availability	Combined Part Availability	Combined Part MTTR	Combined Part MTBF
1	SUP II	1	1	94,252	4	99.99575624%	99.99575624%	4.0	94,252
2	IOS	1	1	10,000	0.100	99.99900001%	99.99900001%	0.1	10,000
3									
4									
5									
6									
7									
8									
9									
10									
11									
12									
13									
14									
15									
16									
17									
18									
19									
20									

Figure 7-10 *The Cisco C5500 Availability HW and SW Results*

As you can see, the Catalyst 5500 switch is a very reliable network device at .99996 availability. This device will contribute only about 22.3 minutes per year of downtime to our example network.

The Cisco 7513 System Availability Calculations for Scenario 1

The Cisco 7513 router is another device that has been designed to provide high availability in networks. With redundant power supplies and processors, the 7513 is nearly reliable enough for a single point of failure. However, with two different 7513s carrying traffic between the ISP network and the Internet, it will become a redundant component in our network. Figure 7-11 shows the 7513 router.

Figure 7-11 *The Cisco 7513 Router*

As with the other devices on this network, we need to draw a RBD for this device in order to make sure we calculate the availability of this system properly. In this case, we have something special because we are going to have two copies of Cisco IOS Software running—one on each processor. Although Figure 7-12 shows the RBD, that particular redundancy nuance is not captured and is instead captured in the actual calculations.

Figure 7-12 *A Cisco 7513 RBD*

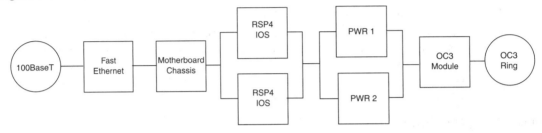

To calculate the availability of a device with redundant CPUs and operating systems, we must again do our RBD and perform a two step calculation process in order to get the parallel/serial components done right. Figure 7-13 shows the calculations for the Cisco 7513 CPU card and its operating system.

As you can see in the diagram, the results of combining the 7513 CPU with Cisco IOS Software provide an MTBF of 21,591 and an MTTR of 0.6 hours. We can plug these results into our system level calculations as a redundant CPU component. Figure 7-14 shows the system level calculation.

As you can see with all of the calculations done for you in the SHARC spreadsheets in Figure 7-14, the availability of the Cisco 7513 in this configuration would be .99994 and create an annual downtime of only 31.9 minutes. This downtime will be reduced dramatically when we combine two 7513 routers in parallel.

Finishing the System Level Calculations for Scenario 1

We have now performed the system level calculations for each of the devices in our network for which we have MTBF and MTTR data. For the remaining network components, we will use assumed availability numbers. Any recalculations required for Scenario 2 will be done in the Scenario 2 section which follows our Scenario 1 computations.

Our final two systems for which we need availability results are the network control computers and the OC-3 ring. For each, we are going to make assumptions as opposed to performing actual calculations.

Figure 7-13 *The Cisco 7513 CPU and IOS Computation*

Figure 7-14 *The Cisco 7513 System Level Computations*

CISCO SYSTEMS

© 1998 Cisco Systems, Inc.

System Hardware Availability and Reliability Calculation Worksheet
For Series-Parallel Configurations

System Description: The Cisco 7513 Series Router

Prepared by: Chris Oggerino
Date: 30-Jan-01

System Availability % =	**99.9939305%**	The fraction of time the system is operational.
System Unavailability % =	**0.00606945%**	Equal to 1-Avail., and is the fraction of time the system is non-operational.
***Annual* Downtime (Min.)** =	**31.9**	Equal to System Unavailability times 525,960 minutes per year.
System MTBF (Hrs.) =	**65,891**	The mean time to go from an operational to a non-operational state
System MTBPR (Hrs.) =	**9,023**	The mean time between any part restoration (including the time to repair).
System MTTR (Hrs.) =	**4.0**	The mean time to repair the system, or the mean time to go from a non-operational to an operational state.

Move to far right for scientific notation →

	Part Description	n (QTY)	m (No. Req.)	Part MTBF (hrs.)	Part MTTR (hrs.)	Part Availability	Combined Part Availability	Combined Part MTTR	Combined Part MTBF
1	Chassis/Motherboard	1	1	114,688	4	99.99651240%	99.99651240%	4.0	114,688
2	OC3 Port Adapter	1	1	217,105	4	99.99815761%	99.99815761%	4.0	217,105
3	CPU and IOS	1	1	21,591	0.600	99.99722114%	99.99999992%	0.3	388,497,659
4	Power Supply	2	1	660,000	4	99.99393394%	100.00000000%	2.0	54,450,660,000
5	100BaseT Adapter	1	1	540,920	4	99.99926052%	99.99926052%	4.0	540,920
6									
7									
8									
9									
10									
11									
12									
13									
14									
15									
16									
17									
18									
19									
20									

The network control computers are expected to be redundant UNIX computer systems. We are assuming an availability of .99999 for this network component. Because this component is so critical, most companies will put in computers with state of the art disk drives and other redundancies, and then they will cluster the computers into redundant groups. Five 9s availability for such a critical function is well within reason if it's done properly.

The OC-3 ring will also be given .99999 availability. Five 9s is reasonable for a fiber ring that includes self-healing. Although we do occasionally hear about OC-3 rings having fiber cuts, it is a press-worthy event and not something that happens very often. Even if you don't agree with these particular assumed numbers, you can use them to learn how to perform the analysis and then switch to different numbers when you analyze your own network.

The Network Availability for Scenario 1

With each component included in our scenario RBD as shown in Figure 7-2, we are ready to perform our network level availability calculations. As when we calculated the availability of systems and networks earlier in this book, we will first calculate the availability of redundant network components and then include them in the end-to-end serial calculations.

Fail-over protocols will be accounted for in the parallel calculations. Human error and standard processes will be added to the entire network calculation in the end. Power considerations will also be accounted for after the end-to-end calculations have been performed.

The Parallel Network Component Calculations for Scenario 1

With each component calculated, we are ready to move on to the next step. Figuring out the availability of those devices that are parallel in our RBD is the next step. We have two areas of the network that include redundancy.

The 7513 Parallel Component

The Cisco 7513 routers are in a standard dual redundant parallel configuration. Calculating the availability of the two 7513 routers in parallel will be easy using our standard parallel calculation. Once that is complete, we are going to need to account for any downtime that might be incurred for the fail-over mechanism. We assume that the OSPF routing protocol is the appropriate protocol. Because we assumed that each fail-over in an OSPF network would cause 35 seconds of downtime, we need to figure out how many failures we will have each year. We can then multiply that by 35 seconds to get our downtime per year.

Normally, I would not even perform these calculations on a data only network. As we discussed, the outage incurred during a fail-over is unlikely to cause any concern by customers as long as the network resumes normal operation within the 35 seconds allotted.

Figure 7-15 *The Cisco 7513 Routers in Parallel Calculations*

$$\text{HW/SW Availability 7513} = .99994$$

$$\text{HW/SW Availability Parallel 7513S} = 1 - [(1 - .99994)(1 - .99994)]$$

$$= .999999996$$

$$\text{MTBF 7513} = 65{,}891$$

$$\text{Hours per year} = 8766$$

$$\frac{8766}{65{,}893} = .133 \text{ failures per year}$$

$$2 \text{ Routers} = .266 \text{ failures per year}$$

$$\text{OSPF recalculation} = 35 \text{ seconds}$$

$$\text{OSPF Downtime} = 35 * .266$$

$$= 9.31 \text{ seconds/year}$$

$$\text{Downtime HW/SW} = 525{,}960 * (1 - .999999996)$$

$$= .0021 \text{ minutes}$$

$$= .126 \text{ seconds}$$

$$\text{Downtime HW/SW/OSPF} = 9.31 + .126*$$

$$= 9.436 \text{ seconds}$$

$$= .16 \text{ minutes}$$

$$\text{Annual Availability} = \frac{(525{,}960 - .16)}{525{,}960}$$

$$= .9999997$$

*Adding times together instead of multiplying availabilities is not a perfect process; however, it is simple and accurate enough for our purposes.

As you can see from the results, two 7513 routers in parallel provide excellent availability of seven, nearly eight 9s. Availability like that is superb for any network.

The AS5300 Parallel Component

The AS5300 calculations are somewhat more difficult because we have three routers with two required for proper operation. To calculate the availability of the three AS5300 routers, we will determine the availability of the three routers, and then we will go ahead and add the downtime for the fail-over mechanism, just as we did with the 7513 calculations.

Figure 7-16 shows the AS5300 calculations.

Figure 7-16 *The Cisco AS5300 Routers in a 2-of-3 Redundancy Scheme*

$$AS\ 5300\ HW/SW = .99987$$

$$2 + 1\ AS\ 5300 = 3 * (0.99987)^2 * (1 - 0.99987) + (0.99987)^3$$

$$= .99999995$$

$$MTBF\ 5300 = 7559$$

$$Hours\ per\ year = 8766$$

$$Annual\ Failures\ per\ router = 1.16\ per\ router$$

$$Total\ AS\ 5300\ Failures\ per\ year = 3.48$$

$$OSPF\ Downtime\ per\ failure = 35\ seconds$$

$$OSPF\ Downtime\ per\ year = 122\ seconds$$

$$= 2.03\ minutes$$

$$Downtime\ HW/SW = 525{,}960 * (1 - .99999995)$$

$$= .026\ minutes$$

$$Total\ Downtime = 2.056\ minutes$$

$$Annual\ Availability = \frac{(525{,}960 - 2.056)}{525{,}960}$$

$$= .999996$$

Two AS5300 routers with a third backup unit provide five 9s availability.

Routers in parallel can really improve the availability when an individual router might have a little more downtime than acceptable. When we go into the next section to compute the serial availability of our network, we are going to be using .9999997 for our parallel 7513 routers and .999996 for the AS5300 routers in a two of three configuration.

The End-to-End Serial Calculations

The next step in computing the availability for this scenario is to perform the end-to-end calculations. With our parallel devices' availability calculated in the preceding sections, we can simply include those results in a standard serial calculation.

Because all the devices we control are at one site, we are next going to perform the end-to-end calculations before we consider power implications. If these devices were in different locations, we would need to include the power contribution to downtime before finishing the end-to-end serial calculations.

Figure 7-17 shows the calculations.

Figure 7-17 *Scenario 1 End-to-End HW,SW and Network Design Calculations*

$$
\begin{aligned}
\text{Sonet Ring} &= \ \ .99999 \\
7513\text{s} &= \ \ .9999997 \\
\text{Network Control} &= \ \ .99999 \\
\text{Catalyst 5500} &= \ \ .99996 \\
5300\text{s} &= \ {}_{\star}.999996 \\
\hline
\text{Total} &= \ \ .99994
\end{aligned}
$$

$$\text{Annual Downtime} = 525{,}960 \ (1 - .99994)$$
$$\cong 31.6 \text{ minutes}$$

As you can see, we arrive at a grand total of .99994 availability and about 31.6 minutes per year of downtime.

Next, we are going to consider power in our calculations.

The Environmental/Power Considerations

All the network devices we are considering are contained within the single ISP site. Normally, environmental or power failures will affect an entire site. That is how we will perform the calculations. As you will see in Scenario 2, we perform the calculations slightly differently if there is more than one site.

In this scenario, we again use 29 minutes as our average annual power outage figure. To make the point, we are going to assume that the ISP does not have any power loss mitigation. This scenario is somewhat contrary to real life in that we are using top notch equipment with redundancy and then not even purchasing a battery backup. It does make for a good tutorial example, however.

In real life, I would most likely just add 29 minutes to the 31.6 minutes we have so far and call it about an hour of downtime per year for this network—excluding human errors. However, the technically correct method for calculating the additional downtime due to power outages needs to include the possibility that the downtime from other causes overlaps the downtime from power. As you will see, the actual results are fairly close to what we would get if we just added them together. Figure 7-18 depicts the proper inclusion of 29 minutes per year of downtime due to a power outage with our .99994 availability thus far in our process.

Figure 7-18 *The Simple ISP Scenario 1 Inclusion of Power Downtime*

$$\text{Availability of Power} = \frac{525,960 - 29}{525,960}$$

$$= .999945$$

$$\text{Availability of Net} = .99994$$

$$\text{Total} = .999945 * .99994$$

$$= .9998855$$

$$\text{Annual Downtime} = 525,960 \, (1 - .999885)$$

$$= 60.5 \text{ minutes}$$

As you can see, we do get a different number (however so slight) by doing the math. Remembering that the more downtime you have the more this difference would be is important. Additionally, the more often you do it the simple way instead of the rigorous way, the more error you introduce into your calculations. With about an hour of downtime excluding human error, we are ready to proceed to the next section and include that final factor for this scenario.

The Human Error/Operations Process Considerations

Human error in this scenario is very easy. Because we haven't determined any particular amount of downtime we expect due to human error in this network, we can simply assume a couple numbers. We will assume that the average amount of time lost as a result of human error on this network will be a three hour outage every 24 months. Without doing the math, seeing that we are going to have about 1.5 hours per year of downtime based on human error is easy.

While some might argue that this number is high and others might argue that this number is low, it will work fine for our purposes. I caution the reader, again, to use these numbers for the purpose of learning how to perform these calculations. Numbers like the one above are arbitrarily assumed by the author in order to show the math and not to describe the real life numbers you might actually see.

Again, we could simply add the human error to our existing hour of downtime and estimate 2.5 hours of downtime per year for this network. However, a rigorous treatment of the numbers is in order if we want to preserve our processes.

Figure 7-19 takes the results of our process so far and includes the human error factor into them. The result is actually the final number for Scenario 1.

Figure 7-19 *The Simple ISP Scenario 1 Final Calculations*

$$\text{Availability of Network} = .999885$$

$$\text{Availability of Human Error} = \frac{2 * 8766}{(2 * 8766) + 3}$$

$$= .999829$$

$$\text{Total Network Availability} = .999714$$

$$\text{Total Annual Downtime} = 525,960 * (1 - .999714)$$

$$\cong 150 \text{ minutes}$$

$$= 2.5 \text{ hours}$$

The results of the rigorous calculations end up matching the results of the approximation and we get a total network downtime for this scenario of 2.5 hours per year.

Summary of Scenario 1

We went through several steps in this example. Each step includes calculations that are used in subsequent steps. The key thing to remember from this example is this: dividing the calculations into manageable parts is what makes it easy. Attempting to put all these calculations into a single step would prove to be impossible. As we move into Scenario 2, you will find that we can use many of the calculations done in Scenario 1.

This situation is typical in the real world. The results from scenario calculations are used in other scenario calculations. This speeds up the work of analyzing multiple scenarios.

Scenario 2 of The Small ISP Example

As we mentioned before performing the Scenario 1 steps, we are going to use those here in Scenario 2. This scenario requires that we include a couple of additional network components. Specifically, the Cisco 800 router and the PSTN availability figures will be required. Additionally, the AS5300 calculations will need to be redone because we are not using that router the same way and also because the redundancy scheme will change.

After calculating the individual components, we will again need to include power, network design, and human error contributions. The power contribution, however, will be simple because we will add the CPE site power contribution directly in with the 800 calculations. The human error contribution will be exactly the same as it was in Scenario 1, but we will have to combine it with a slightly different network scenario.

As we go through the steps for this scenario, we will make sure to visit every step. We will do this even if it is simply to point out that the previous result remains accurate.

System Level Calculations for Scenario 2

As stated in the introduction to this scenario, the system level results for all of the devices remain the same except for the 800 and the 5300 routers. This section shows you the 800 calculations for the first time. We also perform the 5300 calculations based on a different method of operation for that router.

The Cisco 800 ISDN Router Availability Calculations for Scenario 2

The Cisco 800 is a very simple router consisting of a chassis, motherboard, and an external power supply. The Cisco 800 router carries traffic from an Ethernet network in the home to an ISDN connection into the PSTN. In this example, we will not be providing any redundancy options. You could add a battery backup as one form of redundancy, but we will not be doing that in this example. Figure 7-20 shows a picture of the Cisco 800 router.

Figure 7-20 *The Cisco 800 Router*

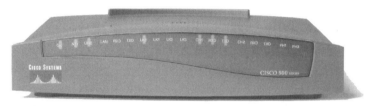

As you can see, this small router is designed for customer premises. The only parts of this product that can really cause any downtime are the motherboard and power supply. Of course Cisco IOS Software runs on the motherboard, and we may have some power failures in the household.

We are going to assume that whenever the Cisco 800 router fails the service provider will give the consumer a new one. This will be accomplished by an onsite delivery and installation of the replacement device. In this case, we are going to assume that the router can be replaced in 24 hours from the time it fails.

Figure 7-21 shows the RBD for this device.

Figure 7-21 *The Cisco 800 RBD*

Table 7-3 shows the MTBF and MTTR numbers required for performing the system availability calculations. As you can see in the table, we have assumed Cisco IOS Software to be a stable version that has been shipping for a while. Cisco IOS Software failures are assumed to fix themselves with a reboot in six or less minutes.

Table 7-3 *The Cisco 800 MTBF and MTTR Assumptions*

System Component	MTBF (hours)	MTTR (hours)
Cisco 800 router	506,756	24
Cisco 800 power supply	2,000,000	24
Cisco 800 IOS	25,000	0.1

With our RBD and our component MTBF and MTTR figures, we are ready to perform the system level availability calculations for this network device. Instead of doing those manually, however, we are going to use the SHARC spreadsheet. Figure 7-22 shows a screenshot of the system level availability computations for the Cisco 800 router.

Figure 7-22 *The Cisco 800 Availability HW, SW Computations*

Cisco Systems

© 1998 Cisco Systems, Inc.

System Hardware Availability and Reliability Calculation Worksheet
For Series-Parallel Configurations

Prepared by: Chris Oggerino
Date: 30–Jan–01

System Description: The Cisco 800 Series Router

System Availability % =	99.9936643**1**%	The fraction of time the system is operational.
System Unavailability % =	0.0063356**9**%	Equal to 1-Avail., and is the fraction of time the system is non-operational.
Annual Downtime (Min.) =	33.3	Equal to System Unavailability times 525,960 minutes per year.
System MTBF (Hrs.) =	23,544	The mean time to go from an operational to a non-operational state.
System MTBPR (Hrs.) =	23,544	The mean time between any part restoration (including the time to repair).
System MTTR (Hrs.) =	1.5	The mean time to repair the system, or the mean time to go from a non-operational to an operational state.

Move to far right for scientific notation →

Part Description	n (QTY)	m (No. Req.)	Part MTBF (hrs.)	Part MTTR (hrs.)	Part Availability	Combined Part Availability	Combined Part MTTR	Combined Part MTBF
1 Chassi/Motherboard	1	1	506,756	24	99.9952642**2**%	99.9952642**2**%	24.0	506,756
2 Power Supply	1	1	2,000,000	24	99.9988000**1**%	99.9988000**1**%	24.0	2,000,000
3 Cisco IOS Software	1	1	25,000	0.100	99.9996000**0**%	99.9996000**0**%	0.1	25,000
4								
5								
6								
7								
8								
9								
10								
11								
12								
13								
14								
15								
16								
17								
18								
19								
20								

The availability for the Cisco 800 router when considering hardware and software is .99994. This availability would cause an annual downtime of 33.3 minutes. Without a battery backup, we will simply assume 29 minutes of power loss at this CPE on an annual basis.

Figure 7-23 shows the calculations to properly combine the availability of the hardware and software along with the availability of power.

Figure 7-23 *The Cisco 800 Availability with Power Considered*

$$
\begin{aligned}
\text{Cisco 800 Availability} &= .99994 \\
\text{Power Availability} &= \frac{525{,}960 - 29}{525{,}960} \\
&= .99994 \\
\text{Cisco 800 with Power Considered} &= .99988 \\
\text{Annual Downtime} &= 525{,}960 * (1 - .99988) \\
&\cong 63 \text{ minutes}
\end{aligned}
$$

As Figure 7-23 shows, our annual downtime will increase from 33.3 minutes to about 63 minutes on average. The device's availability will be included in our network calculations as .99988. Because we have included power problems at the CPE site in these calculations, we will not have to consider them for this device when we get to the power section later.

The Cisco AS5300 Availability for Scenario 2

As you saw from the previous calculation of the AS5300 system level availability in Scenario 1, it can be a very complex device. In this scenario, however, the AS5300 will be terminating ISDN traffic instead of modem traffic. As a result, the modems and the modem carrier cards are not required for the router to operate properly. Therefore, we will no longer include them in our calculations.

As a result, our RBD for the AS5300 changes in this scenario. Figure 7-24 depicts the newer simpler perspective on the AS5300.

Figure 7-24 *The Cisco AS5300 RBD: Scenario 2*

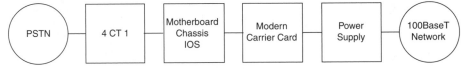

With the RBD completed and an understanding of how the device functions, we are ready to begin our calculations. Because we listed out the MTBF and MTTR for all the required components in Table 7-1 for Scenario 1, we can go directly into our spreadsheet calculations. Figure 7-25 depicts our new calculations based on a simpler use of the AS5300. You should note that the modems will still be in the device and used in the scenario when folks would be dialing into this device using modems like they did in Scenario 1.

Figure 7-25 *The Cisco 5300 Availability HW, SW Computations for Scenario 2*

Cisco Systems
© 1998 Cisco Systems, Inc.

System Hardware Availability and Reliability Calculation Worksheet
For Series-Parallel Configurations

System Description: The Cisco 5300 Series Router

Prepared by: Chris Oggerino
Date: 30-Jan-01

System Availability % =	99.98806072%	The fraction of time the system is operational.
System Unavailability % =	0.01193928%	Equal to 1-Avail., and is the fraction of time the system is non-operational.
Annual Downtime (Min.) =	62.8	Equal to System Unavailability times 525,960 minutes per year.
System MTBF (Hrs.) =	7,761	The mean time to go from an operational to a non-operational state.
System MTBPR (Hrs.) =	7,761	The mean time between any part restoration (including the time to repair).
System MTTR (Hrs.) =	0.9	The mean time to repair the system, or the mean time to go from a non-operational to an operational state.

Move to far right for scientific notation →

Part Description	n (QTY)	m (No. Req.)	Part MTBF (hrs.)	Part MTTR (hrs.)	Part Availability	Combined Part Availability	Combined Part MTTR	Combined Part MTBF
Chassis/Motherboard	1	1	45,218	4	99.99115475%	99.99115475%	4.0	45,218
Power Supply	1	1	500,000	1	99.99980000%	99.99980000%	1.0	500,000
4 T1 Card	1	1	211,152	4	99.99810567%	99.99810567%	4.0	211,152
Cisco IOS Software	1	1	10,000	0.100	99.99900001%	99.99900001%	0.1	10,000

The resulting .99988 availability for the AS5300 will lead to approximately 62.8 minutes of downtime each year due to hardware and software for this device. As with the first time we performed the calculations for the AS5300, we will again include the rest of the factors for availability at a later point in the process.

The Network Availability for Scenario 2

Performing the network availability calculations for this scenario will be easier than the previous scenario because the 7513 calculations are the same. We need only perform the AS5300 calculations because there are two instead of three, and the redundancy is basic parallel, instead of N – 1 of N, or two of three. It is interesting to note that N – 1 of N and parallel redundancy are the same if N is 2 because N – 1 of N becomes one of two.

The Parallel AS5300 Calculations for Scenario 2

With the availability of each AS5300 calculated in the previous step, we can go directly into our calculations to include the redundancy and fail-over times. Figure 7-26 depicts the network design considerations for the AS5300s in Scenario 2.

Figure 7-26 *The Cisco 5300 Redundancy Considerations for Scenario 2*

$$\text{HW/SW Availability} = .99988$$

$$\text{Parallel Availability} = 1 - [(1 - .99988)(1 - .99988)]$$

$$= .999999986$$

$$\text{MTBF 5300} = 77{,}611$$

$$\text{Hours per year} = 8766$$

$$\text{Failures/year/router} = 1.13$$

$$\text{Failures/year} = 2.26$$

$$\text{OSPF Recalculation} = 35 \text{ seconds}$$

$$\text{OSPF Downtime} = 79.1 \text{ seconds}$$

$$\text{Downtime HW/SW} = 525{,}960 * (1 - .999999986)$$

$$= .0074 \text{ minutes}$$

$$= .44 \text{ seconds}$$

$$\text{Downtime HW/SW/OSPF} = 79.54 \text{ seconds}$$

$$= 1.32 \text{ minutes}$$

$$\text{Annual Availability} = \frac{(525{,}960 - 1.32)}{525{,}960}$$

$$= .999997$$

As in the previous scenario, AS5300s in parallel create a highly available point of access for our network. With this calculation performed, we are ready to begin the serial calculations for our network

The End-to-End Serial Calculations

As you will remember by looking at the RBD in Figure 7-3, the end-to-end calculations for this scenario contain a few more devices than in the previous scenario. As with the OC-3 ring and the UNIX systems, the availability we will use for the PSTN will be assumed. For this example, we will use .99995 for the PSTN availability figure.

This scenario encompasses two sites instead of the single ISP site. Two sites require adding the consideration of power before combining the sites in the end-to-end serial calculations.

Figure 7-27 includes the end-the-end calculations for our network devices. Note the addition of the power availability added in the portion of the calculations that represent the devices at the ISP site.

Figure 7-27 *End-to-End Calculations HW,SW and Network Design for Scenario 2*

$$
\begin{aligned}
\text{Sonet Ring} &= .99999 \\
7513\text{s} &= .9999997 \\
\text{Network Control} &= .99999 \\
\text{Catalyst 5500} &= .99996 \\
5300\text{s} &= .999996 \\
\boxed{\text{ISP Site Power Availability} = .999945}\,^* \\
\text{PSTN} &= .99995 \\
800 = *&.999937 \\
\hline
\text{Total} &= .999818
\end{aligned}
$$

* From Scenario 1 calculations

As you can see from Figure 7-27, we simply include the power availability that we calculated for Scenario 1. Because serial availability allows multiplication of all results, we can now move on to the final step, which is accounting for human error. Our final network availability excluding human error comes to .99982. That is 94.67 minutes per year of downtime.

The Human Error/Operations Process Considerations for Scenario 2

Our final calculations for this scenario are to include the same human error figures from Scenario 1. Because our results thus far are slightly different, our result will be different. Regardless, the human error contribution will remain the same.

Figure 7-28 *The Simple ISP Scenario 2 Final Calculations*

Availability of Network = .99982

Availability of Human Error = .999829

Total Network Availability = .99982 * .999829

= .999699

Total Annual Downtime = 525,960 (1 − .999649)

= 184.6 minutes

= 3 hours

As you can see in Figure 7-28, the added components decrease the network availability a little bit. When the final calculations are performed, this scenario incurs about 30 minutes more downtime than Scenario 1. Of course, that is from the perspective of the two different users.

Summary

As you saw after working through two scenarios on the same network, results can be different depending on the customer perspective. Although various network components may be beyond the control of the network designer, they will affect the end users of the network.

Whenever you perform network availability predictions for a network, the most important thing is to determine the perspective you want to examine. After that the calculations become easy.

As we continue with more examples in the next two chapters, the concept of determining the scenarios and thus the calculation process should get easier each time.

An Enterprise Network: An Availability Analysis

This chapter provides the availability predictions for a small enterprise network. The key difference between an enterprise network and a service provider network is that the Internet is not necessarily part of an enterprise network. Additionally, we are typically connecting groups of people together as opposed to connecting a large group of people to a single network.

In our example, we are going to connect two office buildings together. Each office building will have several groups that need to communicate with all the other groups. There will be network services, which need to be accessible to all employees regardless of location. The network diagram in Figure 8-1 describes the basic topology. One thing that may not be obvious in the diagram is that the groups will contain many PCs instead of just the two in the diagrams. Additionally, a larger number of groups is likely.

Obviously, this diagram provides countless different possible scenarios. For our purposes, however, picking a typical scenario from these possibilities will be adequate. What we want to analyze is the availability of the *group application* from the network labeled *Group 1-1*. This calculation will require nearly all the various components to be working. Nearly any other scenario can be derived from this one. If we wanted to measure the availability of mail services from Group 2-1, for example, it would be the same scenario in reverse with only a single modification: the mail server might have a different availability than the application server.

The important thing to note is that we are calculating the availability of a particular path through this network, which we call a scenario. In this example, we don't calculate all of the scenarios, so this might not be entirely obvious.

At any rate, Figure 8-2 shows the reliability block diagram (RBD) depicting the serial/parallel network components between Group 1-1 and the application server. Although they are not specifically shown in the network diagram, the Ethernet segments are serviced by Cisco 1500 hubs. You can see those in the RBD.

Figure 8-1 *A Small Enterprise Network Diagram*

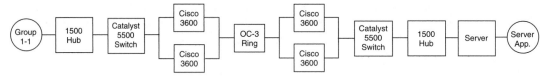

Figure 8-2 *A Small Enterprise Network RBD*

As has become the convention in this book, we will use as many components as possible from previous calculations. This will reduce the amount of work required to perform the calculations. At the same time, you will still be taken through the process and retain learning the availability prediction steps.

Because we have determined the network diagram and the RBD for the scenario we wish to examine, we can proceed with our system level calculations for each component in the network. Once those are complete, we can consider environmental, human error, and network design issues.

System Level Calculations for an Enterprise Network

The system level calculations for the network depicted in Figures 8-1 and 8-2 will be short because we have already calculated or assumed values for most of the devices. The two devices in this network for which we still need to perform calculations are the Cisco 3640 routers and the Cisco 1500 hubs. We begin with the 3640 calculations.

The Cisco 3600 Availability Calculations

The Cisco 3600 series router is a modular router for the purposes of network ports but is limited to a single processor and a single power supply in our configuration. Both the processor and the power supply are part of the chassis and motherboard assembly. It is possible to purchase an external, redundant power supply, but we have not done so in this example. Table 8-1 shows the various components we have selected to use for our 3640 router in order to move the traffic between our buildings.

Table 8-1   *The Cisco 3640 MTBF and MTTR Assumptions*

System Component	MTBF (Hours)	MTTR (Hours)
3640 chassis, CPU, memory	79,738	4.0
3640 Fast Ethernet module	1,197,180	4.0
3640 OC-3 Long Reach	777,776	4.0
Cisco 3640 IOS	10,000	0.1

As you can see in Table 8-1, the individual components for the Cisco 3640 router are reliable and should contribute nicely to a high availability environment. Because all the components are required for the 3640 to operate properly in our network, the router is in a simple serial configuration. This setup eliminates any need to do the RBD for the router. Instead we will go directly into computation of the availability for the hardware and software provided in Figure 8-3.

We use the SHARC spreadsheet to calculate our availability results. The availability result of .99993 is excellent for a router without any redundant components. With that we are ready to move on to the next system.

Figure 8-3 *The 3640 Availability Calculations*

CISCO SYSTEMS

© 1998 Cisco Systems, Inc.

System Hardware Availability and Reliability Calculation Worksheet
For Series-Parallel Configurations

Prepared by: Chris Oggerino
Date: 30-Jan-01

System Description: The Cisco 3640 Router

System Availability % =	**99.99313553%**	The fraction of time the system is operational.
System Unavailability % =	**0.00686447%**	Equal to 1-Avail., and is the fraction of time the system is non-operational.
***Annual* Downtime (Min.) =**	**36.1**	Equal to System Unavailability times 525,960 minutes per year.
System MTBF (Hrs.) =	**8,721**	The mean time to go from an operational to a non-operational state.
System MTBPR (Hrs.) =	**8,721**	The mean time between any part restoration (including the time to repair).
System MTTR (Hrs.) =	**0.6**	The mean time to repair the system, or the mean time to go from a non-operational to an operational state.

Move to far right for scientific notation →

Part Description	n (QTY)	m (No. Req.)	Part MTBF (Hrs.)	Part MTTR (Hrs.)	Part Availability	Combined Part Availability	Combined Part MTTR	Combined Part MTBF
Chassis/Motherboard	1	1	79,738	4	99.99498382%	99.99498382%	4.0	79,738
Ethernet Adapter	1	1	1,197,180	4	99.99966588%	99.99966588%	4.0	1,197,180
OC-3 Adapter	1	1	777,776	4	99.99948572%	99.99948572%	4.0	777,776
Cisco IOS	1	1	10,000	0.100	99.99900001%	99.99900001%	0.1	10,000

The Cisco 1538 Availability Calculations

The Cisco 1538 is a actually a switch. For our purposes, the 1538 will be operated as though it were a hub. This simple device contains only a motherboard and power supply on which we need to perform our calculations. Interestingly enough, the power supply is built into the main chassis, so the MTBF data for the product includes everything we need to know at 290,103 hours. Assuming an MTTR of four hours, our resulting hardware availability will be .999986. With a mature version of Cisco IOS Software the resulting availability would be .999976.

The Downtime from Lost Power for an Enterprise Network

Because we really have two networks in this example, we will calculate the power availability for each network before we begin our end-to-end network calculations. Although we could wait to make these calculations, it is nice to perform them here so that we can include them in our network calculations when we need them.

In Building 1, we will assume that there is no backup in case of a power failure. We will also assume that power fails for 29 minutes each year as we have in our previous examples. In Building 2, we will assume that we have a .99 available battery backup with sufficient power to easily cover the entire 29 minutes.

In Building 1, the power contribution to network downtime will be based on 29 minutes per year of average downtime, which we convert to availability in Figure 8-4.

Figure 8-4 *Building 1: The Power Availability Calculation*

$$\text{Power Availability} = \frac{(525,960 - 29)}{525,960}$$

$$= .999945$$

As you can see, the resulting .999945 is the same as was determined in a previous example, where power was not mitigated. This result will be combined with the rest of the Building 1 figures in the next section.

In Building 2, the power contribution to network downtime will be mitigated by some battery backup capability. The calculations for this building require two steps. The first step will be to determine the mitigation, and the second step will be the availability based on the remaining downtime. Figure 8-5 contains both steps.

Figure 8-5 *Building 2: The Power Availability Calculations*

$$\text{After Power Is Mitigated} = .99 * 29$$
$$= .29 \text{ minutes}$$
$$\text{Power Availability} = \frac{(525{,}960 - .29)}{525{,}960}$$
$$= .99999945$$

As you can see, the resulting contribution due to power loss is significantly minimized by having a battery backup system. One important note is that we are assuming that the battery backup system is installed in such a way that it does not affect the network if it should fail.

With our power availability figures for the two buildings in hand, we are ready to perform the network calculations in the next section.

Network Calculations for an Enterprise Network

By carefully looking at the RBD in Figure 8-2, you can determine that everything to the left of the OC-3 component will be calculated as Building 1. The right side of the OC-3 component will be Building 2. In the calculations for each site, we must also include the fact that the routers between the two sites are in a redundant configuration. Our first step in the network calculations will be to calculate the redundancy of the parallel components at each site. Once we have the parallel component results, we can perform our end-to-end serial calculations for each site. Each of those calculations will have their results affected by the power availability for the site.

With the site availability for both sites calculated, we can add in the OC-3 availability and complete the end-to-end calculations.

The Parallel Component Calculations

In both buildings, we have parallel 3640 routers to access the OC-3 ring, which joins the two sites. Both sites use identically configured 3640 routers. Therefore, we can make a single calculation and use it for both buildings. The calculation for the parallel 3640 routers is a simple application of the parallel availability equation followed up with the consideration for the fail-over mechanism. We will assume that the OSPF routing protocol is used and we absorb 35 seconds of downtime whenever a 3640 incurs a failure.

The calculations in Figure 8-6 show the resulting availability of two 3640 routers in parallel. The availability of the two 3640 routers in parallel works out to over five 9s. We will use this result in our next section where we combine, in serial, all the different components that affect availability in our two buildings.

Figure 8-6   *Redundant 3640 Availability Calculations*

$$3640 \text{ Availability} = .99993$$

$$\text{Parallel } 3640 \text{ Availability} = 1 - [(1 - .99993)^2]$$

$$= .999999995$$

$$3640 \text{ MTBF} = 8721$$

$$\text{Hours per year} = 8766$$

$$3640 \text{ Failures per year} = 2 * \left\lceil \frac{8766}{8721} \right\rceil$$

$$= 2.01$$

$$\text{Downtime per failure} = 35 \text{ seconds}$$

$$\text{OSPF Downtime per year} = 70.35 \text{ seconds}$$

$$= 1.17 \text{ min.}$$

$$\text{OSPF Availability} = \frac{(525{,}960 - 1.17)}{525{,}960}$$

$$= .9999978$$

$$\text{Availability Parallel } 3640 \text{ Component} = .9999978 * .999999995$$

$$= .9999978$$

The Serial Availability Calculations

There are three calculations required for the serial section. Building 1 and Building 2 must each be calculated. Once those calculations are complete, the end-to-end calculation can be completed including the OC-3 ring. Figure 8-7 shows the Building 1 and Building 2 calculations.

Figure 8-7 *Serial Availability Calculations for Buildings 1 and 2*

Building 1

$$1538 \text{ Hub} = \quad .999976$$
$$\text{Cat } 5500 \text{ Switch} = \quad .99996$$
$$\text{Parallel } 3640 \text{ Routers} = \quad .9999978$$
$$\text{Building Power Availability} = {}_{\ast}.999945$$
$$\text{Total Building 1} = \quad .99988$$

Building 2

$$\text{Application Server} = \quad .99999$$
$$1538 \text{ Hub} = \quad .999976$$
$$\text{Cat } 5500 \text{ Switch} = \quad .99996$$
$$\text{Parallel } 3640 \text{ Routers} = \quad .9999978$$
$$\text{Building Power Availability} = {}_{\ast}.99999945$$
$$\text{Total Building 2} = \quad .99992$$

Building 2 results are considerably better than Building 1 results even with an extra device. The battery backup mitigates a tremendous hit to availability.

The final serial availability calculation will be to combine the two building results with the OC-3 availability to get an end-to-end availability exclusive of human error. Figure 8-8 depicts the calculation of this nearly final result.

Figure 8-8 *Serial Availability Calculations for the OC-3 Ring and Both Buildings*

$$\text{Building 1} = \quad .99988$$
$$\text{Building 2} = \quad .99992$$
$$\text{OC-3 Ring} = {}_{\ast}.99999$$
$$\text{Total End-to-End} = \quad .99979$$

$$\text{Total Downtime Excluding Human Error} = \quad 525{,}960 \ast (1 - .99979)$$
$$\cong 110.4 \text{ minutes}$$

Our final results, excluding any contributions to downtime by human error, amount to almost 2 hours per year of downtime at 110.4 minutes.

Human Error and Process Contribution to Downtime in an Enterprise Network

In this final section of calculations, we will finalize our network availability prediction for this scenario for this enterprise network. Starting with 110.4 minutes of downtime before we introduce any human error creates an interesting observation. Nearly every human error that occurs will be more than the downtime for all other reasons combined.

As it turns out, this observation is realistic. Once enterprise networks are operational and the bugs have been worked out, they hardly ever fail. When they do have problems, it is just as likely to be a result of someone changing something as it is for any other reason.

Figure 8-9 shows how we might introduce human error into this network. We assume a human error contribution of four hours every other year.

Figure 8-9   *The Human Error Contribution to Downtime in the Enterprise Network*

$$\text{Network Availability} = .99979$$

$$\text{Human Error Availability} = \frac{(2 * 8766)}{(2 * 8766) + 4}$$

$$= .99977$$

$$\text{Total Enterprise Availability} = .99979 * .99977$$

$$= .99956$$

$$\text{Network Availability} = 525{,}960\,(1 - .999858)$$

$$= 231.4 \text{ minutes}$$

$$= 3.86 \text{ hours}$$

As you can see, the human error contribution to network downtime produces a large percentage increase.

Summary

Enterprise networks are both simpler and more complex than service provider networks when attempting to predict availability. They are simpler because more of the components are under your control and availability is less likely to affect control systems. On the other hand, enterprise networks are likely to include far more scenarios than a typical service provider network. Your work will be significant if you want to perform a complete analysis.

The results of calculating the scenario we chose in this enterprise example are not particularly important. The value we were able to derive in terms of the process and the observation about human error is far more important than the fact we came up with 3.86 hours of annual downtime for the scenario.

CHAPTER 9

A Large VoIP Network: An Availability Analysis

In this final chapter, we will perform our availability predictions on a cable network carrying voice and data traffic. We will be using all of the knowledge we have gained throughout the previous tutorial and example chapters.

The network used in this chapter is partially based on real life networks. However, some parts of one network were used and other parts of another network were used. The design of this network is not included as an example of how to build this type of network. That design would best be left to an network design expert. The design of this network should be considered arbitrary and used only for the purposes of studying availability. I caution the reader here because, as realistic as it may seem, this network may not work in real life because it is a hybrid of two or more real networks. This hybrid network was created to use more components for which MTBF figures were available. It should be obvious that MTBF figures for the various hardware components in the network are required if we are to attempt to predict availability.

As you have seen in the previous chapters, we will go through several steps to arrive at our conclusions. We will calculate availability of components, systems, network segments, and finally network scenarios. Parallel components in systems or network segments will be calculated and included in serial calculations.

As much as possible, all five major contributors to network downtime will be considered. In some cases, however, we will simply make reasonable guesses as to what they might be. I caution you to pay close attention to the process of including these figures as opposed to the actual figures themselves.

With these precautions in mind, we are ready to begin this final example. Our first section describes the network in question and its operation. In this section, we will decide which scenarios exist and for which of those we want predictions. Next, we will move on to performing the availability analysis of the different network systems. As we move through the sections, the different systems will be combined into the various parts of the networks and the different scenarios will be calculated.

A VoIP over Cable Network

The network to be used in this chapter is a cable network. End customers are connected to the network using coax cable, which is the same cable that provides their TV signal. We will call this cabling the Hybrid Fiber Coaxial (HFC) network.

To divide the network into smaller parts, we are going to create four diagrams describing the major components of our network. Those will be what some folks would call the ingress, egress, and control portions of the network. These are each connected to a common backbone. Ingress is called that because traffic normally originates at the customer site and moves into the network. Egress is called that because that can become the final destination of much of the traffic. Control is called that for obvious reasons. The three areas are covered in the next few paragraphs and diagrams.

At the customer site there will be a Cisco router enabling the connection of both regular telephones and computers to the network. Moving inward, data must traverse what we call the cable plant, or HFC plant, to get to the service provider end of the wire—called the *head-end*. The head-end will use Cisco uBR 7246 routers in a "1 of 2" parallel configuration. This traffic will get back-hauled into the ISP backbone using OC-3 into Cisco 12000 routers.

Figure 9-1 shows the HFC ingress portion of the network.

Figure 9-1 *Cable Network Access Section of VoIP Network*

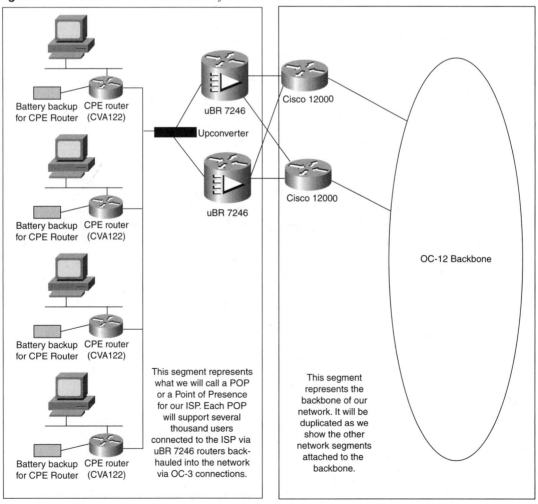

In Figure 9-1, the left side of the figure represents that portion of the network that includes the CPE devices, cable plant, and cable aggregation devices.

The right side of the figure shows the devices that comprise the network backbone. The backbone consists of numerous Cisco 12000 routers.

With the access aggregation depicted, we can now move on to network control and management. As with the access aggregation, the network control must be present on the network backbone and is connected via a pair of Cisco 12000 routers. Figure 9-2 shows how the network control computers are connected to the backbone via a pair of redundant 8540 switch/routers.

Figure 9-2   *Network Control Section of VoIP Network*

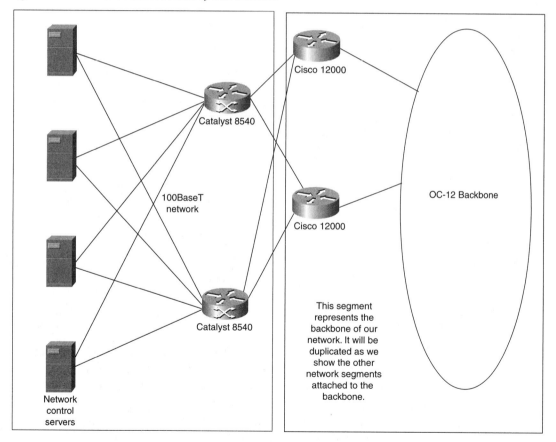

Not obvious from Figure 9-2 is that two of these network control centers will be present on the backbone in different locations to provide the higher availability.

Because telephone traffic is very likely to require destinations not on this network, the network must have access to the PSTN. Figure 9-3 shows the connection from the PSTN to the backbone.

Figure 9-3 *Egress: PSTN to Backbone Section of VoIP Network*

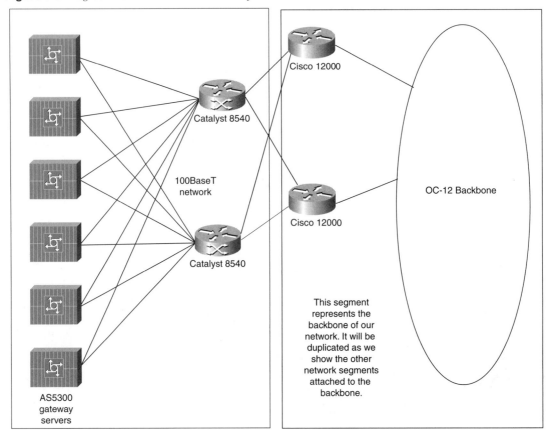

As with the other two sections, all traffic moves between the PSTN, which is connected to the AS5300 routers at the edge and the Cisco 12000 routers on the backbone. The AS5300 and Cisco 12000 routers are connected using Cisco Catalyst 8540 switches.

One final item we did not cover so far is the connection to the Internet from this network. The connection to the Internet will be accomplished via a pair of 8540 switches. These will be connected to the Cisco 12000 routers and to at least two Internet Network Access Point (NAP) sites. Figure 9-4 shows this connection.

Figure 9-4   *Egress: Internet to Backbone Section of VoIP Network*

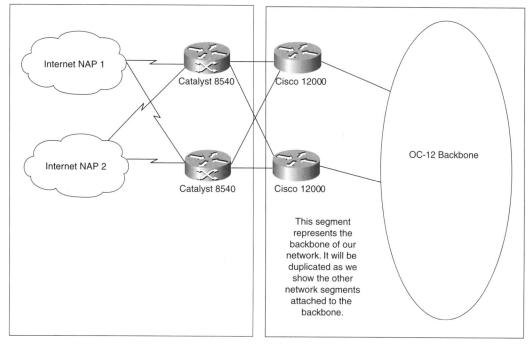

As you can see in Figure 9-4, the connection to the Internet is simple in our model. In real life, this could end up somewhat more complex with the addition of firewalls used to make sure the network was safer.

With these diagrams depicting the smaller parts of the network, we are ready to show a high level view of the entire network. This view is required in order to show the redundancy of the various components. In Figure 9-5, you can see the various parts from above all depicted in abbreviated format.

As you can see in this final figure, the detail is removed in order to show the higher level perspective. As we move into the RBDs, you will find that we need to consider both the high level and the more detailed perspectives. In the following section we will describe the different scenarios and then create the RBDs for them.

Figure 9-5 *High Level Overview of VoIP Network*

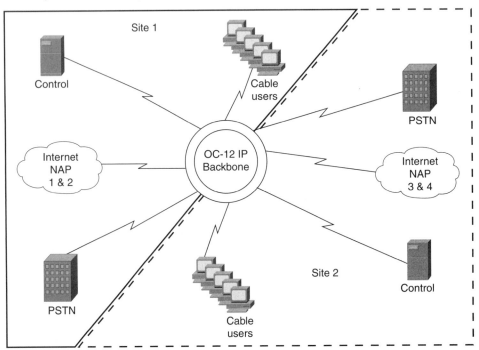

The Availability Scenarios of VoIP over HFC

Because this network carries data, voice, and voice that leaves the network and goes over the PSTN, there will be several different scenarios. In real networks like this one where the network we have diagramed is duplicated in multiple cities by a cable service provider even more scenarios exist. We are going to look at four scenarios, which will be plenty for us to make sure we have an understanding of the availability of this network in the more common scenarios. The four we will consider are

- Data to the Internet
- On net local calling
- Off net local calling
- Off net long distance

The following four subsections will cover the description and reliability block diagrams (RBDs) for each of those scenarios.

Scenario 1: Data to the Internet

This scenario represents the availability of this network from the perspective of the user who is using the network to surf the Internet. Because the users are all connected to the network via the cable, we will need to include the CPE devices, the HFC plant, the head-end, the back-haul systems, the backbone, and finally the actual connections to the Internet. Additionally, the nature of IP over cable requires some network control components. This requires some additional equipment be added to our considerations. Furthermore, we will have several redundancies built into the network. To best understand the requirements for this scenario, we begin by outlining the data flow from the user to the Internet. The user's PC will not be included.

1 Once data leaves the PC, it must traverse the CPE device. We will use a Cisco cable router for this device.

2 After this, the data must traverse the HFC network. At the other end, it will be aggregated by redundant uBR 7246 routers. The up-converters in Figure 9-1 are considered part of the HFC network.

3 The traffic from the uBR 7246 routers is carried over fiber OC-3 connections into Cisco 12000 routers.

4 The 12000 routers deliver traffic to the backbone, which is an OC-12 ring.

5 From this backbone, Internet bound traffic will be delivered to the closest NAP.

Two different, completely redundant network access subsections are on the network. There are also two different redundant network control sections, which are also required to get the packets flowing in the first place.

Figure 9-6 shows the RBD for Scenario 1. As you can see, part of the network is redundantly redundant! Availability professionals would call this, parallel-parallel redundancy.

When we perform the calculations, we will need to start with small blocks in this RBD and then include those in bigger blocks. In the Scenario 1 calculations, we will perform some additional diagramming in order to make this more clear. For now, we want to move on and define the remaining three scenarios.

Figure 9-6   *VoIP: Scenario 1 RBD*

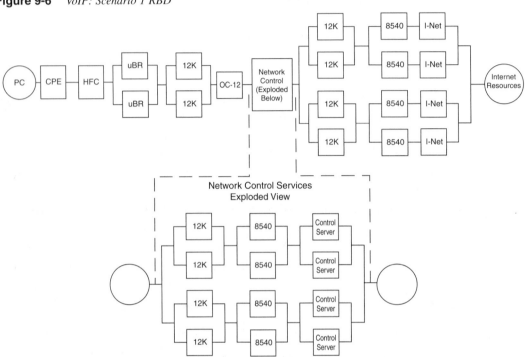

Scenario 2: On Net Local Calling

In some cases, the users on this network will call other users on the network. In the case where both parties of a telephone call subscribe to this network's service, then this scenario represents the availability between those two people.

As with the previous scenario, traffic enters the backbone via the CPE and uBR 7246 routers. We will not assume that the two users are both on the same HFC network segment and will perform the calculations based on a full network traversal. In real life, these types of local calls might be more likely to occur between neighbors and thus on the same segment. In that case, we would not need anything to the right of the network control box in the figure.

Figure 9-7 depicts the RBD for Scenario 2.

Figure 9-7   *VoIP: Scenario 2 RBD*

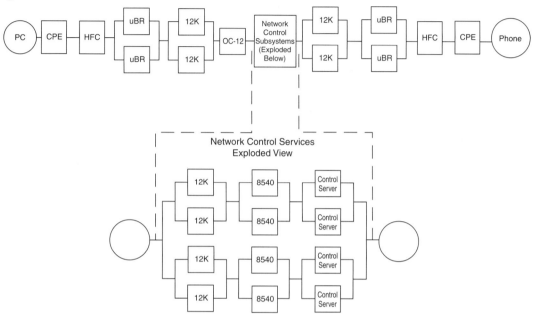

As you can see in Figures 9-6 and 9-7, the network control portion of the network is roughly equal no matter what we are doing. The reason for this is that these servers are required to be operational for any network traffic to flow. Because we are assuming an availability for the UNIX computers, we don't need to distinguish the exact details between DHCP and Call Management type servers. In the real world, you might need to do this, but the calculations would be the same.

Scenario 3: Off Net Local Calling

The data in off net local calling starts in the same place as on net local calling. This data proceeds onto the backbone and requires the network control equipment the same as the on net calling as well. The difference between on and off net occurs when the call leaves the backbone towards a destination. For this, we need to use the equipment depicted in Figure 9-3. Instead of uBR 7246s and CPE routers, we are going to need to account for 8540 switches, AS5300 routers, and the availability of the PSTN.

Figure 9-8 shows the reliability block diagram for this scenario. There are six AS5300 routers all in parallel. These are in a "5 of 6" redundancy configuration. Our calculations will require the (N − 1) + N redundancy equation instead of the basic parallel equation.

Figure 9-8 *VoIP: Scenario 3 RBD*

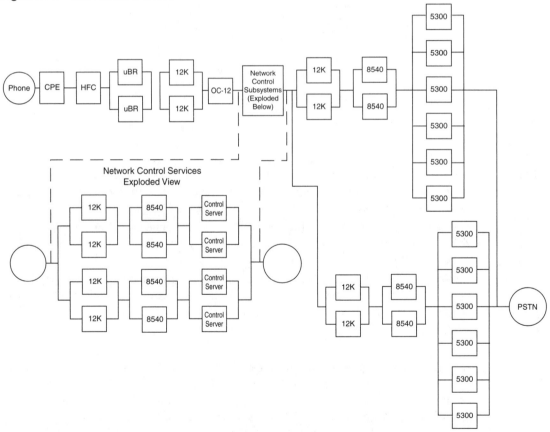

Again, this scenario utilizes the same network control servers and the same backbone. You should be noticing a pattern in our diagrams. In fact, using these patterns makes the calculations of large numbers of scenarios easier. By calculating different sections of the network and noting the results, you can combine sections as appropriate to different scenarios. This arrangement will become completely obvious in our fourth and final scenario.

Scenario 4: Off Net Long Distance Calling

In this final scenario, we are going to change precisely one variable from the previous scenario—the value of the PSTN availability. In local calling, the call is likely to be routed through a single, traditional Class Five telephone switch. At most, local calls normally will go through a Class Five, a Class Four, and then another Class Five switch.

NOTE   For those of you that did not previously know this, Class 4 and Class 5 switches exist inside telephone company networks. Class 5 switches are typically the switches that support individual households. These switches have line cards that support twisted pair wiring that goes to your home. Class 4 switches don't have wiring to individual homes. Class 4 switches are used to connect Class 5 switches together.

When you make a typical, traditional telephone call from your house, your call will likely go from your home into a Class 5 switch, then into a Class 4 switch (or many), and then back into a Class 5 switch and into the destination phone.

The analogy here is like the water company. You get one inch service into your home, but the water mains are six inches. Class 5 switches switch one-inch services; Class 4 switches switch six-inch services.

Long distance calls will start on a Class Five switch, move onto a Class 4 switch and then be moved across a long distance carrier network. At the other end, the Class Four and Class Five switches will be traversed again. The availability of the long distance PSTN is considerably lower than that of a local PSTN network.

For this scenario, we will use the same RBD as we did in Scenario 3 (refer to Figure 9-8), and we will simply assign a different availability to the PSTN component.

A Final Note About Scenarios

As a final note about scenarios, I would like to remind you of one key thought:

> Whenever you are thinking about the availability of a network, you must determine what end-to-end scenario you are considering. Without a thorough understanding of the scenario, network availability predictions are not useful.

With our scenario outlines, we are now ready to move on to the next step where we begin our system level calculations.

The System Level Calculations for VoIP over HFC

As has become part of our process, we begin the availability analysis by predicting the availability of the individual systems used in this network. Although it would be possible to require more than one calculation per system if the scenarios show differing paths through the devices, we were lucky and the paths through the devices were consistent across all of our scenarios.

We will use the SHARC spreadsheet to perform the calculations. On the more complex systems, we will perform RBDs of the systems. With minor exceptions, the hardware and software contributors to downtime will be accounted for in this section and the remaining contributors added on later.

The CPE Router System Level Calculations

The router for which we are going to perform the availability predictions is called the Cisco CVA122. This cable router has both Ethernet and VoIP ports. The CVA122 is a simple router and has only two major hardware components: a motherboard and an external power supply. Most companies installing this device in VoIP network will include a battery backup in order to mitigate power loss to the household. The CVA122 series utilizes the feature of replacing the standard power supply with a combination battery backup/power supply. We will include that device in our calculations. Figure 9-9 shows a picture of the CVA122 series.

Figure 9-9 *The CVA122 Router*

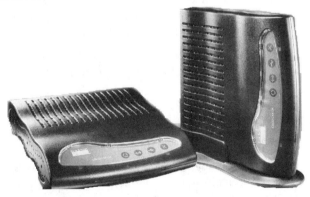

Because the CPE is connected to the rest of the network in a serial method, there will not be any calculations for this device on fail-over times. We will not be including human error for this device. In effect, the calculations for this portion of the network will be complete at the end of this analysis, which includes hardware, software, and power contributions to downtime.

We will only need to include the results from this section in our end-to-end scenarios for this device. We will not need to affect this device with the power, human error, fail-over calculations that we do later. Table 9-1 lists the MTBF and MTTR figures for the CVA122.

Table 9-1   *MTBF and MTTR Figures for the Cisco CVA122*

Product	Description	MTBF	MTTR
CVA122	Cable Voice router	326,928	8
CVA120-UPS	UPS battery backup	300,000	8
Cisco IOS Sofware	Cisco IOS Software for CVA120 series	10,000	0.1

In Figure 9-10, you see the hardware and software calculations for the CVA122 using the SHARC spreadsheet tool.

So far, we have included the hardware and software contribution to downtime for the CVA122.

Including downtime due to power loss is simple for this system if we assume 29 minutes per year of average power outage. In case you have forgotten, we decided to assume 29 minutes annual power downtime in Chapter 4, "Factors that Affect Availability," in the section on including power loss in availability calculations. Because the batteries will keep the router running for much longer than 29 minutes, we can assume that the only time power will b e lost is during the failure of the power supply. We have already included that downtime in our spreadsheet. Note that if the battery backup fails, the entire system fails—in this case.

The figures that we will use when we include the CVA122 system in our network level calculations will be .999938 availability, 9,399 hours MTBF, and 0.6 hours MTTR.

Figure 9-10 *The CVA122 HW,SW Availability Prediction*

CISCO SYSTEMS

© 1998 Cisco Systems, Inc.

System Hardware Availability and Reliability Calculation Worksheet
For Series-Parallel Configurations

System Description: The Cisco CVA122 Router

Prepared by: Chris Oggerino
Date: 27-Mar-01

System Availability % = 99.9938657%   The fraction of time the system is operational.
System Unavailability % = 0.0061143%   Equal to 1-Avail., and is the fraction of time the system is non-operational.
***Annual* Downtime (Min.) =** 32.2   Equal to System Unavailability times 525,960 minutes per year.

System MTBF (Hrs.) = 9,399   The mean time to go from an operational to a non-operational state.
System MTBPR (Hrs.) = 9,399   The mean time between any part restoration (including the time to repair).
System MTTR (Hrs.) = 0.6   The mean time to repair the system, or the mean time to go from a non-operational to an operational state.

Move to far right for scientific notation →

Part Description	n (QTY)	m (No. Req.)	Part MTBF (hrs.)	Part MTTR (hrs.)	Part Availability	Combined Part Availability	Combined Part MTTR	Combined Part MTBF
1 CVA122	1	1	326,928	8	99.99755304%	99.99755304%	8.0	326,928
2 IOS	1	1	10,000	0.100	99.99900001%	99.99900001%	0.1	10,000
3 CVA122-UPS	1	1	300,000	8	99.99733340%	99.99733340%	8.0	300,000
4								
5								
6								
7								
8								
9								
10								
11								
12								
13								
14								
15								
16								
17								
18								
19								
20								

The Head-end Router System Level Calculations

The router used at the head-end of the HFC plant in this network is the Cisco uBR 7246. The uBR 7246 cable router includes the possibility of dual power supplies. The remaining components are not redundant.

Chapter 6 provided an availability analysis of the uBR 7246; however, that was using an Ethernet 100BaseT back-haul instead of OC-3. We will simply need to perform the calculations again using the new components. The RBD in Figure 6-5 from Chapter 6, "Three Cisco Products: An Availability Analysis," will remain the same with the Ethernet section replaced by the OC-3 section.

Table 9-2 shows the MTBF and MTTR values for the uBR 7246 in consideration for this chapter.

Table 9-2   *The uBR 7246 Network Device MTBF and MTTR Figures*

Product	Description	MTBF	MTTR
uBR 7246	Universal broadband router chassis	232,948	4
OC-3 Port Adapter	Intermediate Reach OC-3	357,756[*]	4
MEM-I/O-FLD48M	20 MB Flash memory	333,166	4
NPE-225	CPU for uBR 7246	269,800	4
uBR-MC16C	MC16C cable module	275,046	4
PWR-UBR7200-AC	Power supply	746,269	4
SU7M3-12.0.7SC	Cisco IOS Software	10,000	0.1

*Assumption based on similar adapter.

With the Ethernet port figure replaced by the OC-3 port figure, we are ready to input the data into the SHARC tool in order to get our hardware and software availability figures. Please note that the OC-3 number was derived using a nearly identical part's value. The "OC-3 for the uBR 7246" figures were not available. Again, the figures in this book are demonstrative of real life numbers, but you should verify them with Cisco Systems before using them for your real life calculations.

Figure 9-11 shows a screen capture of the calculations for the availability of this uBR 7246 system done by the SHARC tool.

Figure 9-11 *The uBR 7246 System HW/SW Availability Prediction*

Cisco Systems, Inc.

© 1998 Cisco Systems, Inc.

System Hardware Availability and Reliability Calculation Worksheet
For Series-Parallel Configurations

System Description: The Cisco UBR7246 Router

Prepared by: Chris Oggerino
Date: 05-Feb-01

System Availability % =	99.9920276868%	The fraction of time the system is operational.
System Unavailability % =	0.0079723232%	Equal to 1-Avail., and is the fraction of time the system is non-operational.
Annual Downtime (Min.) =	41.9	Equal to System Unavailability times 525,960 minutes per year.
System MTBF (Hrs.) =	8,516	The mean time to go from an operational to a non-operational state.
System MTBPR (Hrs.) =	8,326	The mean time between any part restoration (including the time to repair).
System MTTR (Hrs.) =	0.7	The mean time to repair the system, or the mean time to go from a non-operational to an operational state.

Move to far right for scientific notation →

Part Description	n (QTY)	m (No. Req.)	Part MTBF (hrs.)	Part MTTR (hrs.)	Part Availability	Combined Part Availability	Combined Part MTTR	Combined Part MTBF
UBR7246 Chassis	1	1	232,948	4	99.9982829%	99.9982829%	4.0	232,948
OC-3 Port Adapter	1	1	357,756	4	99.9988819%	99.9988819%	4.0	357,756
20 MB Memory	1	1	333,166	4	99.9987994%	99.9987994%	4.0	333,166
NPE225	1	1	269,800	4	99.9985174%	99.9985174%	4.0	269,800
UBR-MC16C	1	1	275,046	4	99.9985457%	99.9985457%	4.0	275,046
PWR-UBR7200-AC	2	1	746,299	4	99.9994640%	100.0000000%	2.0	69,615,423,814
IOS	1	1	10,000	0.100	99.9990000%	99.9990000%	0.1	10,000

As you can see in the diagram, the figures that we will use for the rest of our calculations (uBR 7246 Network Component) will be .99992 availability, 8516-hour MTBF, and 0.7-hour MTTR. These numbers include only the hardware and software contributions to downtime.

The Backbone Router System Level Calculations

The router used to create the network backbone for this network is the Cisco 12000 router. This router is a highly available router capable of moving large amounts of data with minimal latency. We previously performed some introductory calculations for the Cisco12000 router in Chapter 6. The hardware configuration of this Cisco 12000, however, will be slightly different in terms of both interfaces and redundant components. Therefore, we will go ahead and perform a new RBD as shown in Figure 9-12.

Figure 9-12 *The Cisco 12000 RBD*

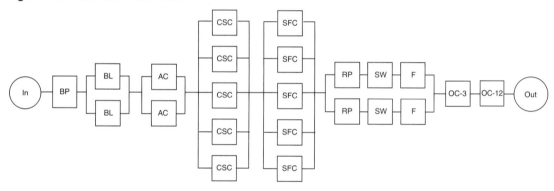

As you can see, this time we are using the full complement of five switch and routing fabrics with N + 1 redundancy in order to maximize the availability of the backbone.

With the RBD completed, our next task is to find the MTBF and MTTR of the various components as listed in Table 9-3.

Table 9-3   *The VoIP Cisco 12000 MTBF and MTTR Figures*

Product	Description	MTBF	MTTR
GSR12012	GSR 12 backplane	620,367	6
GSR12-BLOWER	Blower assembly	570,288	4
PWR-GSR12-AC	AC power supply	316,456	4
GSR12-CSC	Scheduler fabric	272,584	4
GSR12-SFC	Switching fabric	422,115	4
GRP-B	Route processor	87,070	4

Table 9-3 *The VoIP Cisco 12000 MTBF and MTTR Figures (Continued)*

Product	Description	MTBF	MTTR
4OC3/ATM-IR-SC	4 port ATM card	108,304	4
S120Z-12.0.10S	Cisco IOS software	30,000	.1
LC10C12/POS-MM	Multi-Mode OC-12 port	127,124	4
MEM-DFT-GRP/LC-64	Program/route memory	1,984,827	4
MEM-GRP-FL20	20 MB Flash memory	333,166	4

If you note in the RBD, you will see that we have a serial construction inside a parallel component in the form of the four parts of the processing engine. This will require us to perform the calculations in two steps. The first step, represented in Figure 9-13, depicts the availability figures for the processing engine components.

As you can see, we derive a four 9s result, which is the figure we will use in the parallel construction in the system level calculations. The system level calculation in Figure 9-14 includes the results from Figure 9-13 as the "Processing" line.

This two step process is something that you have seen before and should now be comfortable performing yourself. Take a moment to notice how the RBD and the two step process work together to get the final results.

The results for hardware and software contribution to downtime that will be used in the network level calculations for the 12000 are .999922 availability, 53,420 hours MTBF, and 4.2 hours MTTR.

Figure 9-13 *The Cisco 12000 Processing Engine Calculations*

© 1998 Cisco Systems, Inc.

System Hardware Availability and Reliability Calculation Worksheet
For Series-Parallel Configurations

System Description: The Cisco 12000 Route Processor Subsystem

Prepared by: Chris Oggerino
Date: 05-Feb-01

System Availability % =	99.99367084%	The fraction of time the system is operational.
System Unavailability % =	0.00632916%	Equal to 1-Avail., and is the fraction of time the system is non-operational.
***Annual* Downtime (Min.) =**	33.3	Equal to System Unavailability times 525,960 minutes per year.
System MTBF (Hrs.) =	20,694	The mean time to go from an operational to a non-operational state.
System MTBPR (Hrs.) =	20,694	The mean time between any part restoration (including the time to repair).
System MTTR (Hrs.) =	1.3	The mean time to repair the system, or the mean time to go from a non-operational to an operational state.

Move to far right for scientific notation →

Part Description	n (QTY)	m (No. Req.)	Part MTBF (hrs.)	Part MTTR (hrs.)	Part Availability	Combined Part Availability	Combined Part MTTR	Combined Part MTBF
GRP-B	1	1	87,070	4	99.99540621%	99.99540621%	4.0	87,070
MEM-DFT-GRP/LC-64	1	1	1,994,827	4	99.99979847%	99.99979847%	4.0	1,994,827
MEM-GRP-FL20	1	1	333,166	4	99.99879941%	99.99879941%	4.0	333,166
S120Z-12.0.10S	1	1	30,000	0.100	99.99966667%	99.99966667%	0.1	30,000

Figure 9-14 *The Cisco 12000 System Level Calculations*

System Hardware Availability and Reliability Calculation Worksheet
For Series-Parallel Configurations

Prepared by: Chris Oggerino
Date: 05-Feb-01

System Description: The Cisco 12000 Router

System Availability % =	99.9921926%	The fraction of time the system is operational.
System Unavailability % =	0.00780734%	Equal to 1-Avail., and is the fraction of time the system is non-operational.
Annual Downtime (Min.) =	41.1	Equal to System Unavailability times 525,960 minutes per year.
System MTBF (Hrs.) =	53,420	The mean time to go from an operational to a non-operational state.
System MTBPR (Hrs.) =	6,308	The mean time between any part restoration (including the time to repair).
System MTTR (Hrs.) =	4.2	The mean time to repair the system, or the mean time to go from a non-operational to an operational state.

Move to far right for scientific notation →

Part Description	n (QTY)	m (No. Req.)	Part MTBF (hrs.)	Part MTTR (hrs.)	Part Availability	Combined Part Availability	Combined Part MTTR	Combined Part MTBF
1	GSR12012	1	1	620,367	6	99.99903284%	99.99903284%	6.0	620,367
2	GSR12-BLOWER	2	1	570,288	4	99.99929860%	100.0000000%	2.0	40,654,120,656
3	PWR-GSR12-AC	3	2	316,456	4	99.99873602%	99.99999995%	2.0	4,172,841,559
4	GSR12-CSC	5	4	272,584	4	99.99853258%	99.99999978%	2.0	928,843,609
5	GSR12-SFC	5	4	422,115	4	99.99905240%	99.99999991%	2.0	2,227,368,944
6	4OC3ATM-IR-SC	1	1	108,304	4	99.99630683%	99.99630683%	4.0	108,304
7	LC10C12/POS-MM	1	1	127,124	4	99.99685356%	99.99685356%	4.0	127,124
8	Processing	2	1	20,694	1,300	99.93718338%	99.99999961%	0.6	164,729,016

The Switch (8540) System Level Calculations

The router/switch used to connect the computers in the network control area of the network is the Cisco Catalyst 8540 (C8540). This switch is also used in the PSTN connection area and in the Internet connection area. The C8540 switch is a high-end highly available switch appropriate for both LAN and WAN switched connections.

The C8540 can be configured with dual redundant power, switching engines, and routing engines. Figure 9-15 shows a picture of an 8540.

Figure 9-15 *The Cisco Catalyst 8540 Switch/Router*

The first step to calculating the availability of a complex switch like the Catalyst 8540 will be to create the RBD. With several components that are serially configured and installed in parallel, the calculations will be in multiple steps. Note the parallel and serial constructs in the RBD in Figure 9-16.

Figure 9-16 *The Cisco Catalyst 8540 Switch/Router RBD*

The next step to calculate the availability of this switch router is to list the MTBF and MTTR figures for each component. Table 9-4 shows the figures for the Cisco Catalyst 8540.

Table 9-4 *The VoIP Cisco 8540 MTBF and MTTR Figures*

Product	Description	MTBF	MTTR
C8540-CHAS13	8540 chassis	86,568	4
C8540-PWR-AC	Power supply	500,000	4
C8541CSR-RP	Route processor	163,934	4
C8542CSR-SP	Switch processor	72,554	4
C85FE-16F-16K	16 port 100BaseT	166,828	4
C85EGE-2X-16K	2 port Gigabit Ethernet NM	189,090	4
WS-G5484	Gigabit Ethernet adapter	1,000,000	4
S854R3-12.0.10W	Base Cisco IOS software	10,000	.1

With the RBD complete and the MTBF figures, we are ready to begin computing the availability. For this product, we are going to need three steps:

Step 1 Do the computation for the route processing.

Step 2 Do the computation for the switch processing.

Step 3 Combine all the components and obtain our software hardware result.

Figure 9-17 depicts the calculation of the route processor availability. The results will be included in Figure 9-19 as routing.

Figure 9-18 depicts the calculation of the switch processor availability. The results will be included in Figure 9-19 as switching.

Figure 9-19 depicts the software and hardware availability for the 8540. Notice that Figures 9-17 and 9-18 are included in this figure as routing and switching.

The C8540 switch hardware and software figures we will use for our network calculations will be .9999 availability, 41,917-hour MTBF, and 4-hour MTTR.

Figure 9-17 *The Cisco C8540 Routing Engine Calculations*

Cisco Systems, Inc.
© 1998 Cisco Systems, Inc.

System Hardware Availability and Reliability Calculation Worksheet
For Series-Parallel Configurations

Prepared by: Chris Oggerino
Date: 05-Feb-01

System Description: The Cisco C8540 Route Processor Subsystem

System Availability % =	99.99656009%	The fraction of time the system is operational.
System Unavailability % =	0.00343991%	Equal to 1-Avail., and is the fraction of time the system is non-operational.
Annual Downtime (Min.) =	18.1	Equal to System Unavailability times 525,960 minutes per year.
System MTBF (Hrs.) =	9,425	The mean time to go from an operational to a non-operational state.
System MTBPR (Hrs.) =	9,425	The mean time between any part restoration (including the time to repair).
System MTTR (Hrs.) =	0.3	The mean time to repair the system, or the mean time to go from a non-operational to an operational state.

Move to far right for scientific notation →

Part Description	n (QTY.)	m (No. Req.)	Part MTBF (hrs.)	Part MTTR (hrs.)	Part Availability	Combined Part Availability	Combined Part MTTR	Combined Part MTBF
C8541CSR-RP	1	1	163,934	4	99.99756005%	99.99756005%	4.0	163,934
Operating System	1	1	10,000	0.100	99.99900001%	99.99900001%	0.1	10,000

Figure 9-18 *The Cisco C8540 Switching Engine Calculations*

© 1998 Cisco Systems, Inc.

Cisco Systems

System Hardware Availability and Reliability Calculation Worksheet
For Series-Parallel Configurations

Prepared by: Chris Oggerino
Date: 05-Feb-01

System Description: The Cisco C8540 Switch Processor Subsystem

		Explanation
System Availability % =	99.99348723%	The fraction of time the system is operational.
System Unavailability % =	0.00651277%	Equal to 1-Avail., and is the fraction of time the system is non-operational.
Annual Downtime (Min.) =	34.3	Equal to System Unavailability times 525,960 minutes per year.
System MTBF (Hrs.) =	8,789	The mean time to go from an operational to a non-operational state.
System MTBPR (Hrs.) =	8,789	The mean time between any part restoration (including the time to repair).
System MTTR (Hrs.) =	0.6	The mean time to repair the system, or the mean time to go from a non-operational to an operational state.

Move to far right for scientific notation →

Part Description	n (QTY)	m (No. Req.)	Part MTBF (hrs.)	Part MTTR (hrs.)	Part Availability	Combined Part Availability	Combined Part MTTR	Combined Part MTBF
1 C8542CSR-SP	1	1	72,554	4	99.99448717%	99.99448717%	4.0	72,554
2 Operating System	1	1	10,000	0.100	99.99900001%	99.99900001%	0.1	10,000
3								
4								
5								
6								
7								
8								
9								
10								
11								
12								
13								
14								
15								
16								
17								
18								
19								
20								

Figure 9-19 *The Cisco C8540 System Level Calculations*

© 1998 Cisco Systems, Inc.

System Hardware Availability and Reliability Calculation Worksheet
For Series-Parallel Configurations

Prepared by: Chris Oggerino
Date: 05-Feb-01

System Description: The Cisco C8540 Switch Router

System Availability % =	**99.99046632%** The fraction of time the system is operational.
System Unavailability % =	**0.00953368%** Equal to 1-Avail., and is the fraction of time the system is non-operational.
***Annual* Downtime (Min.) =**	**50.1** Equal to System Unavailability times 525,960 minutes per year.
System MTBF (Hrs.) =	**41,917** The mean time to go from an operational to a non-operational state.
System MTBPR (Hrs.) =	**2,139** The mean time between any part restoration (including the time to repair).
System MTTR (Hrs.) =	**4.0** The mean time to repair the system, or the mean time to go from a non-operational to an operational state.

Move to far right for scientific notation →

Part Description	n (QTY)	m (No. Req.)	Part MTBF (hrs.)	Part MTTR (hrs.)	Part Availability	Combined Part Availability	Combined Part MTTR	Combined Part MTBF
C8540 Chassis	1	1	86,568	4	99.99537957%	99.99537957%	4.0	86,568
C8540 Power	2	1	500,000	4	99.99920001%	99.99999999%	2.0	31,250,500,000
Routing	2	1	9,425	0.300	99.99681708%	99.99999990%	0.2	148,060,467
Switching	2	1	8,789	0.600	99.99317375%	99.99999953%	0.3	64,380,890
Gig E NM	1	1	189,090	4	99.99788465%	99.99788465%	4.0	189,090
Gig E Adapter	1	1	1,000,000	4	99.99600000%	99.99600000%	4.0	1,000,000
16 100BaseT Ports	1	1	166,828	4	99.99760238%	99.99760238%	4.0	166,828

The PSTN Gateway System Level Calculations

The interface between the VoIP network and the PSTN is provided by AS5300 routers. The AS5300 is a partially redundant, high performance VoIP router with T1 interfaces that lends itself well to this application.

Because we used the AS5300 in Chapter 7, "A Small ISP Network: An Availability Analysis," you can look there for a picture of the router. The calculations in Chapter 7 were done based on the router's use as a modem access server, so the calculations will need to be redone. However, you will find that they are similar. We will use a similar RBD to the one in Chapter 7, but as you can see in Figure 9-20 the modem digital signal processors, computing chips that act like modems, are replaced by VoIP DSPs.

Figure 9-20 *The Cisco AS5300 Reliability Block Diagram*

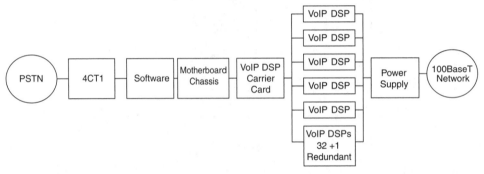

As we did in Chapter 7, we will again treat the AS5300 dual power supply as a single unit with a reduced MTTR because of its design.

The key differences between these calculations and the previous calculations is due to the use of the router. In Chapter 7, the AS5300 was used as a modem access server at a small ISP. In that example, the router was not fully populated with all the modems that it could hold. In this case, the router is in use by a large service provider and all the slots are fully loaded. You can see the difference in that we have switched from a four T1 module to an eight T1 module. We also have double the carrier card and DSP count.

Figure 9-21 depicts the availability calculations for the AS5300 VoIP gateway.

The figures on the spreadsheet show that the availability of the AS5300 for VoIP is almost identical to the data modem version, even with the additional and different components. The results we will be using in our network calculations are .99985 availability, 7326-hour MTBF, and 1.1-hour MTTR. As you might notice when you look at the spreadsheet screenshots, or explore the sheets on the book's CD, the SHARC spreadsheet will allow for a variety of M + N scenarios.

Figure 9-21 *The Cisco AS5300 System Availability Calculations*

Cisco Systems, Inc.
© 1998 Cisco Systems, Inc.

System Hardware Availability and Reliability Calculation Worksheet
For Series-Parallel Configurations

System Description: The Cisco 5300 Series Router

Prepared by: Chris Oggerino
Date: 05-Feb-01

System Availability % =	99.98500417%	The fraction of time the system is operational.
System Unavailability % =	0.01499583%	Equal to 1-Avail., and is the fraction of time the system is non-operational.
Annual Downtime (Min.) =	78.9	Equal to System Unavailability times 525,960 minutes per year.
System MTBF (Hrs.) =	7,326	The mean time to go from an operational to a non-operational state.
System MTBPR (Hrs.) =	5,788	The mean time between any part restoration (including the time to repair).
System MTTR (Hrs.) =	1.1	The mean time to repair the system, or the mean time to go from a non-operational to an operational state.

Move to far right for scientific notation →

Part Description	n (QTY)	m (No. Req.)	Part MTBF (hrs.)	Part MTTR (hrs.)	Part Availability	Combined Part Availability	Combined Part MTTR	Combined Part MTBF
Chassis/Motherboard	1	1	45,218	4	99.99115475%	99.99115475%	4.0	45,218
Carrier Card	2	2	290,930	4	99.99862512%	99.99725025%	4.0	145,465
6 VOIP DSP	33	32	909,378	4	99.99560014%	99.99998998%	2.0	195,806,909
Power Supply	1	1	500,000	1	99.99980000%	99.99980000%	1.0	500,000
8 T1 Card	1	1	181,774	4	99.99779951%	99.99779951%	4.0	181,774
Cisco IOS Software	1	1	10,000	0.100	99.99900001%	99.99900001%	0.1	10,000

The Assumed Availability Figures

The rest of the devices in our network are going to be given assumed availability, MTBF, and MTTR numbers. With component MTBF figures available, we could perform the calculations ourselves. These observed numbers are reasonable, however, and will work fine for our example.

The HFC Component

Our RBDs include an HFC component, the cable company's cable plant. Based on industry observation, we will use an availability of .99986 for this component. MTBF and MTTR will not be required for this component in our calculations.

Internet

In our RBD representing where our network connects to the Internet (refer to Figure 9-6), you can see that there are actually four separate connections to the Internet. We will assume that they go to four different physical connections. We will assume that if a connection to the Internet is working that the Internet itself is working. Our figures for the connections to the Internet will be .99999 availability, 325,000-hour MTBF, and 3.25-hour MTTR.

OC-12 Metropolitan Area Network

We have chosen a ring-based metropolitan-area network (MAN) for our backbone. The operation of this media is such that fiber cuts will result in a ring-wrap. In other words, it would require two separate fiber cuts to take down the backbone. Additionally even with the fiber completely cut, the redundancy of the different supporting services on the network would make it such that two independent networks could potentially operate simultaneously. For this reason, I choose to assume that there hardly will be any downtime due to the OC-12 being down. We will call the availability of this component .999999.

Network Control

The network control components are redundant in a variety of different ways. We will assume that each pair of network control blocks are .99999 available. As with the Internet, this can be achieved with 325,000 hours of MTBF and 3.25 hours of MTTR. In this case, however, it is important to note that this result is based on a pair of UNIX computers as opposed to a single device to which we are connecting.

Local PSTN

For our local PSTN services, we are going to use the same figures as we did for the Internet of .99999 availability, 325,000-hour MTBF, and 3.25-hour MTTR.

Long Distance PSTN

For our long distance PSTN services, we are going to use .999975 availability, 240,000-hour MTBF, and 6-hour MTTR. This takes into account that the telephone company suffers downtime based on different scenarios. The longer the distance, the more equipment that must be working for success.

With these final figures, we are ready to begin network level calculations.

Network Level Availability Calculations

Now that we have computed the availability for each of the boxes in each of our RBDs, we are ready to begin the results into our various network segments. We will do this in steps similar to those we followed for the individual systems. Where appropriate, we will compute subsystems, or parallel segments, and then use those in system level, or serial segments, calculations.

You might note that we are breaking up our work slightly different than in some previous examples: we are not dividing our work by scenario. Eventually, we will do the scenario calculations. However, we will do them after we have calculated most of the smaller network segments. This step will reduce the total amount of work required to perform this particular analysis. It will also make our final calculations easier because many of the parts of the scenarios will have the same results.

Before we begin, inspect Table 9-5, which summarizes the results from the previous section.

Table 9-5 *The VoIP System Level Availability Results*

Network Component	Availability	MTBF	MTTR
CVA122 CPE device	.999938	9399	0.6
uBR 7246 head-end	.99992	8516	0.7
12000 backbone router	.999922	53,420	4.2
C8540 switch router	.9999	41,917	4
AS5300 PSTN gateway	.99985	7326	1.1
OC-12 backbone	.999999	1,000,000	1
The Internet	.99999	325,000	3.25
A pair of network control servers	.99999	325,000	3.25
A local PSTN call	.99999	325,000	3.25
A long distance PSTN call	.999975	240,000	6

It is interesting to note that four 9s of availability can be achieved with widely varying MTBF figures. This is best seen in noting the similarity (and differences) between the results for the uBR 7246 and the 12000.

Calculating Smaller Redundant Segments

The first step will be to perform the calculations on some of the smaller redundant sections of the network. The method we use for selecting our first component is similar to what we did on the Cisco 12000 router calculations. If you remember, we calculated CPU, memory, and operating system results first. That result was used as the parallel device entitled "processing" in the end-to-end system level calculations to achieve our final figures.

Once we have calculated the small serial, segment calculations and the parallel calculations, we will be ready to move onto the scenario calculations. Because we are calculating the parallel constructions in this section, we will be including the fail-over protocols as we go.

Small Serial Network Component Calculations

As it turns out, only one calculation involves serial components, which are lined up in a redundant configuration in the network. That calculation is of the C8540 to Internet connection in Scenario 1.

Instead of performing these calculations manually, we will input the figures from Table 9-5 into our SHARC spreadsheet. The SHARC spreadsheet does a nice job of helping us to compute availability when its input is the MTBF and MTTR for devices in serial or parallel configurations. Figure 9-22 shows the screen shot of this effort.

The result of this calculation is .99989 availability, 37,128-hour MTBF, and 3.9-hour MTTR.

Parallel Network Component Calculations

Nearly all the devices in this network are in some sort of redundant configuration. By computing the availability of each of the parallel constructs in our network, we can compute scenario results with little additional effort. Furthermore, we could use these results to compute additional scenarios should the need arise.

For each of the computations in this area, we will first compute the simple result of the parallel construct in terms of hardware and software. Then we will introduce a reasonable amount of downtime based on fail-over times for the various constructs. For OSPF, we will use 30 seconds per fail-over. For switching, we will use 60 seconds per fail-over.

Parallel Internet Connections

We will perform the parallel Internet computations first because we just finished with the required subcomponent. The C8540 to Internet results will be used here in a parallel construct. The fail-over mechanism will be based on switching because we are assuming dual-homed switches connected to the next upstream portion of the network—the Cisco 12000 routers that connect to the backbone.

To be clear, this calculation includes two C8540 routers and two Internet connections. These will be used again to compute further redundancy because two of these constructs exist in our network. Figure 9-23 depicts the first half of the calculation by utilizing the results from our C8540 to Internet calculation in a parallel construct.

Figure 9-22 *The C8540 to Internet Availability Calculation*

Cisco Systems, Inc.

© 1998 Cisco Systems, Inc.

System Hardware Availability and Reliability Calculation Worksheet
For Series-Parallel Configurations

Prepared by: Chris Oggerino
Date: 05-Feb-01

System Description: The C8540 To Internet HW/SW Availability

System Availability % =	**99.98945835%**	The fraction of time the system is operational.
System Unavailability % =	**0.01054165%**	Equal to 1-Avail., and is the fraction of time the system is non-operational.
***Annual* Downtime (Min.) =**	**55.4**	Equal to System Unavailability times 525,960 minutes per year.
System MTBF (Hrs.) =	**37,128**	The mean time to go from an operational to a non-operational state.
System MTBPR (Hrs.) =	**37,132**	The mean time between any part restoration (including the time to repair).
System MTTR (Hrs.) =	**3.9**	The mean time to repair the system, or the mean time to go from a non-operational to an operational state.

Move to far right for scientific notation →

Part Description	n (QTY)	m (No. Req.)	Part MTBF (hrs.)	Part MTTR (hrs.)	Part Availability	Combined Part Availability	Combined Part MTTR	Combined Part MTBF
C8540	1	1	41,917	4	99.99045824%	99.99045824%	4.0	41,917
Internet	1	1	325,000	3	99.99900001%	99.99900001%	3.2	325,000
3								
4								
5								
6								
7								
8								
9								
10								
11								
12								
13								
14								
15								
16								
17								
18								
19								
20								

Figure 9-23 *Parallel Internet Connection Calculation*

Cisco Systems
© 1998 Cisco Systems, Inc.

System Hardware Availability and Reliability Calculation Worksheet
For Series-Parallel Configurations

Prepared by: Chris Oggerino
Date: 05-Feb-01

System Description: Parallel 8540 to Internet Connection

System Availability % =	99.99998890%	The fraction of time the system is operational.
System Unavailability % =	0.00000110%	Equal to 1-Avail., and is the fraction of time the system is non-operational.
Annual Downtime (Min.) =	< 6 sec.	Equal to System Unavailability times 525,960 minutes per year.
System MTBF (Hrs.) =	176,766,408	The mean time to go from an operational to a non-operational state.
System MTBPR (Hrs.) =	18,566	The mean time between any part restoration (including the time to repair).
System MTTR (Hrs.) =	2.0	The mean time to repair the system, or the mean time to go from a non-operational to an operational state.

Move to far right for scientific notation →

Part Description	n (QTY)	m (No. Req.)	Part MTBF (hrs.)	Part MTTR (hrs.)	Part Availability	Combined Part Availability	Combined Part MTTR	Combined Part MTBF
Parallel 8540 to Internet	2	1	37,128	4	99.98949690%	99.99999890%	2.0	176,766,408
1								
2								
3								
4								
5								
6								
7								
8								
9								
10								
11								
12								
13								
14								
15								
16								
17								
18								
19								
20								

Because we have two devices that might require fail-over and they are running a bridging protocol, we account for the time of the fail-over on the occasional failure of the two devices. Because they each have an MTBF of 37,128 hours and there are 8,766 hours in a year, we should expect them to fail about .236 times per year. Because there are two of them, the average failures per year are .472 and result in .472 minutes of downtime (because there is one minute of downtime per failure). Given this amount of downtime annually due to the fail-over protocol, we can add the fail-over protocol into our spreadsheet as shown in Figure 9-24. Note that we converted .472 minutes into hours in order for the spreadsheet work.

With hardware, software, and fail-over protocol considered, each of our redundant Internet connections will be given a six 9s availability (0.999999) for about half a minute of downtime each year.

An interesting thing to note is that this is only the result for half of our connectivity to the Internet. This connection is used for data, not telephone traffic. This network will have no appreciable loss of connectivity to the Internet. Perhaps we have over-engineered this part of our design.

Parallel Cisco 12000 Routers

Because all the network components are tied together via the backbone and redundant Cisco 12000 routers, we will compute that availability next.

If you remember from our system level calculations, each 12000 weighs in with figures of .999922 availability, 53,420- hour MTBF, and 4.2-hour MTTR. When put in parallel using OSPF as the fail-over protocol, we can see that two Cisco 12000 routers are very reliable. Figure 9-25 combines two steps and shows both the redundant routers as well as the fail-over protocol accounting.

We have used the MTBF of 53,420 hours to compute the annual failures and the resulting amount of time spent failing over via the OSPF protocol, and we included that in line two of our figure. The MTTR is a very small number again and was derived by calculated the number of failures per year based on the number of 12000's (two) and 30 seconds fail-over per failure. Our resulting .2 minute per year of downtime amounts to 12 seconds, which is hardly noticeable—even for voice networking. When we go to our end-to-end calculations, we will use 0.999999 (six 9s) of availability for parallel 12000 constructs.

Parallel Cisco C8540 Switch Routers

Although we already calculated the availability of the Internet via C8540 routers, we have not calculated what availability a pair of 8540 switch routers can provide. This construct uses two different places in our network, so we will need to use this result more than once.

Using the base figures for our C8540 routers, we can put the first line in our spreadsheet and see that the availability of a pair of C8540 switch routers is roughly nine 9s if we don't account for fail-over time. Figure 9-26 shows the spreadsheet screen shot.

Figure 9-24 *Parallel Internet with Fail-over Times*

Cisco Systems, Inc.
© 1998 Cisco Systems, Inc.

System Hardware Availability and Reliability Calculation Worksheet
For Series-Parallel Configurations

Prepared by: Chris Oggerino
Date: 05-Feb-01

System Description: Parallel 8540 to Internet Connection

System Availability % =	99.99990764%	The fraction of time the system is operational.
System Unavailability % =	0.00009236%	Equal to 1-Avail., and is the fraction of time the system is non-operational.
Annual **Downtime (Min.)** =	0.5	Equal to System Unavailability times 525,960 minutes per year.
System MTBF (Hrs.) =	8,766	The mean time to go from an operational to a non-operational state.
System MTBPR (Hrs.) =	5,955	The mean time between any part restoration (including the time to repair).
System MTTR (Hrs.) =	0.0	The mean time to repair the system, or the mean time to go from a non-operational to an operational state.

Move to far right for scientific notation →

Part Description	n (QTY)	m (No. Req.)	Part MTBF (hrs.)	Part MTTR (hrs.)	Part Availability	Combined Part Availability	Combined Part MTTR	Combined Part MTBF
Parallel 8540 to Internet	2	1	37,128	4	99.98949690%	99.99998990%	2.0	176,766,408
Fail-Over	1	1	8,766	0.008	99.99990874%	99.99990874%	0.0	8,766

Comments:

References: Bellcore SR-TSY-001171, Methods and Procedures for System Reliability Analysis
Cisco Quality Document, #7020073-0000, System Hardware Availability and Reliability Calculation Worksheet

Cisco Corporate Quality

Figure 9-25 *Parallel 12000 Routers with Fail-over Times*

Cisco Systems
© 1998 Cisco Systems, Inc.

System Hardware Availability and Reliability Calculation Worksheet
For Series-Parallel Configurations

System Description: Parallel 12000 Routers with OSPF Fail-over

Prepared by: Chris Oggerino
Date: 05-Feb-01

System Availability % =	99.9999516%	The fraction of time the system is operational.
System Unavailability % =	0.0000484%	Equal to 1-Avail., and is the fraction of time the system is non-operational.
Annual Downtime (Min.) =	0.2	Equal to System Unavailability times 525,960 minutes per year.
System MTBF (Hrs.) =	8,766	The mean time to go from an operational to a non-operational state.
System MTBPR (Hrs.) =	6,600	The mean time between any part restoration (including the time to repair).
System MTTR (Hrs.) =	0.0	The mean time to repair the system, or the mean time to go from a non-operational to an operational state.

Move to far right for scientific notation →

Part Description	n (QTY)	m (No. Req.)	Part MTBF (hrs.)	Part MTTR (hrs.)	Part Availability	Combined Part Availability	Combined Part MTTR	Combined Part MTBF
Parallel 12000 Routers	2	1	53.420	4.200	99.9921383%	99.9999938%	2.1	339,779,182
Fail-over Protocol	1	1	8,766	0.003	99.9996578%	99.9996578%	0.0	8,766

Comments:

References: Bellcore SR-TSY-001171, Methods and Procedures for System Reliability Analysis
Cisco Quality Document, #702073-0000, System Hardware Availability and Reliability Calculation Worksheet

Cisco Corporate Quality

Figure 9-26 *Parallel C8540 Switch Routers with Fail-over times*

CISCO SYSTEMS

© 1998 Cisco Systems, Inc.

System Hardware Availability and Reliability Calculation Worksheet
For Series-Parallel Configurations

Prepared by: Chris Oggerino
Date: 05-Feb-01

System Description: Parallel C8540 Routers

System Availability % =	**99.99991924%** The fraction of time the system is operational.
System Unavailability % =	**0.00008076%** Equal to 1-Avail., and is the fraction of time the system is non-operational.
Annual **Downtime (Min.) =**	**0.4** Equal to System Unavailability times 525,960 minutes per year.
System MTBF (Hrs.) =	**8,766** The mean time to go from an operational to a non-operational state.
System MTBPR (Hrs.) =	**6,181** The mean time between any part restoration (including the time to repair).
System MTTR (Hrs.) =	**0.0** The mean time to repair the system, or the mean time to go from a non-operational to an operational state.

Move to far right for scientific notation →

Part Description	n (QTY)	m (No. Req.)	Part MTBF (hrs.)	Part MTTR (hrs.)	Part Availability	Combined Part Availability	Combined Part MTTR	Combined Part MTBF
C8540	2	1	41,917	4	99.99045824%	99.99999909%	2.0	219,671,278
Fail-over	1	1	8,766	0.007	99.99992015%	99.99992015%	0.0	8,766

By dividing 8766 hours per year by the 41,917 hours of MTBF for the C8540, we see that we will get about .21 failures per year. With two devices and a minute per failure, we see that line two of our spreadsheet shows our fail-over time contributes to our annual downtime by reducing nine 9s to six 9s. Six 9s is what we will use for parallel C8540 routers running bridging protocol as their fail-over mechanism.

Parallel AS5300 PSTN Gateway Services

Our PSTN gateway consists of two redundant constructs, each including six redundant AS5300 routers in an N + 1 construct. While there is actually time for fail-over in this construct, we can omit the calculation for the fail-over time because there will be a specific event whenever a failure occurs in this section of the network.

Whenever there is a failure of an AS5300 that supports any users, all of those users will be disconnected. They will be able to immediately redial their telephone call successfully, but they will suffer a disconnect. Measuring the actual time of the fail-over is really about measuring the time it takes the user to decide they have been disconnected and to redial their telephone. Instead, we will compute the number of calls disconnected and make that a note to our calculations. We will assume that the routers are at 50 percent utilization when they fail for this calculation. If we assume that the maximum number of calls simultaneously supported by an AS5300 is 192 and we are running at 50 percent capacity, then 96 calls are disconnected per router failure.

Because there are 12 AS5300 routers in our network and they each have an MTBF of 7326 hours, we can compute the number of telephone call disconnects each year as shown in Figure 9-27.

Figure 9-27 *Calls Disconnected From AS5300 Failures Annually*

$$\text{AS5300 Failures per Year} = \frac{8766}{7326}$$
$$= 1.2$$
$$\text{Total AS5300 Failures} = 12 * 1.2$$
$$= 14.4$$
$$\text{Calls Dropped per Year} = 14.4 * 96$$
$$= 1382.4$$

The result of our calculation shows that with 50 percent loading, we would drop 1382.4 calls per year. This might seem like a lot of dropped calls, but at six minutes per phone call, this network at a 50 percent load would be providing 8,415,360 annual phone calls. We calculate 8,415,360 calls using 8766 hours times 10 calls per hour, times 10 routers, times 96 calls per router. This assumes that we don't put any traffic over the standby routers until they are needed.

Figure 9-28 shows the computation we will use for availability for the PSTN gateway network component.

Figure 9-28 *The AS5300 PSTN Gateway Construct Availability Computations*

CISCO SYSTEMS

© 1998 Cisco Systems, Inc.

System Hardware Availability and Reliability Calculation Worksheet
For Series-Parallel Configurations

System Description: PSTN Gateway: AS5300 N+1 Calculations

Prepared by: Chris Oggerino
Date: 05-Feb-01

System Availability % =	99.99996621%	The fraction of time the system is operational.
System Unavailability % =	0.00003379%	Equal to 1-Avail., and is the fraction of time the system is non-operational.
Annual Downtime (Min.) =	0.2	Equal to System Unavailability times 525,960 minutes per year.
System MTBF (Hrs.) =	1,627,837	The mean time to go from an operational to a non-operational state.
System MTBPR (Hrs.) =	1,221	The mean time between any part restoration (including the time to repair).
System MTTR (Hrs.) =	0.6	The mean time to repair the system, or the mean time to go from a non-operational to an operational state.

Move to far right for scientific notation →

Part Description	n (QTY)	m (No. Req.)	Part MTBF (hrs.)	Part MTTR (hrs.)	Part Availability	Combined Part Availability	Combined Part MTTR	Combined Part MTBF
AS5300	6	5	7,326	1	99.98498724%	99.99996621%	0.6	1,627,837

Our PSTN gateway using 5 + 1 AS5300 routers will be .999999 but will have a side effect of causing 691 dropped calls each year. As we proceed, it might be a good idea to remind ourselves that we have still not computed human error or power loss contributions to annual downtime for the central site equipment.

Parallel uBR 7246 Head-end Construct Availability

Our final parallel calculation will be for the uBR 7246 head-end devices. The uBR 7246 routers present an interesting twist in our calculations because they affect the CPE devices in an interesting way.

Each time a uBR 7246 router fails, we will suffer 20 minutes of downtime for the CPE users attached to that router. This is a result of the Data Over Cable System Interface Specification (DOCSIS) method of connecting our CPE devices to our head-end. When a CPE device connects to a head-end, it must range. This ranging process takes about 20 minutes if you have several thousand CPE devices trying to perform the operation all at the same time.

For each uBR failure, we will attribute 20 minutes to the fail-over contribution to downtime. The spreadsheet in Figure 9-29 shows the calculations for the uBR 7246 router in parallel on the first line and the calculations for the failure protocol on the second line.

The MTTR used for the fail-over time was calculated by multiplying the number of failures per year for the primary uBR 7246 router (1.03) by hours per failure (.33). The result for the head-end network component works out to .99996 availability for our end-to-end calculations.

With this final computation of network component availability, we are ready to move on to computing the availability network services, which will be our final step before moving on to scenario level calculations. The results for the uBR72xx series head-end router will be greatly improved when Cisco releases a new fall-over protocol that eliminates the need for re-ranging. Rumor has it that it is working in their labs at presstime.

Figure 9-29 *The uBR 7246 Redundant Head-End Availability Calculations*

Cisco Systems, Inc.

© 1998 Cisco Systems, Inc.

System Hardware Availability and Reliability Calculation Worksheet
For Series-Parallel Configurations

System Description: Paralle UBR7246 Routers - Head End and Fail-over

Prepared by: Chris Oggerino
Date: 05-Feb-01

System Availability % =	99.99612085%	The fraction of time the system is operational.
System Unavailability % =	0.00387915%	Equal to 1-Avail., and is the fraction of time the system is non-operational.
***Annual* Downtime (Min.)** =	20.4	Equal to System Unavailability times 525,960 minutes per year.
System MTBF (Hrs.) =	8,765	The mean time to go from an operational to a non-operational state.
System MTBPR (Hrs.) =	2,866	The mean time between any part restoration (including the time to repair).
System MTTR (Hrs.) =	0.3	The mean time to repair the system, or the mean time to go from a non-operational to an operational state.

Move to far right for scientific notation →

Part Description	n (QTY)	m (No. Req.)	Part MTBF (hrs.)	Part MTTR (hrs.)	Part Availability	Combined Part Availability	Combined Part MTTR	Combined Part MTBF
UBR7246	2	1	8,516	1	99.9917808085%	99.9999932%	0.3	51,810,127
Fail-over	1	1	8,766	0.340	99.9961215153%	99.9961215153%	0.3	8,766

Major Network Service Construct Availability

Our network includes three major services. The PSTN access, Internet access, and network control services for our network are not only redundant but are completely duplicated. Calculating the scenarios will be easier if we determine the availability of these major services first.

As we did in the previous section, we calculated serial component availability and then used that in parallel equations. We will again perform similar operations for each of our major services in this section.

The Internet Access Service Availability

If you look in the Scenario 1 RBD shown in Figure 9-6, you will see that the Internet is available via two different connections, each of which is redundant all by itself. Previously we calculated the availability of the redundant Internet connection. Here we need to calculate the availability of the Internet to our network considering that we have two of those redundant Internet connections.

To calculate the availability of Internet access services, we need to calculate the availability of the two redundant connections, which are at different sites.

Normally as soon as we started computing the availability of equipment located at different sites, we would have to perform the environmental calculations before combining redundant sites. Because of the distributed property of multiplication, however, we will be able to multiple the power contribution into all four scenarios when we perform the calculations on the redundant network control sections of the network.

Figure 9-30 depicts the calculations for the Internet access service on our network through Steps 1 and 2.

Figure 9-30 *VoIP: The Internet Access Service Availability*

Serial
Parallel 12000 Availability = .999999
Parallel C8540 to Internet = .999999
Backbone to Internet Availability = $(.999999)^2$
= .999998

Parallel
Backbone to Internet in Parallel = $1 - (1 - .999998)^2$
= 1.00000 (rounded)

The availability of the Internet using this design is so reliable that we might as well round the availability to 1.0. Our time lost to fail-over protocols will be accounted for in our end-to-end calculations. Because the two sites are connected together via Cisco 12000 routers over the OC-12 backbone and running OSPF, the calculations are best be done when we calculate all the devices and services together in the scenario calculations.

The Network Control Service Availability

The network control service availability section is common to all scenarios. Therefore, we can include our power calculations and our human error calculations in this section. That will be including both in the entire end-to-end calculations, resulting in one big serial multiplication.

Power Contribution to Downtime

Power will be included by assuming that we have a 99 percent available backup power solution and 24 hours per year of power loss. Power loss will result from power outages, earthquakes, tornadoes, and other environmental problems. Figure 9-31 shows the calculations for power availability at our two sites.

Figure 9-31   *The Environmental Contribution to Downtime*

$$\text{Annual Power Loss} = 24 \text{ hours}$$
$$\text{Power Backup Solution} = .99 \text{ availability}$$
$$\text{Annual Actual Power Outage} = 24 * (1 - .99)$$
$$= .24 \text{ hours}$$
$$\text{Power Availability} = \frac{8766}{8766 + .24}$$
$$= .999973$$

$$\text{Actual Minutes} = 14.4 \text{ Minutes per year}$$

When we introduce power availability into our equation, we will use .999973 as our availability figure.

Human Error Contribution to Downtime

Human error and standard process (or lack thereof) will also be computed into our equation in this section. As with power, we can include it here and it will count for all four scenarios in the end-to-end calculations. The distributed property of multiplication holds for any calculation like this, as long as we make sure we apply it properly. The application of human error and power will occur in the following section.

Let us assume that human error is going to cause downtime of five hours once every two years at Site 1 and six hours every three years at Site 2 in this network. Because all our figures are averages, the calculations for availability of our network with human error considered are simple as illustrated in Figure 9-32.

Figure 9-32 *The Human Error and Standard Process Contribution to Downtime*

Site 1

$$\text{Human Error Availability} = \frac{(8766 * 2)}{((8766 * 2) + 5)}$$

$$= .99971$$

Site 2

$$\text{Human Error Availability} = \frac{(8766 * 3)}{((8766 * 3) + 6)}$$

$$= .99977$$

You may have noticed that I went directly to the solution using the availability equation. You should be able to do that by this point in this book as well.

The results for human error will be .99971 availability for Site 1 and .99977 availability for Site 2. Because both sites are the same, we can apply either number to either site and the answer will be the same.

Network Control Services Results

We now have all of the availability figures required to perform our network control services calculations. Our first step will be to calculate the availability of network control services at the individual sites. Then we will combine those results together using standard parallel construction.

Figure 9-33 depicts the calculations for network control services availability excluding time spent failing over between the two sites.

Figure 9-33 *The Network Control Services Availability*

Parallel 12000 Availability = .999999

Parallel C8540 to Internet = .999999

Parallel Control Server Availability = .999990

Power Availability = .999973

Site 1 Human Error Availability = .99971

Site 2 Human Error Availability = .99977

Site 1 Network Control Services

Availability = .999999 * .999999 * .99999 * .999973 * .99971

= .99967

Site 2 Network Control Services

Availability = .999999 * .999999 * .99999 * .999973 * .99977

= .99973

Network Control Services

Availability = 1 − [(1 − .99967)(1 − .99973)]

= .9999999

Our result of seven 9s is nearly perfect. Even with power and human error causing the two sites to fail occasionally and bring the sites down to as low as three 9s, the two sites together will provide nearly perfect availability for network control services. We will use 0.9999999 availability in our end-to-end results for the network control services in all our scenarios.

As with our Internet access calculations, this network service section will be affected by the fail-over protocol running on the backbone. The Cisco 12000 routers that connect this section to the backbone are part of that network.

The availability predictions for a network with this much redundancy are turning out to be very high so far. When we get to the end-to-end computations and we are forced to include the single points of failure and the lesser redundant components, you will see our overall availability drop dramatically.

PSTN Gateway Services Availability Computations

This final intermediate calculation will compute the availability of the two sites' PSTN access services. Each site has a pair of 12000 routers and C8540 switch routers in serial with a 5 + 1 set of redundant AS5300s.

Because we calculated those individual results earlier, we can go directly into our series-parallel calculations to compute availability for the PSTN access service. Figure 9-34 shows those calculations.

Figure 9-34 *The PSTN Access Services Availability*

Parallel 12000 Availability = .999999

Parallel C8540 Availability = .999999

5 + 1 AS5300 Availability = .999999

Site Availabilty PSTN Access = .999997

$$\text{Parallel Sites} = 1 - [(1 - .999997)^2]$$
$$= 1.0 \text{ rounded}$$

The figures in the diagram show us that our PSTN access will be 100 percent available—with rounding. As with our initial calculations on PSTN availability when we calculated the 5 + 1 availability of our AS5300 routers, we will suffer some disconnected telephone calls during times when equipment fails and fail-over protocols are activated. These call drops are something of which we should be aware.

To keep things simple, let us assume that we will drop twice as many calls as we would in a single site scenario because we have twice as many individual equipment failures. If you remember, we had 1152 dropped calls out of several million total calls based on the AS5300 router predictions. A simple calculation tells us this will result in about 2304 dropped calls each year.

As with the other network services, we will again include the Cisco 12000 routers in this section in the end-to-end network fail-over protocol calculation.

Calculating Scenario Availability

In the preceding section, we calculated the availability for all of the serial and parallel constructs in our network diagrams. We also included all five of the factors for availability. Power was included at Site 1, Site 2, and the CPE site. Human error also was included at both Site 1 and Site 2.

The only thing we omitted to calculate so far was the fail-over contribution to downtime of the backbone 12000 routers. The way we calculate that downtime will be to calculate the failures of the Cisco 12000 routers and attribute 30 seconds of OSPF route recalculation for each failure. Because there are two sites and each site has six 12000 routers, we have 12 Cisco 12000 routers participating in the backbone OSPF area.

Because recalculations on the Cisco 12000 routers will stop connectivity for major services, we account for this loss of connectivity by creating an availability figure for Backbone OSPF as calculated in Figure 9-35.

Figure 9-35 *All Scenarios: The Backbone OSPF Availability*

$$\text{Cisco 12000 MTBF} = 53,420 \text{ hours}$$

$$\text{Failures per Year} = \frac{8766}{53,420}$$

$$= .164$$

$$\text{Total Failures per Year} = .164 * 12$$

$$\text{Total Failures per Year} = 1.968$$

$$\text{Time Lost per Failure} = .5 \text{ minutes}$$

$$\text{Total Minutes Lost} = 1.968 * 5$$

$$= .984$$

$$\text{Annual OSPF Backbone Availability} = \frac{525,960}{525,960 * .984}$$

$$\text{OSPF Backbone} = .999998$$

The result of running 12 Cisco 12000 routers using OSPF over OC-12 media produces an OSPF Backbone availability of .999998. This figure will be included in our scenario calculations.

The Scenario 1 Calculations

Scenario 1 was our CPE to the Internet scenario. This prediction applies to the network users that would be using the network to surf the Internet. Figure 9-36 shows the calculations for this scenario.

Figure 9-36 *The Scenario 1 Calculations*

$$
\begin{aligned}
\text{CVM122} &= & .999938 \\
\text{HFC Network (cable)} &= & .99986 \\
\text{Redundant uBR7246 Routers} &= & .99996 \\
\text{Redundant 12000 Routers} &= & .999999 \\
\text{OC-12 Backbone} &= & .999999 \\
\text{OSPF Backbone} &= & .999998 \\
\text{Network Control Services} &= & .9999999 \\
\text{Internet Access Services} &= & \underline{* \ 1.0} \\
\text{Scenario 1 Availability} &= & .99975 \\
\end{aligned}
$$

Average Annual Downtime = 525,960 (1 − .99975)

$$\approx 131 \text{ minutes}$$

Users utilizing this network to surf the Internet are going to get three and three-quarters 9s of availability. They should see about two hours of downtime each year.

The Scenario 2 Calculations

Scenario 2 was our CPE to CPE telephone call scenario. This prediction applies to the network users that would be using the network to telephone a friend that was also on this network.

Figure 9-37 shows the calculations for this scenario.

Figure 9-37 *The Scenario 2 Calculations*

$$
\begin{aligned}
\text{Ingress} &\begin{cases}
\text{CVA122} = & .999938 \\
\text{HFC} = & .99986 \\
\text{uBRs} = & .99996 \\
\text{12000s} = & .999999 \\
\text{OC-12} = & .999999
\end{cases} \\[1ex]
\text{OSPF Backbone} = & .999998 \\
\text{Network Control} = & .9999999 \\[1ex]
\text{Egress} &\begin{cases}
\text{12000s} = & .999999 \\
\text{uBRs} = & .99996 \\
\text{HFC} = & .99986 \\
\text{CVA 122} = & * \underline{.999938}
\end{cases} \\[1ex]
\text{Scenario 2 Availability} = & .99955
\end{aligned}
$$

Average Annual Downtime = 525,960 (1 − .99955)

$\approx$ 236.7 minutes

$\approx$ 3.9 hours

As you can see, our total downtime is about 3.9 hours with an availability of under four 9s. Luckily, this scenario is unlikely to be used for any critical business use. Improving the CPE device or the HFC network, however, would have dramatic effects on the results for this scenario.

The Scenario 3 and 4 Calculations

Scenarios 3 and 4 are virtually identical. This scenario is where our user makes a telephone to a destination off of our network utilizing the PSTN. Scenario 3 uses the local PSTN and Scenario 4 uses the long distance PSTN availability figures.

Figure 9-38 shows the calculations for both Scenario 3 and 4.

Figure 9-38 *The Scenario 3 and 4 Calculations*

	Scenario 3	**Scenario 4**
CPG =	.999938	.999938
HFC =	.99986	.99986
uBRs =	.99996	.99996
12000s =	.999999	.999999
OC-12 =	.999999	.999999
OSPF Backbone =	.999998	.999998
Network Control =	.9999999	.9999999
Backbone to PSTN Availability =	1.0	1.0
PSTN Local =	* .99999	
PSTN Long Distance =	_____	* .999975
Scenario 3 Availability =	.99974	
Scenario 4 Availability =		.99973
Downtime =	525,960 (1 − .99974)	525,960 (1 − .99973)
Scenario 3 ≅	136.75 minutes	
Scenario 4 ≅		142 minutes

The figures on the diagram show that the two scenarios differ by only 10 minutes per year at 136.75 and 142 minutes per year of downtime. Again, we see the biggest contributor to downtime in these scenarios is the HFC network at only three 9s of availability.

Summary

The calculation of the four scenarios comprised several steps. You might think of calculating the availability of a network scenario as being recursive in nature. Or perhaps you might want to think in terms of concentric circles with each layer going from serial to parallel to serial and back again.

Hopefully, the concept of starting with the smallest components and then working up to the largest network constructs is clear in your mind after this final example.

The Contents of the CD

The CD included with this book contains selected items from within the chapters and a blank version of the System Hardware Availability and Reliability Calculator, or SHARC, spreadsheet. The SHARC spreadsheet included has slightly reduced features compared to the Cisco Systems, Inc., SHARC spreadsheet. You are permitted to use the SHARC spreadsheet for the purposes of learning the materials in this book. Additionally, you can use the SHARC spreadsheet to analyze your own networks.

The license for this free version of the SHARC spreadsheet specifically prohibits commercial use without prior permission from Cisco Systems.

The CD's content is navigable by using a web browser or by your operating system's file manager to browse the CD directly. Three key file types are on the CD. GIF files on the CD can be viewed by using your web browser or a graphics software package with GIF compatibility. There are also PDF files. PDF is a file format from Adobe Systems, Inc. Adobe has free viewers on their web site, a link to their download area is included on the CD. Finally, there are Microsoft Excel Spreadsheets, including the SHARC spreadsheet. You will need to have a copy of Microsoft Excel to use the spreadsheets.

Computer Requirements

The requirements for viewing or running the software on the CD are very basic. In order to view and run the software on the CD as intended, you will need to have a computer running Microsoft Windows. It will need to have a web browser and Microsoft Excel. It should have a screen resolution of no less than 800×600 and no less than 16 colors.

Any CPU, memory, and hard disk capable of running Windows should be able to view and run the software on the CD. None of the pictures or spreadsheets is particularly large.

Enabling macros in your Microsoft Excel software is crucial to get accurate results from the SHARC spreadsheet.

Basic Instructions for Using the CD

Step 1 Insert the CD into your computer's CD drive.

Step 2 The CD should automatically start your computer's default web browser and load the index.htm file. If it does not, then you will need to do so manually.

(a) Browse your computer to the CD drive.

(b) Locate the index.htm file on the CD.

(c) Open that file using your web browsing software.

Step 3 Browse the chapters and click on the files that interest you.

Chapter by Chapter Contents

The materials on the CD are divided into groups based on the chapter in which they appeared. Selections were made based on their inclusion in key parts of each chapter. Reading the parts of the chapters where the files appear in the book will reinforce the key points of the corresponding chapter.

Chapter 1

Chapter 1, "Introduction to High Availability Networking," was introductory in nature. The high availability equation is included on the CD to reinforce the most important equation in the entire book.

Chapter 2

Chapter 2, "The Basic Mathematics of High Availability," was an introduction into the mathematics of high availability. The parallel equation and the serial equation are included from this chapter to reinforce the two key equations used to handle network topology.

Chapter 3

Chapter 3, "Network Topology Fundamentals," refreshed your knowledge on network topology. By relating specific diagrams to the parallel and serial equations, you are reminded of how to interpret network diagrams. Figures 3-1 and 3-3 are included to refresh your memory of a simple network diagram and a diagram of a system that might be the beginning of performing availability analysis.

Chapter 4

Chapter 4, "Factors That Affect Availability," was our first tutorial chapter. This chapter highlighted the five key things that could affect availability of network and how to include them in your calculations. Figures 4-6 and 4-10 reinforce the concept of creating a RBD from a system. Figures 4-11 and 4-12 relate a network diagram and the corresponding network RBD.

Chapter 5

Chapter 5, "Predicting End-to-End Network Availability: The Divide-and-Conquer Method," was a tutorial chapter describing the method we use to make a complex network simpler to analyze. Figures 5-1, 5-2, 5-3, and 5-4 illustrated how a single network diagram can produce several RBDs representing multiple scenarios.

Chapter 6

Chapter 6, "Three Cisco Products: An Availability Analysis," begins our example chapters. Three systems are analyzed for availability. Figures 6-5 and 6-6 show how a complex system can be simplified using a RBD.

Chapter 7

Chapter 7, "A Small ISP Network: An Availability Analysis," was an availability study of a simple network. The first use of the SHARC spreadsheet was included in this chapter. Figures 7-1 and 7-2 illustrate how a network becomes a RBD. Figure 7-6 in the book is represented by a SHARC spreadsheet on the CD. You can experiment with the numbers to see how they might affect the computations done in this chapter by opening the spreadsheet with Microsoft Excel.

Chapter 8

Chapter 8, "An Enterprise Network: An Availability Analysis," continued our examples with an availability study of a network that one might find in a business application as opposed to a service provider network. The network diagram, RBD, and a SHARC spreadsheet representing a network component are included based on Figures 8-1, 8-2, and 8-3.

Chapter 9

Chapter 9, "A Large VoIP Network: An Availability Analysis," represents the culmination of our efforts. In this chapter we expand our use of the SHARC spreadsheet to include calculations of N + 1 network redundancy. We also used a multistep process to compute the availability of subcomponents and then include those results in subsequent calculations. Figures 9-13 and 9-14 show a situation where a processor sub-component is calculated and then subsequently used in a system level calculation. Figure 9-14 also has two lines on which the N + 1 redundancy construct is calculated.

Appendix A

The CD chapter titled Appendix A includes the PDF instructions for the SHARC spreadsheet and a blank version of the spreadsheet. The PDF version of the instructions is nearly identical to the information provided below in "Using the SHARC Spreadsheet."

Technical support is not provided for the SHARC spreadsheet by Cisco Press, Cisco Systems, or by the author of this book. If you have trouble using the spreadsheet, I suggest contacting friends with expertise in Microsoft Excel.

Using the SHARC Spreadsheet

The worksheet was created in Excel 5.0 for Microsoft Office 95, and it is assumed that you have a basic understanding of the Microsoft Excel program. You are reminded of the following:

- The worksheet is protected, or cells locked, in order to guard against the corruption of formulas by misplaced typing.

- The Move command should be avoided as this can destroy formula references. The Copy and Paste commands are generally safe to use. The Paste Special Values command, however, is recommended for pasting so as not to destroy the existing formatting.

- Autocalculation should be turned on.

- Simply using the spacebar key to delete information in the fields does not work. You must actually delete the information. Otherwise, you may see the term, #VALUE! in the fields to the right of your input cells.

- A special software line is included so that smaller MTTR values can be used. This line can be deleted if not required. If you need to enter an MTTR below 1, then you should copy the MTTR from this line into the line where you would like to use a value below 1. Then you simply enter the value. This difference in formatting allows you to see values below 1.0

System Configuration Worksheet Procedure

1 Open the SHARC spreadsheet using Excel.

2 Enter a name for the system at the top.

3 Enter data into the fields as described in Table A-1

Table A-1   *Data to Enter in the SHARC Spreadsheet*

SHARC Column	What to Enter
Enter Part Description	A description of the part. If you have it, the exact part number should be entered here.
Enter Quantity	The total number of this particular part contained in the system.
	If there is just one, enter **1**. For multiple identical parts, the quantity may be any number if the relationship is in-series or 1-to-N redundancy.
Enter Number Required	The minimum number of this particular part that the system requires to function.
	If QTY = 1, then the number required is set equal to "1."
	Redundancy is treated here by entering a number that is less than QTY. For example, if a system configuration includes two power supplies but the system will run fine with only one, then the QTY = 2 and Number Required = 1.
Enter Part MTBF	The part MTBF.
	If you do not have an MTBF for a particular component, then you will need to contact the manufacturer to get one.
Enter Part MTTR	The part MTTR.
	MTTR values vary somewhat depending on the service level employed at the customer site. If you are not sure what MTTR value to use, a good estimate of how long you think it would take to fix the part when it fails (in hours) is the right number to put in this field.

INDEX

A

access aggregation
   small-scale ISP networks, 132
   VoIP networks, 175
analyzing availability
   enterprise networks, 163
      Cisco 1538 routers, 167
      Cisco 3600 routers, 165
   VoIP over HFC networks, 173, 176
      data to the Internet, 179, 218
      network-level availability, 201–202,
         205, 211
      off net local calling, 182, 220
      off net long distance calling, 183, 220
      on net local calling, 180–181, 219
      system-level availability, 184–190,
         193–194, 198
annual reliability, 9–10
AS5300s
   availability
      calculating, 156–158
      in parallel topology, 209
      VoIP over HFC networks, 198
   small-scale ISP networks
      parallel availability calculations, 148
      redundancy, 158
      system level calculations, 135–139
assumed availability figures, VoIP over HFC
   network, 200–201
availability
   cost of, 10
   end-to-end
      predicting with divide-and-conquer
         method, 101–102
      small-scale ISP networks, calculating,
         149–160
   enterprise networks
      analysis of, 163
      Cisco 1538, 167
      Cisco 3600s, 165

equation, 12, 21
   converting between DPM and percentage
      method, 13–14
   parallel availability equation, 24
   serial availability equation, 23
need for, 5–6
network-level, small-scale ISP networks, 147
of multiple components, 23
parallel availability
   estimating, 25
   enterprise networks, 168
   fail-over mechanism, 26
   N+1 redundancy, 27
partial outages, 15
serial availability
   enterprise networks, 169
   estimating, 24
serial/parallel availability, estimating, 28–29
system-level, small-scale ISP networks,
   135–140, 144, 147
VoIP over HFC, 173, 176
   data to the internet, availability analysis,
      179, 218
   network-level availability, 201–202, 205,
      211
   off net local calling, availability analysis,
      182, 220
   off net long distance calling, availability
      analysis, 183, 220
   on net local calling, availability analysis,
      180–181, 219
   system-level availability, 184–194, 198
availability block diagrams
   creating, 29, 31
   uBR 7246, 123

B

backbone
   Cisco 12000 routers, calculating downtime, 218
   VoIP over HFC networks, availability
      calculations, 189–190
backup power supplies, N+M redundancy, 27
battery backup, mitigating power loss, 74–76
Bellcore method of computing MTBF, 47

Bellcore TR-332, 46
bill of materials (BOM), 20
block diagrams, reliability of small-scale ISP
   networks, 143
BOM (bill of materials), 20

C

cable modems
   uBR 7246, 122
      availability block diagram, 123
      head-end construct availability, 211
      MTBF, 124
      MTTR, 124
   uBR 924, availability calculations, 119, 121
calculating
   availability, 21
      DPM method, 10–11
      end-to-end availability, small-scale ISP
         networks, 149–150
      multiple components, 23
      parallel availability, 25
      percentage method, 9–10
      redundant components within a single
         device, 51, 54–55
      serial availability, 24
      serial/parallel availability, 28–29
      SHARC, 131
      simple network devices, 48–51
      system-level, AS5300s, 156–158
      system-level, Cisco 800 routers, 153, 156
   fail-over mechanisms in availability
      predictions, 93, 96–98
   FIT, 20
   MTBF, Cisco IOS software, 59
   MTTR, 12
   N+1 redundancy, 134
   partial outages, 15
   uptime/downtime, 21–22
Catalyst 5500s, system level calculations in
   small-scale ISP networks, 139, 143
Catalyst 8540, availability calculations in VoIP over
   HFC networks, 193–194
catastrophic failures, 44
censored observations, 62

change management, mitigating human error in
   downtime, 92
circuit boards
   FIT, 20
   serial availability, estimating, 24
Cisco 12000 routers
   availability calculations, 125–126
      block diagram, 126, 129
      parallel topology, 205
   downtime in VoIP over HFC network,
      calculating, 218
Cisco 7513 routers, system level calculations in
   small-scale ISP networks, 143–148
Cisco 800 routers, calculating availability, 153, 156
Cisco 8540 switch routers, availability in parallel
   topology, 205
Cisco devices, MTBF, 20
Cisco IOS software
   availability in parallel configuration,
      calculating, 68–69
   MTBF, calculating, 59
   reboot time, 58
Class 4 switches, 183
Class 5 switches, 183
comparing MTBFs, enterprise and service provider
   networks, 62
converting between DPM and percentage methods,
   13–14
cost of availability, 10
CPE (customer premise equipment), 119
   in VoIP over HFC networks
      availability calculations, 184–185
CPUs, calculating redundancy on devices, 144

D

data flow
   parallel topology, 35–36
   parallel/serial topology, 36
   path analysis, 29
      availability block diagrams, 29–31
   serial topology, 33–35
defects per million. *See* DPM
designing networks, goal-oriented, 111, 114

devices
    annual reliability, 9–10
    availability
        equation, 21
        measuring, 19–20
        multiple components, 23
        parallel, 25
        predicting, 46
        serial, 24
        serial/parallel, 28–29
        uptime/downtime, calculating, 21–22
    Cisco 3600 routers, availability analysis, 165
    fail-over mechanisms, 26
    failures, recognition time, 16
    misconfiguration, 81–82
    MTBF
        Cisco products, 20
        predicting, 46–47
    MTTR
        estimating, 20–21
        improving, 50
        predicting, 47–48
    network components, parallel availability
        equation, 24
    parallel availability, calculating, 54
    partial outages, calculating, 15
    serial availability, calculating, 52, 55
    single redundant components, 51, 54–55
    switches, Cisco 1538, availability analysis, 167
    system components, serial availability
        equation, 23
dial tone, loss of, 7
distribution of Cisco IOS software failure, 64
Disturbances Analysis Working Group, 71
divide-and-conquer method, predicting end-to-end
    availability, 101–102
    VoIP network example, 102–110
DOCSIS (Data Over Cable System Interface
    Specification), uBR 7246 fail-over rates, 211

downtime
    calculating, 21–22
    catastrophic failures, 44
    Cisco 12000 routers, VoIP over HFC
        networks, 218
    electrical downtime, 71–78
    environmental factors, 70
    failures per million hours, calculating, 88–92
    FIT (failure in ten billion), 47
    human error as factor, 45, 79
        enterprise networks, 171
        historical analysis, 80–81
        mitigating, 85–92
    misconfiguration as factor, 81–82
    MTTR, estimating, 20–21
    network segments, calculating, 55–56
    small-scale enterprise networks, calculating
        enterprise networks, 167–168
        ISP networks, 150–151
    software as factor, 57
        interfailure method of calculation, 62,
            65–66
        survival method of calculation, 58–62
DPM (defects per million)
    converting to percentage, 13–14
    measuring high availability, 8–11
dropped calls, calculating, 217

E

egress traffic, VoIP over HFC network, 174
electrical downtime, 71–72
    mitigating, 72–73
        with battery backup, 74–75
        with generator backup, 76–78
end-to-end availability
    predicting with divide-and-conquer method,
        101–102
        VoIP network example, 102–111
    small-scale ISP networks, calculating, 149–150,
        159–160

enterprise networks. *See also* ISP networks
  availability analysis, 163–167
  downtime, calculating, 167–168
  human error, effect on availability
    calculations, 171
  MTBF, comparing to service provider
    networks, 62
  network calculations
    parallel components, 168
    serial components, 169
  system-level calculations, 165–167
Enterprise Operational Profiles, 62
environmental factors of downtime, 70
  electrical, 71–72
  mitigating, 72–78
estimating
  MTTR, 20–21
  parallel availability, 25
    N+1 redundancy, 27–28
  serial availability, 24
  serial/parallel availability, 28–29
exponential cost of availability, 10
exponential distribution of failure, 64

F

fail-over mechanisms, 26
  including in availability predictions, 93, 96–98
  load sharing, 93
  standby redundant, 93
"Failure Terminated Test Case", 62
failures
  exponential distribution of, 64
  FIT, 19
  interfailure, lognormal dispersion, 64
  per million hours, calculating, 88, 91–92
failures in 10 billion (FIT), 19
fault tolerance
  annual reliability, 9–10
  DPM, measuring, 10–11
  fail-over mechanisms, 26
  FIT (failures in 10), 19
  improving handling processes, 16
  N+M redundancy, 27

FIT (Failures in Ten Billion), 19, 47
  BOM (bill of materials), 20
  serial availability, estimating, 24
five nines, 9–10

G

gap analysis, calculating failures per million hours,
  88, 91–92
GD (General Deployment) software, 65
generator backup, mitigating power loss, 76–78
goal-oriented network design, 111, 114

H

hardware availability, predicting, 46
  MTBF, 47
  MTTR, 47–48
head-end, 174
  in VoIP over HFC networks, availability
    calculations, 187–189
HFC (hybrid fiber coax) plant, 174
  availability calculations, 173, 176
    data to the Internet, 179, 218
    network-level, 201–202, 205, 211
    off net local calling, 182, 220
    off net long distance calling, 183, 220
    on net local calling, 180–181, 219
    system-level, 184–190, 193–194, 198
  connection to Internet, 176–177
  head end, 174
historical analysis of human error causing
  downtime, 80–81
human error
  affecting enterprise network availability, 171
  as factor in downtime, 79
    historical analysis, 80–81
  contributing to downtime, 45
    small-scale ISP networks, 151–152
  mitigating, 85–92
    change management phase, 92

I-J

improving
  MTTR, 50
  network availability, operations process, 86–88, 91–92
incorporating process contributions to downtime, 82–85
ingress traffic, HFC network scenario, 174
installation, contribution to downtime, 81–82
interfailure
  calculating MTBF, 62, 65–66
  lognormal dispersion, 64
Internet
  access service, availability in VoIP over HFC network, 213–214
  online purchasing, registration process, 5–6
ISP networks, small-scale, 131–132, 134
  downtime, calculating, 150–151
  end-to-end availability calculations, 159–160
  Internet access with ISDN router, 152–153, 156–160
  Internet access with modem, 135–152
  network-level availability, 147–152
  reliability block diagram, 143
  single point of failure, 139–140
  system-level calculations, 135–139, 143–144

K-L

Kececioglu's Reliability Engineering Handbook, 65

large-scale VoIP over HFC networks, availability analysis, 173, 176
  connection to Internet, 176–177
  data to the Internet, 179, 219
  network-level, 201–202, 205, 209–211
  off net local calling, 182, 220
  off net long distance calling, 183, 220
  on net local calling, 180–181, 219
  system-level, 184–190, 193–194, 198
load sharing, fail-over mechanisms, 93
lognormal dispersion of interfailure times, 64
loss of dial tone, 7

loss of power
  enterprise networks, 167–168
  mitigating, 72–73
    with battery backup, 74–75
    with generator backup, 76–78

M

"mean survival time" studies, 60
meantime between failure (MTBF), 9
measuring
  availability
    partial outages, 15
    Parts Count Method, 19–20
  high availability, 8
    DPM method, 10–11
    percentage method, 9–10
medical emergencies, 911 phone calls, 8
Mil-Hdbk-217 specification for computing MTBF, 46–47
misconfiguration, contribution to downtime, 81–82
mitigating
  human error as downtime factor, 85–92
    change management phase, 92
  power loss, 72–73
    with battery backup, 74–75
    with generator backup, 76–78
modems. See cable modems
MTBF (Mean Time Between Failure), 9–11
  in Cisco devices, 20
  predicting for hardware
    TR-332 method, 47
    Telcordia Parts Count Method, 46
  software, calculating, 57
    interfailure method, 62, 65–66
    survival method, 58–62
  uBR 7246, 124
  uBR 924, 120
MTTF (Mean Time To Failure), 11
MTTR (Mean Time To Repair), 12
  estimating, 20–21
  improving, 50
  of uBR 924, 120
  predicting for hardware, TR-332 method, 47–48
  uBR 7246, 124

N

N+1 redundancy, calculating, 134
N+M redundancy, 27
NATKIT, 60
NERC (North American Electric Reliability
    Council), 71–72
network availability, improving with operations
    process, 86–92
network components, parallel availability
    equation, 24
network control service, availability in VoIP over
    HFC network, 214–215
network control/management, VoIP network, 175
network design, goal-oriented, 111, 114
network segments, 55–56
network-level availability
    small-scale ISP networks, 147–152
    VoIP over HFC network, 201–202, 205,
        209–211
        parallel AS5300 PSTN gateway
            services, 209
        parallel components, 202
        parallel Internet connections, 202, 205
        parallel routers, 205
        parallel switch routers, 205
        parallel uBR 7246 head-end
            construct availability, 211
        redundant segments, 202
        serial components, 202
networks
    small-scale ISP
        Internet access with ISDN router,
            152–153, 156–160
        Internet access with modem, 135–139,
            143–144, 147–152
    voice, regulation of, 8

O

off net local calling, VoIP over HFC networks,
    182, 220
off net long distance calling, VoIP over HFC
    networks, 183, 220
on net local calling, VoIP over HFC networks,
    180–181, 219
online purchasing, registration process, 5–6
operating systems, calculating redundancy on
    devices, 144
operations process for increasing network
    availability, 86–88, 91–92

P-Q

parallel availability
    AS5300s, calculating, 148
    Cisco 7513, calculating, 147–148
    equation, 24
    estimating, 25
    fail-over mechanism, 26
    in enterprise networks, 168
    N+1 availability, 27–28
parallel components
    availability, calculating, 54
    VoIP over HFC network, 202, 205,
        209–211
parallel topologies, 35–36
parallel/serial topologies, 36
parallel-parallel redundancy, 179
partial failures, 15, 44
Parts Count Method, 19–20
path analysis, 29
    availability block diagrams, 29–31
percentage method
    conversion to DPM, 13–14
    measuring high availability, 8–10
    uptime/downtime, calculating, 21–22
POTS (plain old telephone service), loss of dial
    tone, 7
power loss, mitigating, 72–73
    with battery backup, 74–76
    with generator backup, 76–78

predicting availability
    downtime
        human error as factor, 45
        incorporating process contributions, 82–85
        end-to-end network availability, divide-and-conquer method, 101–102
            VoIP network example, 102–110
        enterprise network availability
            downtime calculations, 167–168
            human error calculations, 171
            network calculations, 168–170
            system-level calculations, 165–167
        hardware availability, 46
            MTBF, 46–47
            MTTR, 47–48
        including fail-over mechanisms, 93, 96–98
    process contributions to downtime, 81–85
PSTN (private switched telephone network) service, availability in VoIP over HFC network, 217
purchasing online, registration process, 5–6

reliability
    annual, 9–10
    block diagrams, small-scale ISP networks, 143
    cost of, 10
    measuring, Parts Count Method, 19–20
    partial outages, calculating, 15
    telephone service, 7
repair, MTTR, 20–21
restrictions, SHARC, 131
rounding off numbers, SHARC spreadsheet, 139
routers
    backbone (VoIP over HFC network), 189–190
    Cisco 12000
        availability, calculating, 125–126
        availability block diagram, 126, 129
        downtime, calculating, 218
    Cisco 3600, availability analysis, 165
    CPE (VoIP over HFC network), 184
    head-end (VoIP over HFC network), 187–189
    reboot time, 58
routing protocols, selecting, 44

R

RBDs (reliability block diagrams)
    creating, 104–106, 110
        for network segments, 55–56
    VoIP over HFC network
        data to the Internet, 179
        on net local calling, 180
reboot time, Cisco routers, 58
recognition time, device failure, 16
redundancy
    AS5300s, small-scale ISP networks, 158
    Cisco 5500s as single point of failure, 139–140
    fail-over mechanisms, 26
    MTBF, 9–10
    N+M, 27
        SHARC spreadsheet, 27
    parallel-parallel, 179
regulation of telephone service, 8
regulation of voice networks, 8

S

scenarios, creating RBDs, 104–106, 110
selecting network topology, 44
serial availability
    calculating, 23
    estimating, 24
    in enterprise networks, 169
serial availability equation
serial components
    availability
        calculating, 52, 55
    VoIP over HFC network
        availability calculations, 202
serial topologies, 33, 35
serial/parallel availability, estimating, 28–29
service construct availability (VoIP over HFC networks)
    Internet access service, 213–214
    network control service, 214–215
    PSTN service, 217
service contracts, estimating MTTR, 20–21
service outages, 44

service provider networks, 163. *See also* enterprise networks
   MTBF, comparing to enterprise networks, 62
SHARC (System Hardware Availability and Reliability Calculator), 27, 131, 139
shopping online, registration process, 5–6
simple network devices, calculating availability, 48–51
simple parallel availability, N+1 redundancy, 27–28
single point of failure
   cost of eliminating, 35–36
   small-scale ISP networks, 139–140
small-scale enterprise networks
   availability analysis, 163
      Cisco 1538, 167
      Cisco 3600s, 165
   downtime, calculating, 167–168
small-scale ISP networks, 131–134
   downtime, calculating, 150–151
   end-to-end availability, calculating, 159–160
   network-level availability, 147–152
   reliability block diagram, 143
   single point of failure, 139–140
   system-level calculations
      AS5300s, 135–139
      Catalyst 5500s, 139, 143
      Cisco 7513, 143–144
software
   as factor in system availability, 67–68
   Cisco IOS, calculating MTBF, 59
   GD (General Deployment), 65
   MTBF, calculating, 57–62
   parallel configuration, 68–69
   partial failures, 44
   service outages, 44
spreadsheets, SHARC, 131
   rounding off numbers, 139
standby redundant fail-over mechanisms, 93
survival method, calculating software MTBF, 58–62
switches
   Catalyst 5500, system availability calculations for small-scale ISP networks, 139, 143
   Cisco 1538, availability analysis, 167
   Class 4/5, 183
   in VoIP over HFC networks, availability calculations, 193–194
system components, serial availability equation, 23

system-level calculations
   in enterprise networks, 165–167
   SHARC, 131
   small-scale ISP networks, 153, 156, 158
      AS5300s, 135–139
      Catalyst 5500, 139, 143
      Cisco 7513, 143–144
   software as factor, 67–68
   VoIP over HFC network, CPE router, 184–190, 193–194, 198

T

Telcordia Parts Count Method, 19–20, 46
telephone networks
   loss of dial tone, 7
   service regulations, 8
topologies
   parallel, 35–36
   parallel/serial, 36
   selecting, 44
   serial, 33, 35
TR-332 method of predicting MTBF, 47
traffic
   data flow
      in parallel topology, 35–36
      in parallel/serial topology, 36
      in serial topology, 33, 35
   egress, VoIP over HFC network, 174
   ingress, HFC network scenario, 174
   load sharing fail-over mechanisms, 93
   path analysis, 29
      availability block diagrams, 29–31

U

uBR 7246, 122
   availability block diagram, 123
   head-end construct availability
      in VoIP over HFC networks, 211
   MTBF, 124
   MTTR, 124
uBR 924, availability calculations, 119, 121
UPSs (uninterruptible power supplies), N+M redundancy, 27

uptime, calculating, 21–22
utilities, SHARC, 27

V-Z

voice networks, regulation of, 8
VoIP over HFC network
    assumed availability figures, 200–201
    availability calculations, 173, 176
        data to the Internet, 179, 219
        network-level, 201–202, 205, 209–211
        off net local calling, 182, 220
        off net long distance calling, 183, 220
        on net local calling, 180–181, 219
        system-level, 184–190, 193–194, 198
    connection to Internet, 176–177
    head-end, 174
    service construct availability
        Internet access, 213–214
        network control service, 214–215
        PSTN service, 217

Web sites
    NERC, 71
    Telcordia, 19